C000040952

Fragrance of the Earth

Then an old man, a keeper of an inn, said,
Speak to us of Eating and Drinking.
And he said:
Would that you could live on the fragrance of the earth,
and like an air plant be sustained by the light.

Kahlil Gibran, *The Prophet*

Nada Saleh

Fragrance of the Earth

LEBANESE HOME COOKING

Foreword by Albert Roux

Photographs by Barbara and Zafer Baran

SAQI
BOOKS

For Ziad

Original wood engravings by Fiodor Domogatsky
Book design by Misha Anikst

British Library Cataloguing-in-Publication Data
A catalogue record for this book is available from the British Library

ISBN 0 86356 256 6 (hb)
ISBN 0 86356 056 3 (pbk)

© Nada Saleh, 1996

This edition first published 1996
Saqi Books
26 Westbourne Grove, London W2 5RH

Printed in Hong Kong

Contents

Acknowledgments

I wish to express my deep gratitude to Yankit So, whose warm friendship never failed me throughout the various stages of my work, and who supported and encouraged me with her valuable advice.

I am also indebted to Diane and Michel Khlat for their kind, continuous support, and for introducing me to authoritative people in the food business.

To Patrick Holford for teaching me the nutritional value of food.

My heartfelt thanks to Albert Roux for reading my manuscript and writing a generous appreciation and to Claudia Roden, who took the time to look at my work despite her busy schedule working on her new book.

My special thanks to Rachid Rahme for his pertinent medical advice, and to Talal Farah for his valuable information, used in some parts of the book.

All my thanks to Barbara and Zafer Baran for the magnificent photographs they have produced, and to Misha Anikst for his fine design.

My thanks for the continuous support of Françoise Peretti, Elizabeth Harwood and Hilda Phillips Flack.

I would also like to mention my debt to Nayla Obeid, Graham Handley, Tony and Zeina Kiwan, the management and staff of the Lebanese Restaurant, Nada Anid, Marie Taktouk, Anna Captan, Souad Mokbel Wensley, Nawaf Salam, Ghazi Youssef, Vouty Mattar and my sisters, Rafat Bouchacra and Samira Sayegh. To George Chucrallah for re-testing some of my recipes, and to Kate Miles-Kingston for her patient typing and her advice.

My gratitude to my husband Nabil for his advice and patience and to my daughter Nour for her assistance throughout and for drawing my attention to the story of Daniel from the Bible which is mentioned in the book.

Finally I would like to thank Mai Ghoussoub and André Gaspard whose efforts and faith in my work made this publication possible.

Foreword

by Albert Roux

First I must declare an interest: I am a lover of fine Lebanese cuisine and what follows in Nada Saleh's book is a delightful collection of recipes.

Some of the dishes you will find simple to prepare and some more complicated but all are delicious and, combined with a fascinating insight into their history, the anecdotes and the tempting photography, this book will be equally at home on your kitchen book-shelf and on your coffee table.

Glossary

Amino acids: Units that form protein. To function well, the body requires 22 amino acids. Essential amino acids are not produced by the body, so they must be supplied from food. These are histidine, isoleucine, leucine, lysine, methionine, phenylalanine, thionine, tryptophan and valine.

Aniseed (*yansoun*): The aromatic seed of a plant that contains the oil used in the making of arak. The seeds and the powder are used to flavour biscuits, puddings and jams. Aniseed is also made into infusions to aid digestion and calm the nerves.

Antioxidant: A substance that reduces or prevents oxidation in cells.

Beta-carotene: Occurs in many plants and converts into vitamin A in the body. Good for eyesight and skin.

Caraway (*karawiya*): A herb with yellowish white flowers. The ground seeds are used to flavour savoury dishes and the sweet *mughli* (a pudding of different spices and ground rice).

Carbohydrates: An important source of energy. Carbohydrates are composed of carbon, hydrogen and oxygen. They are divided into two types: complex carbohydrates (found in vegetables, fresh and dried fruits, nuts, etc) and simple carbohydrates (found in refined and processed sugars).

Carcinogen: Any element that induces, over a long period, the development of cancer in living cells.

Cardamom (*heil*): An expensive spice which belongs to the ginger family. It is used to add a distinctive flavour to stock and to help remove the rank odour of meat and chicken. It is also used with ground coffee to give a special taste.

Carob molasses (*dibs kharroub*): A thick syrup obtained from the pods of leguminous (carob) trees which do not necessarily require watering. It is used instead of sugar and also as a sweet delicacy when mixed with *tahini*.

Cassia (*kirfeh*): Comes from the laurel tree and was introduced into Europe by the Phoenicians and the inhabitants of the Arabian peninsula. It is an essential spice. I have used either ground cassia or cassia bark in my recipes because of the strong flavour. When unavailable, cinnamon can be used in its place.

Cholesterol: A fatty substance produced by the liver. Bad cholesterol (LDL) in the blood is associated with heart disease and vessel atherosclerosis. There is also good cholesterol (HDL), with proven protective properties.

Clove (*kibsh kronfol*): The dried flower bud of a small evergreen tree. It has a strong smell and flavour and is used in small amounts to enhance the taste of stock.

Complete protein: Foods that provide all essential amino acids, sufficient to meet the body's needs.

Cracked wheat (*burghol*): A staple wheat grain that has been boiled, dried and cracked into coarse and fine particles. The coarse variety is used to make *moujaddara* and in fillings for courgettes, vine leaves, etc. The fine variety is used to make *kibbeh* and *tabbouleh*.

Cream of sesame (*tahini*): A thick creamy liquid obtained from sesame seeds. It has a delicious flavour and is widely used in dips, savoury dishes, sauces and some sweets. It is also eaten along with the popular *dibs kharroub*.

Cumin: A small aromatic plant which yields pink or white flowers. It is highly flavoured and is said to aid digestion. It is added to pulse and bean dishes in varying quantities depending on the household.

Fats: A concentrated source of energy. Fats form the bulk of lipid (fat) deposition in obesity. They are divided into three types: saturated fatty acids (linked to atherosclerosis and found mainly in meat, butter, cream, egg yolk, coconut and palm oils); monounsaturated fatty acids (found in olives, olive oil and peanut oil) and polyunsaturated fatty acids (found in oils such as safflower, corn and sunflower).

Fibre: A bulk-forming substance made of husks, cellulose, lignin, hemicelluloses, pentosans, gums and pectins. It relieves constipation, stimulates gut motion, regulates bowel action and enhances digestion.

Gluten: A protein found in wheat, rye, oats and barley, associated with food allergy in susceptible patients.

Hay diet: A diet developed by Dr William Howard Hay which is based on combining certain foods that do not conflict with each other in digestion. Its basic principle is not to mix carbohydrates with proteins and acid fruits.

Kawarma: A delicacy made of lamb meat preserved in fat. The meat is cut into small cubes (1 cm/1/2 in or less), seasoned with sea salt and allspice and left for a day. Then it is fried in the fat and put in jars to use instead of fresh meat, especially at times when meat is scarce and expensive.

Kishk: A combination of *burghol* processed with milk and yoghurt; its preparation requires several stages. *Kishk* is a traditional staple food of the mountain villages.

Mahlab: An aromatic spice obtained from the kernel of the black cherry. It is added to some sweets. To obtain the maximum flavour, buy whole and grind in a mortar.

Mastic (*miskee*): A resin or gum obtained from a small evergreen tree. It is used to enhance and add a distinctive taste to milk puddings, fig jam and *shawarma*.

Mezze: A traditional combination of appetizers, comprising several small dishes such as *tabbouleh*, *hoummos*, *fattoush*, olives, *labneh*, *baba ghannouj*, etc.

Minerals: Crucial elements in the metabolism of cells and organs. Important for nerve function, bone and blood formation.

Munee: Provisions of different spices, dried vegetables, pickles, sackfuls of beans and legumes, oil, olives, etc.

Olive oil: A monounsaturated fat with recognized beneficial effects in lowering blood cholesterol and preventing heart disease. Recent reports suggest that olive oil may reduce the risk of breast cancer and delay the ageing process.

In Lebanon olive oil is used extensively, especially where olive trees grow. In this book extra virgin olive oil is used in both salads and cooking. It is both tasty and healthy; when cooked, it conserves a full-bodied flavour.

Omega 3: A polyunsaturate essential fatty acid that helps prevent atherosclerosis, found in oily fish and some plants, such as purslane.

Orange-blossom water (*ma al-zahr*): Distilled from the blossoms of the Seville orange tree. It is added to sweets to enliven the flavour. A few drops are added to boiled water to produce a calming, digestive drink known as white coffee (*kahwe baida*).

Pine-nuts: The edible seed of the pine tree. Pale beige in colour with an oblong shape, pine-nuts are used extensively to garnish savoury dishes and in some sweets.

Pomegranate syrup (*dibs al-roumman*): Made of the juice extracted from the pomegranate. The juice is then boiled until it thickens and its colour changes from red to burgundy brown. It has a succulent flavour which gives a lift to savoury dishes.

Protein: Long chains of amino acids necessary for the growth and repair of cells and tissues. Proteins are also needed for the production of hormones, enzymes and antibodies. Proteins are found in meat, fish, poultry, eggs, dairy products, soya beans, pulses and dried peas. Proteins obtained from vegetables must be properly combined and varied to obtain all the essential amino acids (for example, eating rice with beans or lentils). This book includes many recipes that provide the correct combinations of proteins (for example, *makhlouta*).

Rosewater (*ma al-ward*): An essence obtained from the strongest-scented rose petals, *ward al-jouri*; the petals are pink in colour and mostly found in Tripoli (north Lebanon) and the Bekaa Valley.

Sahlab: A starchy powder obtained from the tubers of wild orchids. It is used in the preparation of a hot drink, consumed traditionally in the early hours of the morning, and as an ice cream.

Semolina (*smeed*): Made of durum wheat and used in sweets.

Sesame seeds (*simsom*): The plant grows in the Middle and Far East but may have originated in Africa or India. The tiny flat seeds are highly nutritious and are added to sweet pastries, bread and *zaatar*. The creamy liquid *tahini* is obtained from the seeds.

Sumak: Comes from the berries of a shrub which grows wild in Lebanon's mountains. The unripened berries are dried, then ground. It provides a sour, lemony taste. In the past it was very useful as a substitute for lemon when lemons were out of season and expensive. *Sumak* is an essential part of *zaatar* mixture.

Thyme (*zaatar*): A mixture of dried crushed thyme, dried crushed *sumak*, toasted sesame seeds and a little sea salt. This is then mixed with olive oil and spread over bread to be eaten as a sandwich and is also used in *mankoushi*.

Turmeric (*ikdeh safra*): A member of the ginger family which grows in the Middle East. It has a mild flavour and is used, mostly for its yellow colour, in some desserts and in a variety of savoury recipes.

Vitamins: Constituents of diet that are essential in body metabolism. They are catalysts or activators. An adequate balance is provided in Lebanese cuisine. Vitamin deficiencies lead to recognized disease entities.

Recommendations for Good Health

1. If necessary, change your eating habits to include wholefoods (for example, brown rice, wholemeal pasta and bread) in your diet. Avoid processed foods.
2. Wash but do not soak vegetables for prolonged periods in water to prevent the loss of vitamins.
3. When cooking vegetables, use small amounts of water.
4. Steam vegetables, and cook potatoes with their skins on, to retain nutrients.
5. Chew food thoroughly; digestion starts in the mouth.
6. Eat plenty of fresh fruit and vegetables.
7. Ensure your diet is rich in mineral salts, which play an important role in the regulation of all body activities. These minerals are:
   calcium: dairy produce (e.g. milk, cheese and yoghurt), nuts, seeds, dried beans, broccoli, spinach, whitebait, and canned sardines with bones;
   phosporus: fish, poultry, meat, wholegrains, eggs, nuts, seeds;
   potassium: bananas, figs, dates, watercress, green leafy vegetables, sunflower seeds, potatoes;
   chlorine: olives, salt (in reasonable quantities);
   sodium: salt, seafood, artichokes, meat.
8. Include foods rich in monounsaturated fatty acids (olive oil) whenever possible. Also unsaturated fats (found in vegetable oils, wheatgerm, walnuts, almonds, pecans, avocados and seeds).
9. Boost your immunity and enhance your well-being by including foods rich in antioxidants in your daily diet:
   vitamin A: liver, carrots, beetroot, broccoli, pumpkin, spinach, eggs, dairy produce, fruit;
   vitamin C: peppers, green leafy vegetables, tomatoes, cauliflower, citrus fruits, guavas, kiwis;
   vitamin E: nuts, seeds, and vegetable oils such as those made of safflower, sunflower, corn and peanuts;
   selenium: garlic, onions, tuna fish and shellfish, wholegrains.
10. Drink plenty of water (about 6–8 glasses per day).
11. Decrease your intake of high-sugar foods and of stimulants such as coffee and alcohol.

12. Avoid the carbonized parts of food as they can be carcinogenic.
13. Include onions, garlic, olive oil and yoghurt in your daily diet.
14. Cook food in covered pots to conserve freshness and vitamin content.
15. Do not use aluminium pots or foil in contact with direct heat. High aluminium content in food, consumed over a prolonged period, has been linked to brain damage and loss of memory.
16. Exercise daily: 30 minutes brisk walk in fresh air is adequate.

Finally always remember that Ibn al-Nafis, a 13th-century Syrian physician, would never prescribe medicine when diet sufficed.

Introduction

Beirut, the mid-1960s...

'Fish, fresh fish.' I woke up to the repeated cries knowing it was 7 o'clock on a Wednesday morning. That was when the fisherman used to stand beneath the balcony of my father's house, yelling the praises of his fish to make my mother aware of his presence.

Summoned by my mother's nod through the window to come up to the first floor, he would place a large, shallow wicker basket full of a variety of Mediterranean fish on the outside landing of our typical 19th-century house and prepare himself for some hard bargaining.

It was my grandmother, not my mother, who would challenge his asking price, no matter what that price was. He, for his part, always made sure to ask more than he would eventually be content with. The fierce bargaining session would invariably end up with my grandmother's seeming victory. 'This is the freshest fish you'll ever find; see you next Wednesday,' he would say before departing, adding some reassurance about the quality of his wares.

We were a large family and the whole contents of the fisherman's basket would habitually be prepared by my mother for our Wednesday lunch. I used to watch her calmly presiding over her kitchen, declining any help with this familiar but important ceremonial.

On Fridays we ate *moujaddara* (purée of lentils and rice) and *fattoush* (mixed salad with purslane and toasted bread). We knew, before any health pundits said so, that *moujaddara* was extremely nourishing; my grandmother called it 'knees' nails' (*massamir al-rukab*). We now know that lentils are high in protein and fibre, rich in B vitamins and low in fat.

Whether at home in Beirut or in the countryside, *kibbeh* was our Sunday meal. *Kibbeh* is a traditional dish made of *burghol*, meat and onions pounded together in a huge stone mortar. Its origin, like that of *tabbouleh*, is indisputably Lebanese. *Hoummos* may be claimed by several Mediterranean countries, vegetables stuffed with meat and rice may be arrogated in turn by Persian, Turkish or Byzantine cuisine, but *kibbeh* and *tabbouleh* are part of Lebanon's cooking heritage and folklore.

Weather permitting, we would drive on Sundays in the early sunlight in the direction of the Shouf Mountains. As we reached the outskirts of our native town, Mukhtara, we would be struck by the silence, broken only by the regular sound of water dripping on the rocks on its way to the valley in a thin and shiny meandering string. We could hear the leaves of the swaying poplars whispering and breathe the soothing scents of wood, earth and leaves. Calm and charm enveloped every soul. The houses, which are scattered in no apparent order, seemed uninhabited until a vague silhouette emerged through the door to roam silently in the small adjacent kitchen garden, where parsley, mint, tomatoes, basil and lavender grew next to flowers and fruit trees.

Uphill, along the road, was the modest retreat of a feudal Druse leader who used to isolate himself and meditate, burning Indian incense, far from the demanding political dependants who crowded his Italianate ancient palace nearby. As we followed the curved path, still going uphill, we would pass two churches, one for the Maronites and the other for the Melkites. From afar we could see a man in black with a white turban walking next to a slowly trotting donkey. His costume and head-dress were typical of a Druse holy man (*sheikh*). To my father's greetings he would invariably answer, '*Sabahnakom bil-kheir,* (May this day be of goodness to you all).' In Mukhtara, we would feel eyes watching us from behind the drawn flimsy curtains. Mountain people are cautious: they observe until they recognize you.

We would pick up my uncle and other relatives and head straight for Ain Murshid, the picnic spot. It was a large wooded area where poplars had pride of place, an indication that water was plentiful. The site gradually narrowed, leading us to the source, which springs beneath a huge curved rock and immediately drops down in a precipitous fall. We used to sit in the cool next to the spring and in no time the *mezze* (appetizers) were spread out: They mainly comprised *hoummos, tabbouleh, labneh* (cream cheese made from yoghurt), olives and lots of bread, an accompaniment to every meal, and freshly cut or picked vegetables. These were followed by *kibbeh* as well as *meshwi* (grilled meat), one of the many culinary legacies left by the Ottomans, or possibly before them by the Crusaders.

Locally grown fresh fruits in season were then served, sometimes along with *muhallabiyah* or *baluza*. The former is a kind of pudding attributed to a 7th-century emir, Muhlab Ibn Safra, and the latter is a Persian recipe comprising wheat, water and honey, or, more often, molasses mixed with sesame cream or fig jam. Abundant Turkish coffee was provided in an attractive traditional coffee-pot, and afterwards the grounds in the cup had to be read.

Few of our company drank alcohol; when they did it was *arak* (anisette). Most of us were content to quench our thirst from the spring, using an earthenware jug with a narrow neck, handle and spout, probably handed down from antiquity.

Sites such as Ain Murshid made one realize that food at its best combines a way of life with nature. Nature has not been very generous to the inhabitants of Lebanon. Soil suitable for agriculture is limited. Nevertheless, the Lebanese have traditionally managed to use basic and sometimes very ordinary ingredients to make noble food. *Kibbeh* is in reality a clever way of making poor-quality meat deliciously edible. Grains, beans and pulses are prepared with imagination but in such a way that they retain their highly nutritious properties. Bread used to be prepared at home in a variety of shapes and sizes. The dough was sent to the neighbourhood bakery, but a small piece was put aside in a wooden container to be used to start off another batch. The same principle applied in making yoghurt.

Some dishes to be served cold were dressed with olive oil only—these were called *tabikh bi-zeit*. The traditional way of cooking was with clarified butter (*samneh*); recently, vegetable oils other than olive oil have been introduced. Those vegetable oils were wrongly assumed to be healthier than olive oil, but recent studies show that olive oil is to be preferred as it is monounsaturated and, unlike other vegetable oils, does not oxidize in a matter of seconds. Olive oil is, of course, used extensively in Lebanon in places where olive trees grow. Not only is the olive tree deemed sacred—a belief derived from interpretations of the Bible, the Gospels and the Quran—but it is also valued for its yield of olives, oil, soap and wood.

This book is an attempt to present what I have learnt from books and from experiments in my kitchen. Some people think that Middle Eastern meals are too rich and heavy. I have tried to meet the challenge of showing how they can be made lighter and healthier while keeping their traditional flavour.

Besides enjoyment, food must supply our bodies with a variety of nutrients as providers of energy, cell renewal and hence longevity. A deficiency—as well as an excess—can disrupt the metabolism and be detrimental to health and well-being.

Some dishes are healthy and simple and others can be made more so quite easily and without the need to become obsessive about health. Fortunately Middle Eastern dishes, particularly the Lebanese ones, lend themselves very readily to these possibilities.

Vegetables, Grains and Pulses

Thammuz came next behind
Whose annual wound in Lebanon allured
The Syrian damsels to lament his fate
In amorous ditties all a summer's day
While smooth Adonis from his native rock
Ran purple to the sea, supposed with blood
Of Thammuz yearly wounded.

Milton, *Paradise Lost*, 1:446

In ancient times the recurring wonder of spring was attributed to the gods by men who were close to nature and lived off the produce of the earth.

Sumer, Babylon and Assyria worshipped Thammuz, who died every year and rose again in spring (they sat 'weeping for Thammuz', Ezekiel 8:14). The legend travelled west, and the Greeks named the god Adonis.

Thammuz, or Adonis, was revered in a temple (its ruins still stand) in the heights above Byblos, now in Lebanon. It was destroyed at Constantine's order when he became weary of the pagan ceremonies and the licentiousness that accompanied them every spring.

The history of certain places seems to emanate from them and sharpen the senses. Sitting on one of the fallen columns of the temple, it did not require any great effort of the imagination to 'see' the legend of Adonis enacted in front of me. I could visualize Aphrodite rushing to help the fallen Adonis, gored to death by a wild boar while hunting; I could see her being pricked by a thorn and her blood dyeing the white anemone red, while Adonis's blood 'ran purple to the sea', forming what is now the Adonis River. 'Do not cry, Aphrodite,' I was tempted to say. 'Adonis will be brought back to life with the new blossoming of the produce of the earth. Those who lamented in Byblos will soon walk in procession to his temple and celebrate his resurrection, and they will worship him as the god of vegetation.'

In Lebanon we sow corn grains in small pots filled with earth just in time for them to sprout at Easter. The sprouting grains are not to be eaten, but are a symbol of rebirth, celebrating the emergence of the new crops.

Another tribute is paid to the ancient gods, albeit unwittingly, for we call fruit and vegetables that are not watered during the dry season *baal*, the ancient local name for the god of rain and fertility.

Vegetables, grains and pulses form the basis of the daily diet of the Lebanese, whether they live in the country or a city. In September, when this produce is abundant and cheap, every family joins in the ritual of amassing the *munee* (provisions), which gives people a sense of security. The *munee* consists of sackfuls of *burghol* (cracked wheat), lentils, beans and chick-peas, less perishable products such as onions and garlic braided into long ropes, tough-skinned potatoes, olives (styled as *sultan al-sofra*, or 'sultan of the table'), olive oil, *kishk* (a combination of *burghol* and milk), *labneh* (cream cheese made from yoghurt), spices, *debs* (molasses, made either from carob or from grapes), jam preserves (apples, apricots, figs . . .), as well as sun-dried vegetables and herbs, such as green beans, okra, courgettes and tomatoes (the last two are sliced and slightly salted), mint and thyme. Tomatoes are also prepared as condensed purée to be used in *yakhne* (stew).

Vegetables such as cucumbers, turnips, beetroots, cauliflowers, green and chilli peppers, carrots, okra, baby aubergines, fresh thyme and vine leaves are pickled in glass jars, either in vinegar or in lightly salted boiled water, and topped with a fine layer of olive oil to keep out the air and prevent spoilage. An expensive delicacy is baby aubergines, stuffed with garlic, walnuts and almonds, and preserved in oil.

Throughout the country these provisions are saved for the 'dead' seasons, and also for the hard times that have regularly afflicted Lebanon.

The stored grains and pulses are matched and mixed in an imaginative way with the vegetables, transforming a poor peasant diet into delicious and healthy meals, glorious in their simplicity and goodness.

Vegetables, grains and pulses are variously combined and prepared with olive oil and lemon juice, then presented as salads, stews, fried or boiled dishes such as the irresistible *tabbouleh*, the sublime *fattoush*, the delicious *moujaddara*, the satisfying potato salad, or the tasty and simply cooked *bamia bi-zeit*. This diet is substantially the food eaten daily by the Lebanese throughout the country for their lunch or dinner, for parties or for *mezze* (appetizers).

The Lebanese are vegetable-lovers. I still have vivid memories of the southern coastal strip, with its rich soil, where all types of citrus fruits and bananas grow, among them lettuces, spring onions, radishes, parsley and mint. Fifteen years of war on Lebanese soil have wrought suffering and misery, but a few good things have resulted, among them the return of many Lebanese to the villages and boroughs they deserted when they were lured by the attractions of the capital; the return to a simpler life; and the rediscovery of the basic, plain food of their parents and ancestors.

People in the West have become increasingly aware of health, in particular of the need to include more vegetables, grains and pulses in their daily diet; consequently their attention has been drawn to the Lebanese culinary regime. Nutritionists list it as one of the healthiest, and it is suitable for everyone, including vegetarians. The plant foods that are central to the Lebanese diet supply a wealth of nutritional needs, being remarkably rich in roughage, vitamin C, protein, complex carbohydrate, B complex vitamins, iron and trace minerals.

The nutritional value of vegetables and grains is highlighted by the story of Daniel in the Old Testament (Daniel 1:1-21). He was carried as a young hostage with three companions from Jerusalem to Babylon by King Nebuchadnezzar. The king ordered his guard to feed them with royal food, rich in meat and wine, so that they would grow strong and become wise men. Daniel and his companions, who had to follow God's laws, asked the guard to give them vegetables and water only. The guard was at first afraid to do so but then he agreed to give them a ten-day trial. After this period he found that Daniel and his companions were fitter than the men who were eating the royal food, so he allowed them to continue eating as they pleased for the entire three-year period of their captivity. At the end of this time, Daniel and his companions had indeed grown healthier and wiser!

*Let food be your medicine
and medicine your food.*

Hippocrates

Cracked Wheat Salad
Tabbouleh

This is an exotic and mouth-watering salad, in which the dominant ingredient is parsley, used by the ancient Greeks for its medicinal purposes and mentioned by Homer in the *Odyssey*. *Tabbouleh* has such pride of place in Lebanese cuisine that the purchaser of some houses in the district of Mar Maroun, then outside Beirut's walls (occupied during the 19th century by the French poet Lamartine), converted them into a restaurant which he named Le jardin de *tabbouleh*.

Tabbouleh, sometimes called the energy salad, is said to have originated from the random pickings of whatever the kitchen garden offered. In mountain villages, parsley, mint any hour the hosts quickly gather the vegetables to prepare *tabbouleh* and serve it with tender vine leaves, also picked freshly from the garden. Its popularity has spread to the West, but in Europe the *burghol* (cracked wheat) component is dominant and parsley is used in very small amounts. This version of *tabbouleh* should thus be called *burghol* salad.

In Lebanon *tabbouleh* is prepared for any occasion, but it has long been a favourite for Sunday picnic lunch. It is eaten with the meshwi of chicken and lamb kebabs. Besides being succulent, *tabbouleh* provides a wealth of the antioxidant vitamins A and C.

Ingredients

1 bunch of parsley (about 200 g/7 oz), yielding
    about 50 g (2 oz) chopped parsley
75 g (2½ oz) fine *burghol*
250 g (9 oz) rinsed, finely chopped ripe tomatoes
2 medium spring onions (trim both ends, remove green
    end retaining about 5 cm/2 in), finely chopped
1 tsp salt or to taste
¼ tsp freshly milled black pepper
a pinch of cinnamon (optional)
2¾ tbs lemon juice
3–4 tbs extra virgin olive oil
a large handful of mint leaves, rinsed,
    drained, finely chopped

Undo the bunch of parsley and gather the sprigs into small bundles so that the leaves are packed together at the same level. Place each bundle on your chopping surface, grip the upper part of the parsley firmly with one hand, and with the other, use a sharp knife to cut off the stalks; save these to flavour stock or fish. Chop the rest of the parsley, rinse and drain.

Wash the *burghol*, drain quickly, squeeze out excess water and place in a salad bowl. Cover the *burghol* with the tomatoes, allowing it to absorb the tomato juices. Meanwhile, sprinkle the onion with the salt, black pepper and cinnamon (if used) and rub these in with your fingers (they reduce the sharpness of the onion), then add to the *burghol* and tomato in the bowl. Add the lemon juice, oil, mint and parsley, and mix well; taste and adjust the seasonings. If the *tabbouleh* is not moist enough, mix in about 1½ tbs water.

Serve immediately with leaves of cos lettuce or (if tender) cabbage. To eat, pile the *tabbouleh* into the hollow of a leaf.

Bread Salad
Fattoush

Fattoush is a substantial salad which combines the greens and vegetables found in all kitchen gardens in Lebanon, and is second in popularity to *tabbouleh*. It consists of purslane (which comes in bunches like watercress, but has a light green colour, thick pear shape and smooth, matt, slippery leaves, with a unique mild flavour; it is an important herb for *fattoush* but its season is short), parsley, tomatoes, cos lettuce, cucumber, radishes, spring onions, mint and toasted bread, flavoured with lemon juice, olive oil and *sumak*, which has a pleasant sour taste. These ingredients provide a wealth of nutrients and antioxidants that increase vitality and protect the body from illnesses and premature ageing. The salad is characterized by the distinctive tastes of *sumak* and purslane.

The preparation of *fattoush* is easy but it takes a little time. In my recipe I have added some chopped rocket leaves and a few cauliflower florets cut into tiny pieces the size of chick-peas; these give the salad a deeper flavour, especially when purslane is out of season.

Purslane, when in season, can be found at all Lebanese and Greek grocers.

Ingredients

1 clove of garlic, peeled
1¼ tsp salt or to taste
4 tbs lemon juice
4 tbs extra virgin olive oil
1 tbs *sumak*
285 g (10 oz) ripe tomatoes, rinsed and chopped into 1¼ cm (½ in) cubes
4–5 large spring onions, trimmed, rinsed, thinly sliced
6 radishes, trimmed, rinsed, coarsely chopped or thinly sliced
2 cauliflower florets, rinsed and cut into tiny pieces (optional)
1 green pepper, seeded, rinsed and coarsely chopped
1 baby cucumber, rinsed, cut lengthwise and sliced
a handful of rocket leaves (about 45 g/1½ oz), rinsed and chopped
¼ tsp freshly milled black pepper
half a bunch of parsley (about 85 g/3 oz with stems on), leaves stripped off, rinsed
    and used whole or coarsely chopped
a handful of mint leaves, rinsed and chopped
half a head of cos lettuce (8 leaves), rinsed well, drained and shredded into 11/4 cm
    (1/2 in) ribbons
1½ medium-sized pitta breads, toasted until crisp, torn up into small pieces

In a large salad bowl, crush the garlic with ¼ the amount of salt, until smooth and creamy; add the lemon juice and 1 tbs only of the oil. Add the *sumak* and the tomatoes, sprinkled with the remaining salt to bring out their full flavour. Add the spring onions, the radishes, the cauliflower florets (if used), the green pepper, the cucumber and the rocket leaves and season with the black pepper. Add the parsley, mint and lettuce. Set aside for a minute.

In a separate small bowl toss the toasted bread in the remaining oil, coating it on all sides; this will keep it crunchy for longer. Add to the reserved salad mixture and toss well with the other ingredients. Taste, adjust the seasonings and add more oil if necessary.

Serve immediately as a main dish, a starter or as an accompaniment to other dishes.

The various components of *fattoush* can be prepared in advance, but do not combine them until just before serving.

Cabbage Salad
Salatet malfouf

Cabbage salad normally accompanies the national dish, *kibbeh*. In Lebanon cabbage has moister, more tender leaves than those grown in Europe. It is therefore more suited for salads and for eating with *tabbouleh*.

The Romans, who incidentally introduced cabbage to Britain, regarded it as a panacea against the discomforts of high living as well as a neutralizer of the effects of alcohol. The Roman censor Marcus Cato strongly advised the inclusion of raw cabbage in the diet as a prophylactic. He himself lived to the age of 85, living proof of its efficacy. Cabbage is an excellent source of the antioxidant vitamin C and of iron, and scientists from various countries are engaged in research into its curative properties. There is already strong evidence that it stimulates the immune system, can lower the risk of cancer and kills bacteria and viruses.

In this recipe I have added tomatoes to give moisture to the salad and top up the nutritional intake.

Ingredients

1 clove of garlic, peeled
1 tsp salt or to taste
3⅔ tbs extra virgin olive oil
2½–3 tbs lemon juice
115 g (4 oz) tomatoes, rinsed and chopped into 1¼ cm (½ in) pieces
½ head cabbage (preferably white),
   rinsed and very thinly shredded

In a bowl, crush the garlic with the salt. Add the oil and the lemon juice. Add the tomatoes and finally the shredded cabbage. Toss, coating them thoroughly with the dressing. Taste and adjust the seasonings. Serve immediately. Eat with *kibbeh*, *kibbet al-samak* or *moújaddara*.

Bread salad (*fattoush*)

Variation: Add some cooked or freshly shredded beetroot or substitute it for the tomatoes.

Purslane and Tomato Salad
Salatet al-bakli

The peppery purslane has grown for centuries in the Middle East. It is a valuable herb, containing a high concentration of Omega 3 (*see glossary*) and vitamin C and having natural diuretic properties. Purslane blends well with other herbs and its distinctive taste crowns the famous Lebanese *fattoush*. It is also used as a filling in *fatayer*. Its leaves are delicate and bruise very quickly, so they must be rinsed very gently. This exceptionally healthy salad is delicious and goes well with grain dishes.

Ingredients

1 clove of garlic peeled and crushed
2–3 tbs extra virgin olive oil
2 tbs lemon juice
1 onion (about 115 g/4 oz) peeled, cut into thin slices; or
    4 spring onions, both ends trimmed, rinsed and cut thickly
225 g (8 oz) tomatoes, rinsed and quartered
$1^{1}/_{4}$ tsp salt, or to taste
1 tsp sumak (optional)
2 bunches (about 400 g/14 oz) of purslane; strip off leaves keeping
    very tender stems, rinse, drain

In a salad bowl, add the garlic, oil, lemon juice, onions and tomatoes, seasoned all over with the salt to bring out more of their flavour. Sprinkle on the sumak if used. Stir well. Add the purslane and toss gently.

Serve as an accompaniment to fish, chicken or pulse dishes. Eat with a good whole-meal bread and a few green olives.

Oriental Salad
Salata arabieh

Salata arabieh is prepared with a combination of many of the vegetables found in abundance in Lebanon. Here they create an extremely nourishing and refreshing salad, rich in the antioxidants A and C, along with other valuable vitamins and minerals. The ingredients are crunchy, moist cos lettuce, wonderful sun-ripened tomatoes, strongly flavoured onions, juicy cucumber and aromatic mint, all tossed in the classic anti-viral Lebanese dressing—lemon juice, garlic and olive oil.

In this salad I use cos lettuce, native to the Mediterranean, which spread into the rest of Europe from Italy only in the 16th century. It is believed that eating lettuce induces sleep. The Persian Kings of around 500 bc ate it and the Egyptians at the time of the Pharaohs represented it in some of their paintings.

Ingredients

1 clove of garlic, peeled
1 tsp salt, or to taste
2$\frac{1}{2}$ tbs lemon juice
2–3 tbs extra virgin olive oil
400 g (14 oz) tomatoes, rinsed and cut into 1$\frac{1}{4}$ cm ($\frac{1}{2}$ in) cubes
3 large spring onions, trimmed, rinsed and thinly sliced
a handful of mint leaves, rinsed and chopped (or 2 tsp dried crushed mint)
a few radishes (about 8), rinsed and sliced
1 baby cucumber, rinsed and sliced
$\frac{1}{4}$ tsp freshly milled black pepper
1 small head of cos lettuce (about 8–10 leaves),
    rinsed, drained, shredded into 1$\frac{1}{4}$ cm ($\frac{1}{2}$ in) ribbons
45 g (1$\frac{1}{2}$ oz) parsley leaves, rinsed, drained

In a salad bowl crush the garlic with ¼ tsp of the salt until a smooth paste. Add the lemon juice, oil, and tomatoes, sprinkled with the remaining salt to bring out their flavour; add the onions, mint (fresh or dried), radishes and cucumber. Stir well. Season with the black pepper. Finally add the cos lettuce and the parsley leaves. Toss them well. Serve and eat accompanied with chicken kebab.

Thyme Salad
Salatet al-zaatar al-akhdar

Thyme, fresh or dried, is loved by the Lebanese. This invigorating and aromatic salad is very simple to prepare when one variety of fresh thyme is in season. For this recipe, I have used the thyme that has dense, elongated, pointed, green tender leaves.

Another variety of thyme is a bushy shrub with strongly flavoured leaves, which bears green blooms with a touch of white. It is picked, dried, crushed and stored in an airtight container after being mixed with *sumak*, toasted sesame seeds and a little salt, to be used for *manakish* or eaten mixed in olive oil with pitta bread as a sandwich.

Since it is believed in Lebanon that thyme strengthens the memory, most students used to consume it in large quantities before their exams. Thyme is said to stimulate the circulation and aid in the digestion of fatty foods.

This recipe uses fresh thyme, which is different in appearance and taste from the English one, and is normally served as a part of the *mezze* or as an accompaniment to other dishes. When in season, starting in May, you can buy it in bunches from all Lebanese or Greek grocers.

Ingredients

1 clove of garlic, peeled
1 tsp salt, or to taste
2½ tbs extra virgin olive oil
2–3 tbs lemon juice
85 g (3 oz) onion, peeled and sliced or finely chopped
1 bunch of fresh thyme (about 200 g/7 oz); strip off
    leaves and very tender stems only, rinse and drain

In a bowl crush the garlic with the salt until smooth. Add the oil and the lemon juice and stir vigorously to combine well. Add the onions and the thyme and toss them well. Serve with pitta bread and a side dish of green olives.

Note: If you like, you can garnish the salad with about 12 pitted green olives.

Tomato and Onion Salad
Salata bi-banadoura wa-bassal

If the fridge is empty of greens, this is the salad to prepare. Onions or spring onions can be used.

In Lebanon during the dry season tomatoes are not watered, so they are called *baal*, the Phoenician name for the god of fertility. Another name derived from Baal is Baalbeck (with its famous Roman temple built in the 2nd century AD), which was renamed Heliopolis by the Greeks.

Tomatoes, also called love apples, are flavourful and highly valued for their antioxidant vitamins A and C. Onions, praised as a natural antibiotic, were greatly valued by the Greeks for their curative powers. In Lebanon, onions are eaten raw in large quantities and are also used to flavour and enliven most dishes.

Ingredients

1 clove of garlic, peeled

1¼ tsp salt, or to taste

3–4 tbs extra virgin olive oil

1½ tbs lemon juice

550 g (1¼ lb) tomatoes, rinsed and cut into 2 cm (¾ in) pieces

1 medium-sized onion, peeled and finely chopped; or 4 large spring onions, trimmed, rinsed and sliced

In a salad bowl, crush the garlic with ¼ the amount of salt until smooth. Add the oil and lemon juice and stir. Add the tomatoes, sprinkled with the remaining salt, and finally the onions. Toss them well with the dressing. Serve immediately. It is delicious eaten with grilled *kafta* and pitta bread.

Artichoke Salad

Salatet ardichowki

The artichoke, this wonderful exotic vegetable, is native to the Mediterranean. Its Arabic name, *al-kharshuf*, is the origin of both the Italian name, *carciofo* and the Spanish name, *alcachofa*.

In 1533 the Florentine Catherine de' Medici brought the artichoke to France with her dowry when she married the heir to the throne. Afterwards Henry VIII took to it, not surprisingly, for its alleged aphrodisiac qualities.

Artichoke has a subtle, sweet taste and is an excellent source of fibre and vitamin C. In Lebanon artichokes are prepared in various ways, of which this artichoke salad is one.

Ingredients

6 to 8 fresh artichokes, rinsed

1 clove of garlic, peeled

I tsp salt, or to taste

2–3 tbs lemon juice

2½–3 tbs extra virgin olive oil

a handful of parsley leaves (about 2 heaped tbs), rinsed, drained and finely chopped

½ tsp cayenne pepper (optional)

Cut off and discard the stalk close to the base of each artichoke. Place the artichokes in one large or two smaller saucepans. Cover with boiling salted water. Bring to the boil and simmer for 30–40 minutes, or until the bases of the artichokes are tender. Remove from the water and drain, base up, in a colander.

Gently remove all outer leaves (the fleshy ends of these can be eaten separately as an appetizer) until you reach the heart of the artichoke with the choke in the middle. With a spoon or a sharp knife gently remove the choke and discard. Rub each heart with lemon to prevent discolouration, and cut crosswise to make four equal pieces. Continue until all artichokes are ready.

In a salad bowl crush the garlic with the salt until a smooth paste; add the lemon juice and stir gently. Toss the pieces of artichoke. Add the olive oil, stir, taste and adjust the seasonings. Finally sprinkle with parsley and cayenne pepper, if used.

Serve as an accompaniment to a protein dish.

Note: The artichokes can be steamed for about 20 minutes until tender; this will retain more of their nutrients.

Monk's Salad

Batinjan al-raheb

This superbly healthy salad is attributed to a head monk (*raheb*), who was inordinately fond of aubergines that had been grilled, scooped out of their skins and puréed, then garnished with green peppers, tomatoes and onions, and topped with olive oil. It is said that the monk gave orders to the convent's cook to prepare this dish whenever aubergine was in season (i.e. summer). I am sure that the monk not only liked this dish but also recognized its excellent nutritional value.

Ingredients

2–3 small aubergines, about 900 g (2 lb), rinsed
1 large clove of garlic, peeled and crushed
1½ tsp salt, or to taste
2 tbs lemon juice
1 green pepper, rinsed, de-seeded and finely chopped
200 g (7 oz) tomatoes, washed and finely chopped
3 large spring onions, trimmed, rinsed, thinly sliced
a handful of parsley leaves (about 2 heaped tbs) rinsed, drained
3 tbs extra virgin olive oil
½ tsp chilli pepper (optional)

Slit the skin of each aubergine once or twice. Put the aubergines on a baking sheet and place it under a pre-heated grill. Cook for about 15–20 minutes or until the flesh is blackened and blistered and the pulp is soft.

Meanwhile on a serving platter mash the garlic with the salt. Remove the cooked aubergines from the grill, cool slightly and scrape the pulp from skin. Add this to the garlic in the platter and, with a fork, mash and mix with the garlic (this can be done in a blender but make sure you do not purée it too much). Add the lemon juice, work it well into the aubergine and spread mixture evenly. Arrange green pepper, tomatoes, spring onions and parsley all over the mashed aubergine pulp. Cover with oil and sprinkle with chilli pepper, if used. Serve and eat with wholemeal pitta bread.

Note: When fresh sour pomegranate is in season, garnish the dish with its seeds to top up the flavour and the nutrients.

Green Bean Salad
Salatet loubieh

The green bean is also known as the French bean because it was taken from France to England in 1594. It is favoured for its crispy pod and flavoursome seeds.

Inhabitants of villages in Lebanon used to pick the *loubieh* in September, dry it and store it as a supply for winter. Like most salads this one is easy to prepare and makes an excellent accompaniment to barbecued food.

I like to steam green beans, to retain the maximum nutrients.

Ingredients

225 g (8 oz) green beans, topped, tailed, strings removed and rinsed
1 small clove of garlic, peeled
1 tsp salt or to taste
2–3 tbs lemon juice
85 g (3 oz) onion, peeled, sliced into half-moon shapes
3 tbs extra virgin olive oil
¼ tsp freshly milled black pepper (optional)

Arrange the green beans over a stainless steel steaming basket and set into a saucepan over 2½ cm (1 in) of boiling water. Cover tightly and cook until tender but not very soft (about 10–12 minutes), to retain their nutrients and flavour. Meanwhile in a salad bowl crush the garlic with the salt. Add the lemon juice and then the onions and oil.

Remove the beans from the steamer, add to the salad bowl and toss well with the dressing and onions. Serve warm or cold with pitta bread and *shish kebab*.

Vegetable Salad
Salatet al-khodar

This salad is prepared with whatever seasonal vegetables you have to hand. *Salatet al-khodar* is bursting with valuable antioxidants and fibre that may help to prevent cancer and other degenerative diseases.

Ingredients

275–335 g (10–12 oz) potatoes, washed but unpeeled
225 g (8 oz) green beans, topped and tailed and rinsed
1 medium-sized carrot, peeled and thickly sliced
4 florets of cauliflower, rinsed
4 florets of broccoli, rinsed
1 medium-sized marrow, rinsed and thickly sliced
1 clove of garlic, peeled and crushed
1 tsp salt, or to taste
2–3 tbs extra virgin olive oil
3 tbs lemon juice
½ bunch watercress, rinsed; strip off the leaves with tender stems

Put the potatoes into a saucepan and add sufficient boiling water to cover. Cook the potatoes for about 15 minutes or until tender (different kinds vary as to time). Remove from the saucepan, cool slightly and cut into 1¼ cm (½ in) cubes and reserve. Save some of the liquid to steam the vegetables.

Put a stainless steel disk in the same saucepan with 2½ cm (1 in) of water and place on it the beans, carrot slices, florets of cauliflower and broccoli and slices of marrow and steam for about 8–10 minutes or until tender but not overcooked.

Meanwhile in a serving bowl mash the garlic with the salt, add the olive oil and lemon juice and stir well. Add the reserved potatoes and toss with the oil dressing, then add the steamed vegetables. Toss gently. Garnish with the watercress, which adds a peppery flavour to the salad as well as an abundance of mineral salts such as iron, iodine, calcium sulphate and vitamin C.

Serve warm or cold. Eat on its own or as an accompaniment to whitebait. For variety add cooked beetroot.

Potato Salad
Salatet al-batata

It is said that the 17th-century Emir of Lebanon, Fakhreddin, introduced the potato to the country after returning from exile in Tuscany. Since that time, potatoes have been extensively used in Lebanese cuisine. The Arabic name is *batata*, the name given to the sweet potato in the Caribbean, the area where the potato originated. Potatoes are very nutritious and, when boiled, low in calories. In my recipe the potatoes are left unpeeled to retain most of their nutrients and flavour.

Ingredients

450 g (1 lb) potatoes, well rinsed, unpeeled

For the dressing
1 clove garlic, peeled
¾ tsp salt, or to taste
1–1½ tbs extra virgin olive oil
1 tbs lemon juice
¼ tsp cinnamon
¼ tsp freshly milled black pepper
½ tsp paprika (optional)
2 tbs chopped parsley

Put the potatoes into a saucepan and add sufficient boiling water to cover; return to the boil, reduce the heat to medium, cover and simmer until tender (about 10–15 minutes or longer, depending on the variety). Remove potatoes, drain and let cool slightly.

Meanwhile prepare the dressing. In a serving bowl crush the garlic with the salt. Add the oil, lemon juice, cinnamon and black pepper; stir well. Cut the potatoes into 1¼ cm (½ in) cubes, add them to the dressing and toss gently. Sprinkle with the paprika, if used, and the parsley. Eat with baked fish.

Potato Salad with Cream of Sesame
Salatet al-batata bi-tahini

An interesting combination of flavours produces this tasty salad, which is both highly nutritious and filling. *Salatet al-batata bi-tahini* is easy to prepare and makes an excellent dish for a variety of occasions. Potatoes are blended with *tahini* cream (*see below*). *Tahini* is basically ground sesame seeds, and is widely used in the Middle East to give added flavour, even to sweet dishes.

Ingredients

450 g (1 lb) potatoes, well washed, unpeeled

For the sauce
1 clove of garlic, peeled

1 tsp salt, or to taste
4 tbs *tahini*
4 tbs lemon juice
4 tbs water
½ tsp paprika (optional)
1 heaped tbs parsley, chopped, rinsed, drained

Put the potatoes in a saucepan and add boiling water to cover, return to boil, cover and simmer over moderate heat until they are tender (about 10–15 minutes or longer, depending on the variety).

Meanwhile prepare the sauce. In a bowl crush the garlic with the salt until smooth. Add the *tahini* and lemon juice and whisk well. Add the water and keep whisking the sauce until it forms a liquid like cream.

When the potatoes are ready, drain, cool slightly and cut into 1¼ cm (½ in) cubes, toss with the *tahini* sauce; sprinkle with paprika, if used, and chopped parsley. Serve immediately or cover and chill.

Chick-Pea Salad
Balila

The preparation of *balila* is simplicity itself. The chick-pea originated in Western Asia and is one of the most nutritious beans, rich in protein, carbohydrates, fibre and valuable vitamins and minerals; but it is free of gluten, of which some people are intolerant. This salad, which is popular throughout the Middle East, is served as part of the *mezze* and eaten with bread. Traditionally *balila* is prepared without lemon juice, but if you wish, add about 1½ tbs of lemon juice.

Ingredients

225 g (8 oz) chick-peas, picked over, soaked overnight, rinsed and drained
about 1.4–1.7 l (2½–3 pints) water
1 clove garlic, peeled, crushed
1 tsp salt, or to taste
1 tbs light *tahini* (optional)
3–4 tbs extra virgin olive oil or to taste
1 tsp ground cumin (optional)

Drain the beans and rinse under running water; drain again and place in a large saucepan covered with water over medium–high heat. Skim the foam from the surface of the water and bring to the boil. Reduce the heat to medium–low, cover and simmer until very soft, about 1½–2 hours. Alternatively, cook in a pressure cooker, following the maker's instructions, for about 40 minutes.

Drain the chick-peas, reserving 3 tbs of the cooking liquid. Meanwhile place the garlic, salt and *tahini* (if used) in a serving bowl; add the reserved cooking liquid and the chick-peas, crushing part of them lightly. Drizzle the olive oil all over and toss. Season with cumin, if used.

Serve immediately. Eat with wholemeal bread, onions and watercress.

Brown Bean Salad
Foul m'dammas

Foul m'dammas is the staple food of the poor, but it occupies an honoured place in Lebanese cuisine. It is traditionally either eaten at breakfast with pitta bread, and washed down with cups of Turkish coffee, or is part of the *mezze*, where it is served with *tabbouleh*, *hoummos*, *baba ghannouj* and many other dishes.

The humble brown bean (*foul*), is thought to have garnished the Pharaoh's table in Egypt, where it originated. In Lebanon *foul* preparation differs slightly from that used in Egypt. It is simple to prepare, flavourful and healthy.

Ingredients

200 g (7 oz) dry *foul*, picked over, soaked overnight, drained and rinsed
600 ml (21 fl oz) water
1 tsp salt
5 tbs extra virgin olive oil
1–2 cloves garlic, peeled
3–4 tbs lemon juice
3 tbs chopped parsley, rinsed, drained
½ tsp paprika (optional)

Put the dry beans and the water in a pan over a high heat. Add the salt and 1 tbs of the oil, and bring to the boil. Reduce the heat to low, cover and simmer for about 40–45 minutes or until the *foul* are tender.

Meanwhile in a bowl crush the garlic. Add the *foul*, with the reduced liquid, probably about half a cup, and stir well, mashing the *foul* lightly to coat with the garlic. Add the lemon juice, stir and top with the remaining olive oil.

Sprinkle with the parsley and paprika if used. Serve hot. Eat with wholemeal pitta bread, onions and radishes.

Variation: To make *foul moutamam* (*foul* with chick-peas), prepare half the amount of chick-pea salad and place on top of the brown bean salad. Eat with wholemeal bread and onions.

Brown bean salad (*foul moutamam*)

Butter Bean Salad
Salatet al-fassoulia al-baida

Butter beans have a delicious and distinctive flavour and are nourishing while being low in fat and high in fibre, essential for the efficient functioning of the digestive system. The succulent butter bean salad is one of my favourites, as it is for many Lebanese. Eat with a good-quality wholemeal bread to provide a balance of nutrients and satisfy the appetite.

Ingredients

225 g (8 oz) butter beans, soaked 6 hours in water, rinsed, drained
1.1–1.4 l (2–2½ pints) water
1 clove of garlic, peeled, crushed to a smooth paste
¾ tsp salt, or to taste
3 tbs lemon juice
2 tbs extra virgin olive oil
a handful of parsley leaves, finely chopped and rinsed
¼ tsp cayenne pepper (optional)

In a large pan over medium heat place the beans and the water, skim the foam from the surface of the water, bring to the boil and reduce the heat to moderately low; cover and simmer beans until tender but not disintegrating, about 40–60 minutes.

Meanwhile in a salad bowl combine the garlic, salt, lemon juice and oil, drain the beans, add and toss gently with the combined ingredients. Sprinkle with the parsley and cayenne pepper if used. Serve and eat with wholemeal pitta bread and a mixture of vegetables such as spring onions and radishes.

Variation: Add 1 large diced steamed carrot or about 55 g (2 oz) of coarsely chopped rocket leaves.

Lentil Salad
Salatet al-adas

Archaeological finds indicate that lentils were widespread from China to Europe in ancient times. After all, Esau sold his birthright for a plate of red lentils!

The lentil, sometimes called 'the poor man's dish', has fortunately turned out to be an excellent provider of protein, fibre and a variety of minerals. It is low in fat as well as cholesterol-free.

Lentils come in various colours: green, brown and orange-red when split. This salad calls for brown lentils. It is tasty and requires few ingredients, so whenever the cupboard begins to look bare and I am too lazy to go shopping, lentil salad comes first to my mind.

Ingredients

200 g (7 oz) brown lentils, picked over and rinsed
650–700 ml (23–25 fl oz) water
1 tsp salt, or to taste
1 clove of garlic, peeled
2–3 tbs lemon juice
3–4 tbs extra virgin olive oil
½ tsp cumin, or to taste

Combine the lentils and water in a saucepan, add ½ tsp salt and bring to the boil over a high heat. Reduce to moderate heat, cover and simmer lentils for about 35–45 minutes (time varies with origin of produce). Check the water level at intervals and if necessary add a little boiling water.

Meanwhile in a salad bowl crush the garlic with the remaining salt. Add the lentils with their reduced liquid to the garlic in the salad bowl and stir well, mashing lightly. Add the lemon juice and olive oil and stir again. Sprinkle with the cumin.

Serve hot or warm. Eat with wholemeal pitta bread and lots of spring onions.

Note: If desired, garnish with a handful of finely chopped parsley leaves.

'Fried' Potatoes
Batata 'mikli'

Fried potatoes are irresistible and loved by old and young alike. In Lebanon fried potatoes come with *mezze*, on request, or as an accompaniment to *shawarma* (lamb and chicken kebab).

Because fried potatoes have a high fat content and take a long time to cook on a gas ring, I decided to try the oven. The potatoes are left unpeeled and cut as if they were to be fried, then combined with olive oil, but in a diminutive amount compared to the oil used for frying. My daughter Nour and her friends assure me that potatoes cooked in this way are superior in taste to ordinary fried potatoes and crunchier. They are also lighter. I recommend you give them a try: potatoes are healthy and filling.

Ingredients

4–5 tbs extra virgin olive oil
1 kg (2¼ lb) potatoes, unpeeled but washed and scrubbed
salt to taste (optional)

Pre-heat the oven to 220° C (425° F/gas mark 8). On a chopping board cut the potatoes lengthwise into 1¼ cm (½ in) slices, then cut each slice, as best you can, into uniform sticks. Put these in the oil and turn them well, to coat them all over with oil, then arrange evenly on a baking sheet and put in the oven. Bake for 50 minutes or until golden and crunchy.

Serve hot, sprinkled with salt if used.

Fried Cauliflower
Arnabit mikli

Cauliflower was grown in Egypt as early as 400 BC and in Syria as early as 200 BC. This recipe is a delicious way of preparing cauliflower. Traditionally the florets are boiled for quite some time in water, which means that many of the nutrients are lost. In my recipe they are steamed, but then have to be deep-fried.

Ingredients

450 g (1 lb) cauliflower florets, stems peeled, rinsed
1 tsp salt
olive oil for deep-frying

Put 2½ cm (1 in) of water into a saucepan, bring to the boil and carefully place a steaming basket in the pan. Spread the cauliflower out in the basket. Cover and steam over moderate heat for 5–7 minutes or until tender. Remove cauliflower from steamer and allow to cool slightly.

Meanwhile in a frying pan heat the oil until hot but not smoking (about 190° C/375° F) and fry the cauliflower florets until golden colour. Remove from pan and drain on kitchen paper. Arrange on a serving dish.

Serve hot or cold. Eat with wholemeal pitta bread, dipping it in *tahini* sauce.

Fried Aubergine
Batinjan mikli

The aubergine is native to India; it reached Arabia, then Spain, through Arab traders during the Middle Ages, and arrived in France as late as the eighteenth century. It is rich in fibre and low in fat, which counterbalances the amount of oil it absorbs when being fried. It is said, without definitive medical evidence, that aubergine is beneficial in the prevention of cancer and damage to the arteries.

Aubergines are available all year round in different shapes and sizes. Aubergine dishes, prepared and enjoyed all around the Mediterranean, are deeply satisfying and full of flavour. The versatility of the aubergine means that it blends harmoniously with almost any ingredient.

This easy recipe provides a magnificent accompaniment to barbecued dishes. Traditionally the aubergine is thinly sliced lengthwise and fried. Because of its spongy texture, it soaks up a fair amount of oil; with the recent trend towards healthy eating, a number of people choose to grill the vegetables rather than fry them. Whichever method you choose, select a firm aubergine, dark in colour, with a smooth, shiny skin. To grill, brush the slices of aubergine with oil on both sides and cook under a pre-heated grill about 10 cm (4 in) from the heat until golden brown on both sides.

Ingredients

675 g (1½ lb) aubergines, rinsed
salt to taste
oil for deep-frying

With a sharp knife, cut through and discard the stem ends of the aubergines, cut aubergines lengthwise into ½ cm (¼ in) slices, sprinkle generously with salt and allow them to stand in a colander for at least 40 minutes, to draw out their bitter juices and to prevent the absorption of too much oil. Rinse the aubergine slices and pat dry between sheets of kitchen paper. Into a frying pan pour about ½ cm (¼ in) of oil, place over moderate heat; when oil is hot but not smoking sauté the aubergines until lightly browned on both sides. Remove with a slotted spoon and drain on kitchen papers. Sprinkle with salt and eat with bread.

Okra in Oil
Bamieh bi-zeit

Okra originated in Africa and is one of the oldest vegetables known. This is a traditional okra dish; another is a homely stew with diced lamb, eaten with rice, generally at lunchtime.

While the okra, tomatoes, coriander, onions and garlic are simmering over a low flame, the okra releases a glutinous substance, which thickens the sauce.

In this tasty and healthful recipe, okra is grilled instead of fried.

Ingredients

550 g (1¼ lb) okra, rinsed, top pointed stem peeled (not cut) off
225 g (8 oz) onions, peeled and thinly sliced into half moon shapes
8–10 large cloves of garlic, peeled, cut into two
1½ tsp salt, or to taste
2 tbs extra virgin olive oil
85 g (3 oz) coriander, roots cut off, rinsed and finely chopped

550 g (1¼ lb) ripe tomatoes, rinsed, quartered
½ tsp cinnamon
½ tsp allspice
¼ tsp black pepper
5–6 tbs boiling water
3½ tbs lemon juice

Pre-heat the grill, rinse the okra, drain in a colander and put on a baking sheet. Grill for 3–5 minutes, then remove and reserve. Into a pan put the onions, garlic, ½ tsp of the salt and the oil, mix thoroughly to coat. Place the pan over moderately high heat, cover and allow to cook undisturbed for 3 minutes. After that reduce the heat to medium, uncover and stir occasionally until the onions and garlic are transparent and slightly golden in colour (about 5 more minutes). The onion juices will coat the pan and caramelize, which adds to the flavour. Add the coriander, stir for a minute to bring out its full flavour, add the tomatoes. Season with the remaining salt, the cinnamon, the allspice and the black pepper. Add the reserved okra and the water, cover and simmer over medium heat for 20–25 minutes or until tender. Remove the lid, pour the lemon juice all over, cover for one minute and transfer to a serving dish.

Eat warm or cold, with radishes and wholemeal pitta bread.

Variation: For a lighter dish, place 200 ml (about 7 fl oz) of water along with the onions in a pan, bring to the boil, cover and simmer over medium heat for 6–8 minutes; add all remaining ingredients except for the oil—add ½ tbs only—and cook until okra is soft and flavours have blended (about 20–30 minutes).

Broad Beans in Oil
Foul akhdar bi-zeit

The broad bean, also known as the *fava* bean, is popular in the Mediterranean where it originated. In Lebanon the inner beans of young, tender broad beans are eaten as an appetizer, but this is not advisable because raw or undercooked beans can cause favism, an acute anaemia.

Broad beans are an excellent food, rich in fibre, with an abundance of the B vitamins and also many minerals such as iron, phosphorus and magnesium. This superbly aromatic dish is very easy to prepare and much appreciated by the Lebanese as an accompaniment to other dishes.

Ingredients

2 tbs extra virgin olive oil
2 medium onions (about 255 g/9 oz) peeled, finely chopped

500 g (1 lb 2 oz) broad beans, topped, tailed, string removed, cut into pieces 2½ cm (1 in) long

3–4 large garlic cloves, peeled and crushed

½ bunch of fresh coriander (about 100 g/3½ oz), roots cut off, tough stems removed, rinsed, drained, chopped

1 tsp flour

1 tsp salt or to taste

¼ tsp cinnamon

¼ tsp freshly milled black pepper

a pinch of allspice

150 ml (a little under ⅓ pint) hot water

2 tbs lemon juice

Heat the oil in a medium-sized pan over moderately high heat, add the onions and sauté until pale and transparent, stirring all the time (about a minute). Add the beans, cover, reduce heat to medium and let them sweat in their own juices for 8 minutes. Uncover the pan, add the garlic, coriander and flour, stir them with the beans for a few seconds. Season with salt, cinnamon, black pepper and allspice, add the water, cover and simmer gently over medium–low heat for 15 minutes or until tender. When time is up turn the heat off, add the lemon juice, stir; cover the pan again and let it stand for 2 minutes to allow the flavours to mellow.

Serve warm or at room temperature. Eat with wholemeal bread to top up the nutrients.

Green Beans in Oil
Loubieh bi-zeit

Loubieh bi-zeit is nutritious, very tasty and quite popular all over Lebanon. It is prepared with onions and garlic, cooked in oil and left to simmer over a low flame with equal amounts of fresh green beans and juicy tomatoes. It can be prepared ahead of time.

Ingredients

2–3 tbs extra virgin olive oil

200 g (7 oz) onions, peeled and thinly sliced into half-moon shapes

6–7 cloves garlic, peeled and slivered

450 g (1 lb) green beans, topped and tailed, strings removed and rinsed

1¼ tsp salt, or to taste

¼ tsp freshly milled black pepper

¼ tsp cinnamon

¼ tsp allspice

450 g (1 lb) ripe tomatoes, peeled (optional) and thickly sliced

Heat the oil in a saucepan. When it is hot but not smoking, add the onions and garlic and cook over moderately high heat for about 2–3 minutes or until golden brown in colour. Add the green beans, sprinkle with the salt, pepper, cinnamon and allspice. Reduce the heat to moderately low. Cover and let the beans sweat for about 15 minutes, stirring once or twice without disturbing the onions. Add the tomatoes, cover and simmer over moderately low heat for about 20 minutes, allowing the beans to cook in the juices of the tomatoes.

Serve warm or cold. Eat with pitta bread.

Wild Chicory in Oil
Hindbeh bi-zeit

This is a simple peasant dish loved by almost everyone. The wild chicory that grows in Lebanon is dark green in colour, elongated in shape, with a curly edge and a mild bitterness that is reduced by boiling. Wild chicory, believed to have medicinal properties, is a good source of iron and folic acid. It is sold in bunches at Lebanese and Cypriot grocers.

The traditional recipe calls for a large quantity of onions to be browned until crisp, which means that a large amount of oil is necessary. In my recipe the onions are steamed to reduce their bulk, then sautéed gently in a small amount of olive oil. The taste may not be exactly the same as the traditional recipe, but it is delicious, healthy and far lower in calories.

Ingredients

1 kg (2 lb 2 oz) wild chicory, about 2$\frac{1}{2}$ cm (1 in) cut off the roots
30 ml (2 tbs) extra virgin olive oil
3 medium onions (about 400 g/14 oz), peeled, thinly sliced,
    steamed for 4–5 minutes, cool
$\frac{1}{2}$ tsp salt or to taste
$\frac{1}{4}$ tsp freshly milled black pepper
a pinch of allspice (optional)
4 tbs lemon juice or to taste

Wash the wild chicory in plenty of water, but do not leave to soak or nutrients will be lost. Drain. Bring a large pan of water to the boil, add $\frac{1}{2}$ tbs of salt and put the chicory in it, bring back to the boil and boil rapidly for 1 minute. Remove from the water, drain and leave to cool.

Meanwhile heat the oil in a medium pan over moderate heat; when oil is hot but not smoking add the steamed onions, cover with a lid, cook for about 1$\frac{1}{2}$ minutes undisturbed, uncover and cook until onions are brown in colour, but not burnt, stirring occasionally. Remove half the amount to a side dish. After that, lightly squeeze excess water from the chicory, chop coarsely and add to the onions in the pan. Sauté for a minute or so, stirring constantly, season with salt, black pepper and allspice if used. Stir them well and turn the heat off; add the lemon juice and the remaining browned onions to the chicory in the pan and stir them well again to blend. Arrange on a platter.

Serve warm or at room temperature. Eat with wholemeal bread and a few green olives.

Sweet Peppers with Tomatoes
M'tabbakat al-flaifleh

This interesting dish is rich in vitamins A and C and silicon, an organic mineral important for a beautiful complexion and shiny hair.

No oil at all is used in this recipe, which therefore answers perfectly to 20th-century demands for a healthy lifestyle. *M'tabbakat al-flaifleh* is an excellent accompaniment to grilled fish, chicken or lamb.

Ingredients

2 green peppers, de-seeded and cut into strips, rinsed
1 red pepper, de-seeded and cut into strips, rinsed
4 medium-sized tomatoes, rinsed, cubed
1 medium-sized onion (about 115 g/4 oz) peeled and sliced
1 large clove of garlic, peeled, crushed
1 tsp salt, or to taste
¼ tsp freshly milled black pepper
4–6 tbs hot water

In a saucepan combine the peppers, tomatoes, onions and garlic. Season with the salt and freshly milled black pepper; add the water and bring to the boil, then reduce the heat to moderately low. Cover and simmer until tender, about 20 minutes.

Transfer to a serving dish.
Serve with grilled chicken *kebab*.

Aubergine Moussaka
Batinjan m'tabbak bi-zeit)

With its attractive contrasting colours, this nutritious and very tasty Lebanese preparation is inspired by an Ottoman recipe and is unlike the Greek recipe, despite the similarity in names. The aubergines, onions, garlic and chick-peas are sautéed in a generous amount of olive oil, then simmered with fresh, ripe tomatoes, heightened by spices and the delicious, fragrant pomegranate syrup. A multitude of glorious flavours swim through the rich tomato sauce. In this recipe, use small aubergines; if not available cut large ones into 1¼ cm (½ in) cubes, then follow the instructions below.

Ingredients

12 baby aubergines (about 450 g/1 lb), rinsed
4 tbs olive oil
1 onion (about 250 g/9 oz) peeled, thinly sliced
10–12 small cloves of garlic, peeled and left whole or thickly slivered
115 g (4 oz) chick-peas, soaked overnight, rinsed, drained and pre-cooked for 1 hour
1½ tbs pomegranate syrup (optional)
450 g (1 lb) tomatoes, rinsed and quartered
1½ tsp salt or to taste
½ tsp cinnamon
½ tsp allspice
¼ tsp freshly milled black pepper
200 ml (⅓ pint) water

Trim the green tops of the aubergines, leaving one half of the stem intact; peel, leaving lengthwise stripes about 1¼ cm (½ in) wide, as prepared traditionally. In a pan heat 3 tbs of oil over medium heat and sauté the aubergines for a minute or two or until golden brown. With a slotted spoon remove to a side dish and reserve. To the pan add the remaining oil, the onions and the garlic and sauté, stirring constantly until pale in colour and soft (about 2–3 minutes), adding more oil if necessary. Add the chick-peas and stir occasionally for 5 minutes longer, add the pomegranate syrup, if used. Return the reserved aubergines to the pan. Add the tomatoes, sprinkle with the salt, cinnamon, allspice and black pepper and add the water, bring to the boil and quickly reduce the heat to moderately low. Cover and simmer for 30–40 minutes.

Serve warm or cold. Eat with wholemeal bread as a starter or a main dish, or serve as part of a large buffet.

Potatoes with Garlic and Coriander
M'tabbakat al-batata bi-kouzbara

This is a very tasty dish of the utmost simplicity, originally from south Lebanon. The robust flavours of fresh spices and olive oil are pleasant and marry well with the potatoes. Traditionally the potatoes are peeled, cubed and fried in oil until golden, along with the remaining ingredients. In this recipe I do not fry or peel the potatoes as their skin contains a substance that may prevent cancer and other diseases. If you like potatoes crisp, roast them unpeeled in a hot oven, then follow the recipe for the other steps.

Ingredients

900 g (2 lb) potatoes, washed, unpeeled
1 tsp salt, or to taste
3 tbs extra virgin olive oil
¼ tsp freshly milled black pepper
¼ tsp cinnamon
3 cloves of garlic, peeled and crushed
¼ bunch of coriander (about 2 oz); roots cut off, rinsed, drained, chopped finely
2 tbs lemon juice
¼ tsp cayenne pepper (optional)

Pre-heat oven to 220° C (425° F/gas mark 7). Cut potatoes into small pieces, about 1¼ cm (½ in) cubes, sprinkle all over with the salt, add the oil, mix until the potatoes are coated evenly with the oil. Place in the oven and bake for 30–40 minutes. Remove potatoes from oven; sprinkle all over with the black pepper and cinnamon. Add the garlic, coriander and lemon juice, gently mix them to prevent breaking the potatoes, return the potatoes to the oven, reduce heat to 200° C (400° F/gas mark 6), cook for a further 10 minutes, or more if you like them crisper.

Serve hot or cold.

Chick-Pea Dip
Hoummos

This dish is rich in B vitamins and minerals. It is extremely popular in the Middle East and, nowadays, known and welcomed all over the world. It is simple to prepare and freezes well when prepared without the garlic. The chick-peas are combined with the light variety of *tahini*, a creamy paste of sesame seeds and oil sold in health shops and supermarkets. The delicious flavour and texture contribute greatly to the appeal of this dish.

Ingredients

225 g (8 oz) dried chick-peas (soaked overnight, rinsed)
1.5–1.75 l (2½–3 pints) water
5 tbs light *tahini*
125–150 ml (4½–5 fl oz) lemon juice
2 cloves garlic, peeled, crushed
1½ tsp salt, or to taste
about 5 tbs cooking liquid (from chick-peas)
¼ tsp cayenne pepper (optional)
2 tbs extra virgin olive oil

Drain the beans and place in a large pan with cold water; skim the foam from the surface and bring to the boil, reduce heat to low, cover and simmer until chick-peas are very soft, about 1½–2 hours. Drain, reserving about half a cup of the cooking liquid and a handful of whole chick-peas to garnish the *hoummos*.

Place the beans, *tahini*, lemon juice, garlic and salt in a food processor; purée until a uniform and smooth consistency, gradually adding the reserved cooking liquid as necessary. Taste and adjust the seasonings, spread over a plate and garnish with the reserved whole chick-peas. Sprinkle with cayenne pepper if desired, and a drizzle of extra virgin olive oil. Eat with wholemeal bread and cos lettuce.

Note: A pressure-cooker will shorten the cooking time, use less water and reduce the loss of nutrients. If you are using one always follow the instructions for your pressure-cooker.

Aubergine Dip
M'tabal al-batinjan

A popular Lebanese classic, *m'tabal al-batinjan* is served cold as part of the *mezze*, together with other tempting dishes. Aubergine can be grilled, baked, charred over an open fire or even steamed; however cooked, it will retain its distinctive taste. This dish is extremely simple to prepare, but is rich in fibre, vitamins and minerals, with a good combination of texture and flavour. *Tahini*, a smooth paste, is added to the puréed flesh along with lemon juice, enhancing its taste and topping up the minerals.

As *tahini* is high in calories, you may like to substitute half the amount with low-fat yoghurt.

Ingredients

675 g (1½ lb) aubergines
1 clove garlic, peeled
¾ tsp salt, or to taste
2½ tbs light *tahini*
3–4 tbs lemon juice
a handful of parsley leaves (about 2 tbs) chopped, rinsed
¼ tsp cayenne pepper
1–2 tbs extra virgin olive oil (optional)

Slit the skin of each aubergine once or twice. Put them on a baking sheet and place under a pre-heated grill 10 cm (4 in) away from the heat. Grill for 20–30 minutes, or until the skin is blackened and blistered and the pulp is soft, turning them once.

Meanwhile in a glass bowl mash the garlic with the salt. Remove aubergine from grill, cool slightly and scrape the pulp from skin, place pulp in a blender and purée for a few

Aubergine dip (*m'tabal al-batinjan*)

seconds only. Remove from blender, add to the garlic and mix, add the *tahini*, stir, and finally add the lemon juice, mix well, taste and adjust the seasonings.

Decorate with parsley, sprinkle with cayenne pepper if desired. Pour olive oil all over if used. Serve and eat with wholemeal bread or cos lettuce leaves.

Note: Decorate the surface of the aubergine dip evenly with the seeds of sour pomegranates when these are in season.

Pumpkin Dip
Laktin m'tabal bi-tahini

Pumpkin is low in fat and an excellent source of the potent antioxidant beta-carotene. This dip is nourishing, tasty, inexpensive and very easy to prepare.

Ingredients

675 g (1½ lb) pumpkin, peeled, de-seeded, cut into 5 cm (2 in) pieces
1 large clove of garlic, peeled
1 tsp salt, or to taste
3 tbs light *tahini*
3 tbs lemon juice

Pour 2½ cm (1 in) of hot water into a saucepan, bring the water to the boil and carefully place a steaming container in the saucepan. Spread the pumpkin pieces, cover, and over moderate heat cook 10 minutes or until tender. Meanwhile in a serving bowl crush the garlic with the salt until a smooth paste. Reserve.

Remove the tender pumpkin pieces, drain, allow to cool and then purée in a blender. Add to the reserved garlic in the bowl, add the *tahini* and lemon juice, mix well, taste and adjust the seasonings. Garnish with parsley.

Eat with cos lettuce and wholemeal bread.

Falafel

Laktin m'tabal bi-tahiniFalafel are an Egyptian speciality, also known as taamia; they are very popular in the Middle East and much enjoyed by the Lebanese in the form of take-away sandwiches. The gloriously rich, fragrant falafel are a delicious combination of puréed chick-peas and broad beans, complemented by a powerful mixture of fresh spices and herbs and made into round cakes; a little raising agent is added to puff up the patties and they are then fried until brown and crisp.

Falafel are ideal as a starter and make an excellent meal for vegetarians. When friends are round for dinner I like to serve a dish of *falafel*, placing each patty in a baby pitta bread pocket with 1 tbs of *tahini* and a mixture of fresh vegetables to enhance the taste.

Ingredients

170 g (6 oz) chick-peas, soaked overnight, rinsed and drained
85 g (3 oz) dried, skinned fava beans, soaked overnight, rinsed and drained
2 large sprigs coriander, leaves only (about 8 g/^{1}/$_4$ oz), rinsed, drained, patted dry
parsley leaves (8 g/^{1}/$_4$ oz) , rinsed, drained and patted dry
a quarter of an onion (about 45 g/1^1/$_2$ oz), preferably white
1 large spring onion, both ends trimmed, yielding 30 g (1 oz), rinsed
4 cloves garlic, peeled, slivered
1 green pepper (about 140 g/5 oz), rinsed, de-seeded, quartered, patted dry
1 red pepper (about 140 g/5 oz), rinsed, de-seeded, quartered, patted dry
1–2 red chilli peppers, de-seeded, rinsed, patted dry
1^3/$_4$ tsp salt, or to taste
2^1/$_2$ tsp ground cumin
2 tsp ground coriander
^{1}/$_4$ tsp black pepper
¼ tsp cayenne pepper or to taste
^{1}/$_2$–^{3}/$_4$ tsp baking soda
4–5 tbs sesame seeds (optional)
good quality peanut oil for deep-frying

Place the chick-peas and fava beans in a blender with the coriander, parsley, onion, garlic, and green, red and chilli peppers. Season with the salt, cumin, ground coriander, black and cayenne peppers. Purée until smooth. Remove the moist dough and place in a bowl, mix and cover with a cloth and allow to stand for at least 1 hour.

Just before frying, mix the baking soda thoroughly. In a small frying saucepan, heat the oil to 190° C (350° F). While the oil is heating make the *falafel* patties: take a small portion of the mixture at a time, flatten and press lightly between the palms of your hands to form a patty 2½ cm (1 in) in diameter; dip one side in the sesame seeds. Gently drop the patties in the hot oil two or three at a time, and allow to fry undisturbed until set, then turn them and fry until golden brown. Remove with a slotted spoon and drain on kitchen paper.

Serve immediately. Eat with *tahini* sauce, a mixture of finely chopped spring onions, chopped tomatoes, sliced radishes and diced cucumber and turnip pickles and wholemeal bread.

Artichokes, Broad Beans and Swiss Chard
Ardichowki bi-foul wa-silk

This wholesome, delicious and filling dish combines varied textures and flavours and is highly nutritious and full of B vitamins, iron and fibre. It is an easy recipe and can be prepared ahead of time; in fact, it tastes even better the next day. Like most Lebanese dishes, if well stored, it will keep for 3–4 days.

Ardichowki bi-foul wa-silk is frequently made in Lebanon, especially when these vegetables are in season, otherwise with frozen artichokes and broad beans are used. Fresh produce naturally has a better taste, although it takes longer to prepare. *Ardichowki bi-foul wa-silk* can be served as a side dish or on its own with pitta bread and a piece of white cheese such as *feta*.

Ingredients

1 tbs extra virgin olive oil
150 g (5½ oz) onions, peeled and chopped
4 cloves of garlic, peeled and crushed
4 sprigs of coriander (about 55 g/2 oz), roots cut off, tough stems
    removed and discarded, rinsed and chopped
675 g (1½ lb) broad beans, podded (makes 280–356 g/10–12 oz)
3½ tbs lemon juice
½ tsp sugar (optional)
225 g (9 oz) silver beet, ends cut off, rinsed, sliced in 1¼ cm (½ in) ribbons
4 artichoke hearts, each cut crosswise into 4 pieces
¼ tsp white pepper
¼ tsp cinnamon
½ tsp allspice
½ tsp salt, or to taste
200–250 ml (7–8 fl oz) boiling water

In a saucepan heat the oil. Add the onions and cook over a high heat for ½ minute, stirring frequently. Reduce the heat to moderate. Continue cooking the onions until golden in colour; add the garlic, stirring frequently for a few seconds. Add the coriander and stir for another few seconds to bring out its full flavour. Add the broad beans and stir; add 1 tbs lemon juice and the sugar, if used, and stir again.

Add the silver beet, cover and let the mixture sweat for 4–5 minutes over moderately low heat. Add the artichokes and sprinkle with the white pepper, cinnamon, allspice and finally the salt. Add the boiling water and cook for 15–20 minutes over moderately low heat. 3 minutes before the end of cooking add the remaining lemon juice. Serve warm or cold. Eat with wholemeal pitta bread.

Black-Eyed Beans with Silver Beet
Fassoulia bi-silk

This is a highly nutritious meal, rich in protein, fibre and iron. The black-eyed bean, native to Africa and Asia, is low in fat and has no cholesterol. Here it is combined with one of the oldest known vegetables, the silver beet, and perfumed with herbs and spices to give the dish its distinct flavour. It is ideal for vegetarians as well as for people following the Hay diet.

Ingredients

225 g (8 oz) black-eyed beans, soaked for 6 hours
    or overnight, rinsed and drained
1½ tbs extra virgin olive oil
1 onion (about 200 g/7 oz), peeled and finely chopped
3 cloves of garlic, peeled and crushed
4 sprigs of coriander, roots cut off, tough stems removed, rinsed and drained
1 bunch silver beet (about 450 g/1 lb), about 2½ cm (1 in) cut off the ends, rinsed,
    sliced into 1¼ cm (½ in) ribbons
¼ tsp black pepper
¼ tsp white pepper
¾ tsp salt, or to taste

Set a pan over medium–high heat, add the beans and cold water to cover by 6 cm (2½ in); skim the foam from the surface of the water and bring to the boil. Reduce the heat to moderately low, cover and simmer the beans until tender, about 1–1¼ hours.

Meanwhile set a large, deep-frying pan over medium–high heat, add the oil; when oil is hot but not smoking add the onions, sauté until soft (about 2–3 minutes), add the garlic and stir for a few seconds; add the coriander and stir for a few seconds longer. Add the silver beet in batches, stirring until it has reduced in size, then stir occasionally for another 4 minutes or so, season with the black pepper and white pepper; to this mixture add the cooked soft beans and their reduced liquid, which should be about ¼ cup (2 fl oz) or a little less. Stir, cover and simmer for 5 minutes. Add the lemon juice, stir gently and turn off the heat.

Serve warm or cold with wholemeal bread and some white cheese.

Mixed Grains and Beans
Makhlouta

A feast and a real peasant dish, *makhlouta* is an excellent source of complex carbohydrates, fibre, B vitamins and minerals, as well as essential amino acids. This dish is prepared during the cold winter in Lebanese villages; it provides energy and natural heating, and is a most effective way of preventing colds. Departing from the traditional recipe, I have not fried the onions. About 2 heaped tablespoons of *kawarma* (*see glossary*) are sometimes added to give extra flavour and body. *Makhlouta* keeps well in the fridge for up to 3–4 days.

Ingredients

115 g (4 oz) kidney beans, soaked overnight, rinsed, drained
115 g (4 oz) large white beans, soaked overnight, rinsed, drained
85 g (3 oz) chick-peas, soaked overnight, rinsed, drained
1.66–1.75 l (2¾–3 pints) water
115 g (4 oz) brown lentils, picked over, rinsed several times, drained
½ tbs extra virgin olive oil
285 g (10 oz) onion, peeled and finely chopped
115 g (4 oz) coarse *burghol*, rinsed and drained
1½ tsp salt, or to taste
¼ tsp freshly milled black pepper
¼ tsp white pepper
1½ tsp cumin, or to taste

In a large pan, place the kidney beans, large white beans, chick-peas and water over a high heat. Skim off the foam from the surface of the water and bring to the boil, cover and simmer for at least 5 minutes; reduce heat to medium–low and cook until tender (about 60 minutes). When the cooking time is over, add the lentils, oil and onions, bring to the boil, cover and simmer over a moderately low heat for 15 minutes. Then add the *burghol*, season with salt, black pepper, white pepper and cumin, stir, cover and simmer for 15 minutes or until tender and the water has evaporated. Taste and adjust the seasonings.

Serve with a salad such as cabbage or a mixture of grilled vegetables such as aubergines and courgettes.

Variation: Sauté about 225 g (8 oz) lean ground meat, preferably lamb, until nicely browned; add to the bean mixture at the same time as you add the *burghol*.

Red Kidney Beans in Tomato Sauce

Fassoulia hamra bi-roub al-banadoura

Beans are popular with healthy eaters and vegetarians. They are low in fat and sugar and rich in soluble fibre, which makes them useful for diabetics and slimmers. Red kidney beans contain valuable B vitamins and minerals such as magnesium. Eaten at the same time with whole grains, they make a complete protein meal. As in many other recipes in the book I have simplified this appetizing dish, making it healthier by omitting the frying and cutting down on the use of oil.

Ingredients

200 g (7 oz) red kidney beans, soaked overnight
1.1 l (2 pints) water
2–3 tbs tomato purée
1 medium onion (about 140 g/5 oz) peeled, finely chopped
3 cloves of garlic, peeled, crushed
¼ tsp cinnamon
¼ tsp freshly milled black pepper
1 tsp olive oil
1 tsp salt, or to taste

Place the beans in a large pan, cover with cold water. Skim the foam from the surface of the water and boil rapidly for at least 5 minutes to destroy the toxins. Reduce the heat to moderately low, cover and simmer for 60 minutes or until the beans are tender. When cooking time is up and beans are tender, add the tomato purée, onion, garlic, cinnamon, black pepper, oil and salt. Bring back to the boil, cover and simmer over medium–low heat for 20–25 minutes longer.

Serve hot on a bed of rice, preferably brown.

Butter Beans in Tomato Sauce

Fassoulia baida bi-salset al-banadoura

Butter beans have a distinctive flavour and, like other beans, they are very good food, providing a lot of nourishment. Butter beans in tomato sauce are delicious and very simple to make. In this dish I have again deviated from tradition by omitting the oil. This makes the dish very low in fat. With brown rice it becomes a complete protein meal.

Ingredients

255 g (9 oz) butter beans, soaked for 6–8 hours
850 ml (1½ pints) cold water
1 medium-sized onion (about 125 g/4½ oz) peeled, finely chopped
6 cloves of garlic, peeled and crushed
a handful of coriander leaves with only tender stems,
    rinsed, coarsely chopped
2–3 tbs tomato concentrate
1½ tsp salt, or to taste
½ tsp cinnamon
¼ tsp freshly milled black pepper

Drain the beans, rinse under cold running water, drain again and place in a large pan. Cover with water, skim the foam from the surface of the water, bring to the boil, cover and simmer over medium–low heat for 45–50 minutes, or until the beans are tender. When cooking time is over add the onions, garlic, coriander, tomato concentrate, salt, cinnamon and black pepper; cover and cook for 20 to 30 minutes longer.

    Serve hot. Eat with vermicelli rice.

Note: You can add 1 tsp of olive oil at the same time as you add the onions.

Cracked Wheat with Tomatoes

Burghol bi-banadoura

Cracked wheat or *burghol* is a wheat grain that is boiled, dried and cracked into coarse and fine particles. It is an important grain in Lebanese cuisine and has been known in the Middle East since centuries before Christ. Traditionally *burghol* was more common than rice, especially in the villages, and it is sometimes added to pulses and stuffed vegetables instead of rice. *Burghol* is nourishing, has a nutty flavour and provides lots of energy. *Burghol bi-banadoura* is inexpensive, simple and quick to prepare.

Ingredients

1 tbs extra virgin olive oil
1 small onion, about 100 g (3 oz), peeled, finely chopped
170 g (6 oz) ripe tomatoes, rinsed, skinned, chopped
200 g (7 oz) coarse *burghol*, rinsed once, drained
300 ml (½ pint) water
½ tsp cinnamon
¼ tsp allspice
1 tsp salt, or to taste

In a small pan heat the oil, add the onions and sauté until pale and transparent; add the tomatoes, stir for a few seconds and add the water, bring to the boil, cover and allow to simmer for 5 minutes over medium heat; add the *burghol*, season with the cinnamon, allspice and salt. Cover and reduce the heat to medium–low, cook for about 8–10 minutes or until the *burghol* is soft and the water has evaporated.

Serve hot with yoghurt and wholemeal bread.

Pumpkin Kibbeh
Kibbet al-laktin

This succulent vegetarian version of the traditional *kibbeh* combines the colourful, carotene-rich pumpkin with *burghol*; flour is added to give firmness to the moist dough. Different aromatic spices are mixed in to bring out the full taste.

Kibbet al-laktin, a Lebanese village creation, was, to my astonishment, unknown to many Lebanese until very recently, when people became more aware of healthy eating and began to look for a substitute for meat. Pumpkin *kibbeh* needs a little patience. A simpler way of preparing it is to sandwich the filling between two layers of *kibbeh* dough. Prepare also as patties, grill and serve topped with the filling. Whichever way you make it, pumpkin *kibbeh* brims with lots of healthful ingredients.

Ingredients

55 g (2 oz) chick-peas, soaked overnight, rinsed, drained (optional)

For the dough
600 g (1 lb 5 oz) pumpkin, peeled, seeded, cut in thick pieces
    (will come to about 420 g/15 oz)
1 onion (about 100 g/3½ oz) peeled, quartered
I tsp salt, or to taste
½ tsp cinnamon

½ tsp allspice
¹/₂ tsp freshly milled black pepper
140 g (5 oz) fine *burghol*, do not rinse
75 g (2½ oz) wholemeal flour

For the filling
1 tbs extra virgin olive oil
1 onion (about 125 g/4½ oz), peeled, finely chopped
75 g (2½ oz) coarsely chopped walnuts
3 tbs sour pomegranate seeds (optional)
slices of aubergine (about 200 g/7 oz) grilled, cut up into tiny pieces.
2 tbs pomegranate syrup
½ tsp salt, or to taste
½ tsp cinnamon
olive oil for deep-frying

In a saucepan place the chick-peas, add cold water to cover by 5 cm (2 in). Skim the foam, bring to the boil, cover and cook over medium–low heat for 1½ hours or until tender. Drain, split each chick-pea in half and reserve.

Meanwhile pour 2½ cm (1 in) of water into a saucepan, place a steaming basket in the pan, bring the water to the boil and arrange the pumpkin pieces on the basket. Cover the saucepan tightly and over a moderate heat cook until tender (about 10–15 minutes). Remove, drain in a colander and reserve.

In a blender place the onion, salt, cinnamon, allspice and black pepper; purée until smooth and creamy. Remove and place in a mixing bowl, add the *burghol* and rub well with the onion. Then use the back of a jug to press the pumpkin in the colander and squeeze out excess water; transfer the pumpkin to the mixing bowl; add the flour and knead, mixing thoroughly with puréed onions and *burghol* to form a moist dough. Taste and adjust the seasonings. Cover with a clean cloth and leave to stand for at least 40 minutes, until firm. This will make the shaping of *kibbeh* shells easier.

To prepare filling, set a frying pan over medium high heat, add the oil, onion and salt, and mix to coat the onion with the oil; cover with a lid, allow a minute or two, remove the lid, reduce heat to medium–low and stir constantly until onions are golden in colour; add the reserved chick-peas, if used. Stir for about 2 minutes and add the walnuts, pomegranate seeds if used, the cut-up aubergine, pomegranate syrup, salt and cinnamon. Stir well and remove from heat.

To shape *kibbeh* shells, moisten hands lightly with cold water, take a small portion of *kibbeh* mixture and roll each portion between the palms of the hands to form a short cigar shape; hold firmly in one palm, and with the index finger of the other hand poke a hole into the centre of the *kibbeh*. Work around the inside with your finger until you have a thin shell.

Place a heaped tablespoon of the filling mixture in each *kibbeh* shell and gently reshape and smooth to enclose the filling within an oval shape, moistening fingers as necessary with cold water.

When all the shells are ready, pour the oil into a small, deep-frying pan and heat to 190° C (350° F). You will see the oil moving but do not allow it to smoke (check by dropping a piece of bread into it, which should immediately rise to the surface). Gently lower 3 or 4 *kibbeh* shells at a time into the hot oil and fry until brown and crusty (about 3 minutes). Repeat until all are done. Remove and drain on kitchen paper.

Serve warm or at room temperature. Eat with aubergine dip.

Potato Kibbeh Patties

Aqrass kibbet al-batata

This enjoyable traditional dish, which relies on the flavour of fresh local produce, combines mashed potatoes with *burghol*, onions, spices and the dominant aromatic coriander. It can be grilled, shallow-fried or baked as in *kibbet al-samak* or *kibbeh sayniyeh*. The patties make an unusual and interesting starter.

Ingredients

450 g (1 lb 1 oz) potatoes
1 medium-sized onion (about 115 g/4 oz)
    peeled, coarsely chopped
$\frac{1}{4}$ tsp freshly milled black pepper
$\frac{1}{2}$ tsp cinnamon
$\frac{1}{2}$ tsp allspice
1 tsp salt, or to taste
about $\frac{3}{4}$ bunch of coriander (about 150 g/5$\frac{1}{2}$ oz),
    roots cut off and discarded, rinsed, drained and
    patted dry between sheets of kitchen paper
a pinch of nutmeg (optional)
125 g (4$\frac{1}{2}$ oz) fine *burghol*, do not rinse
50 g (2 oz) flour

Scrub gently, but do not peel, the potatoes, place in a pan and cover with boiling water. Cook until potatoes are tender (about 15–20 minutes depending on the variety).

Meanwhile rub the onions with the black pepper, cinnamon, allspice and salt, place in a blender along with the coriander and purée until smooth. Reserve this mixture.

Remove the potatoes from pan, allow to cool a little, peel and press through a fine sieve or mash until you have a smooth texture; sprinkle with the nutmeg, if used, incorporate the reserved coriander mixture, the *burghol* and the flour and mix thoroughly (or run in a blender) to form a soft dough. Let it stand for 30 minutes until firm. Then make the potato patties. Take small portions at a time and, with moistened hands, shape each portion into 4 cm (1½ in) patties; repeat with the remaining mixture in the same way. Pre-heat the grill, allow the baking sheet to heat under the grill for a few minutes, remove carefully and brush generously with olive oil, arrange the patties and cook 10 cm (4 in) from the heat for about 6–8 minutes or until lightly browned on both sides.

Serve hot or cold. Eat with *fattoush* or cabbage salad.

Variation: You need for the filling:
1 large aubergine (about 450 g/1 lb)
olive oil for baking and frying
1 medium-sized onion
    (about 115 g/4 oz) peeled, finely chopped
coarsely chopped walnuts (about 100 g/3½ oz)
2 tbs pomegranate syrup
1 tsp salt, or to taste
½ tsp cinnamon
¼ tsp allspice
¼ tsp freshly milled black pepper
¼ tsp cayenne pepper (optional)

Pre-heat the oven to 220° C (425° F/gas mark 7). Peel aubergine and cut into 1¼ cm (½ in) cubes. Toss with enough oil to coat well and spread over a baking sheet. Place in the oven and bake until deep golden in colour and soft (about 30 minutes).

In a medium-sized frying pan toss the onions to coat well with 1 tbs of olive oil, cover with a lid and cook over medium heat for 1 minute. Uncover and stir, reduce the heat to medium–low and cook the onions until soft, stirring occasionally, for about 2 minutes. Add the walnuts and the pomegranate syrup, season with salt, cinnamon, allspice, black pepper and cayenne pepper if used, stir well and turn the heat off. Reserve this mixture. Remove the aubergine from the oven, drain on kitchen paper, then add to the reserved mixture in the frying pan; mix well. Serve a little of this mixture over each *kibbeh* patty, or use as a filling if you choose to prepare potato *kibbeh* as described in *Kibbeh sayniyeh*.

Lentils and Rice
Moudardra

Well-balanced in taste, nutrition and simplicity, this dish provides warmth in winter and is satisfying all year round. In this recipe, the lentils do not require soaking and combine perfectly with the rice. *Moudardra* is traditionally prepared with white rice; I use brown rice, which marries wonderfully in texture and flavour and also makes a healthy meal that is rich in essential amino acids. For further nutritional completeness and balance, eat it with a vitamin C-rich vegetable salad.

Ingredients

1 tbs olive oil
1 onion (about 125 g/4 oz), peeled and finely chopped
200 g (7 oz) brown lentils,
    picked over, rinsed several times
125 g (4 oz) brown rice, rinsed once
850 ml–1 l (1½–1¾ pints) water
1 tsp salt, or to taste
¼ tsp allspice
¼ tsp freshly milled black pepper
a pinch of cinnamon (optional)

Set a pan over medium–high heat and add the oil. When oil is hot but not smoking add the onions and sauté until golden brown, stirring frequently, for about 2–3 minutes. Add the lentils and stir for 10 seconds, add the brown rice and stir for another 10 seconds, add the water and the salt. Bring to the boil, reduce heat to medium–low, cover and simmer for 30–40 minutes. Half-way through cooking, season with the allspice, black pepper and cinnamon (if used). When cooking time is up, transfer the *moudardra* to a platter.

Serve warm or at room temperature. Eat with *fattoush* or tomato and onion salad.

Note: Garnish with fried onions if desired. To fry onions check the recipe of Thick Red Lentil Soup.

Lentils and Rice
Moujaddara

This humble dish is found mainly on the dining tables of Lebanese Christian communities during Lent; and also on Wednesday and Friday during weeks when the Eastern Church forbade the eating of meat, a precept that remained in force until recently.

Moujaddara contains valuable B vitamins and minerals, together with abundant protein and fibre. It is a perfect meal for vegetarians and the health-conscious. Eating it with a vitamin C-rich salad such as *fattoush* or cabbage and a piece of white or low-fat cheese provides an excellent nutritional balance.

The traditional method of making *moujaddara* uses a large quantity of oil to fry the onions until they are dark brown in colour (this will deepen the taste). I omit this procedure to limit the calorie intake and eliminate harmful free-radicals; a further benefit is that my recipe is less time-consuming. To top up the nutritional value, I use brown rice. Some say that the secret of a good *moujaddara* lies in the browning of the onions, but I think that the slight improvement in taste does not justify the possible harmful effects or the effort.

Ingredients

200 g (7 oz) brown lentils
85 g (3 oz) organic brown rice, rinsed once, drained
1.7 l (3 pints) water
2 medium-sized onions (about 200 g/7 oz) peeled
    and coarsely sliced (about ½ cm/¼ in)
1½ tbs extra virgin olive oil
1½ tsp salt, or to taste
¼ tsp freshly milled black pepper

In a pan place the lentils, rice and onions, cover with cold water, add the oil and half the amount of salt and bring to the boil. Reduce the heat to moderate, cover and simmer for 35–40 minutes or until tender.

When the cooking time is up, strain the lentils and rice with their liquid through a vegetable mill, or blend in a liquidizer, until creamy. Return this mixture to the same pan. Season with the remaining salt and the black pepper and reheat, stirring occasionally. Bring to the boil. Reduce heat to moderate and cook for 15–20 minutes or until it thickens and the flavours mellow, stirring occasionally to prevent sticking.

Pour the mixture over individual dishes or a large serving dish, allow to cool. Serve. Eat with cabbage salad, wholemeal bread and white or spring onions.

Vermicelli Rice
Roz bi-shaiirya

The Arabs introduced rice into Europe through Spain. In the Middle East rice has almost the character of a sacrament and is served almost every day. It provides the basis of the Lebanese cuisine and symbolizes good fortune; for that reason a bride is showered with it for good luck. I love rice and it revives memories of my childhood, when after school I hurried to the kitchen to eat it straight from the pot. At that time I knew only white rice. Afterwards, when I settled in England, I discovered the qualities of brown rice, which is superior to white as a source of fibre and energy. I have used it in this book in recipes in which its flavour is well assimilated with other ingredients. In some other recipes I favour the use of white rice, especially the aromatic basmati. Note that brown rice takes longer to cook, and therefore needs more water.

Ingredients

1 tbs extra virgin olive oil
1 vermicelli nest (about 35 g/1¼ oz), broken
    between the hands into small pieces

200 g (7 oz) brown rice, rinsed once
500 ml (17 fl oz) water
1 tsp salt

Set a medium-sized heavy pan over medium–high heat. Heat the oil but do not allow to smoke; add the vermicelli, sauté, stirring constantly until they are golden brown in colour (do not burn). Then, with a spoon push back the vermicelli and pour off most of the oil in the pan; add the rice and stir with the vermicelli, add the water, season with salt and bring to the boil; cover and simmer over medium–low heat for 35 minutes or until rice is tender and water is absorbed. Keep pan covered and undisturbed for one minute.

Serve hot on its own or with yoghurt.

Note: If using white rice you will need 400 ml (14 fl oz) water and a cooking time of 8–10 minutes over medium–low heat.

Fish Rice
Roz al-samak

A delicately seasoned rice often served with fish. The dish is distinguished by its use of strongly scented saffron (one of the most expensive spices). Saffron is thought to have travelled everywhere with Phoenician traders, particularly to Spain, and is said to have anti-inflammatory properties. It imparts a strong flavour and should be used sparingly, otherwise it will overpower the dish. Turmeric adds colour and pine-nuts enhance the taste and top up the nutrients.

Ingredients

2 tbs extra virgin olive oil
55 g (2 oz) pine nuts
200 g (7 oz) onions, peeled and sliced into half-moon shapes
200 g (7 oz) white rice (preferably basmati), rinsed once and drained
400 ml (14 fl oz) water
a pinch of saffron threads
¼ tsp of turmeric
1 tsp salt or to taste

Heat the olive oil and sauté the pine-nuts until slightly golden in colour. Remove with a slotted spoon allowing the oil to drip back into the pan and reserve.

Add the onions to the pan and coat them all over with oil. Sauté for 2 minutes over high heat, reduce heat to medium and continue to sauté the onions until golden in colour, stirring occasionally. Add the saffron threads and turmeric and stir gently for a few seconds to bring out the flavour. Add the rice, return the reserved pine-nuts to the pan and stir for ½ minute. Add the water, season with salt and bring to the boil, reduce heat to medium–low, cover and simmer for 10 minutes or until rice is soft and water has been absorbed.

Serve immediately on its own, with a salad, or with fish stew or *tagen*.

Spinach with Rice
Sabanekh bi-roz

Another delicious meal made of a mixture of natural ingredients, aromatic herbs and spices, pleasant to the palate, nourishing and remarkably light to digest. Spinach with Rice is one of the finest and simplest of meals. It is inexpensive, has a high content of iron—which is recommended for vegetarians—and is prepared with a small amount of oil, which is advantageous for slimmers; in addition, the combination fits the rules of the Hay diet.

Ingredients

1 tbs extra-virgin olive oil
170 g (6 oz) onion, peeled, finely chopped
6 sprigs of coriander, roots cut off, tough ends removed, rinsed and chopped
675 g (1 lb 8 oz) spinach, tough stems removed,   washed several times, drained and chopped
200 g (7 oz) rice, preferably basmati
½ tsp cinnamon
¼ tsp black pepper
½ tsp allspice
200–250 ml (7–8 fl oz) water
1¼ tsp salt or to taste

Set a medium-sized, thick-bottomed pan over high heat. Heat the oil, add the onions and cook until soft (about 2–3 minutes), stirring constantly. Add the coriander, reduce the heat to medium and sauté with the onions, stirring for about ½ minute longer; add the spinach in batches at a time. As the spinach reduces in size, add the rice, stir gently and season with the cinnamon, black pepper and allspice; stir, then add the water and salt. Bring to the boil, reduce heat to medium–low, cover and simmer for 10 minutes or until rice is soft. Turn the heat off and leave the pan covered for 2 minutes before serving.

Eat on its own or accompanied by yoghurt, if desired, and a piece of white cheese.

Potatoes and Rice
Batata bi-roz

This is another simple and highly nourishing recipe. It is warming comforting and thus suitable for the elderly, but also energizing for athletes and active people. *Batata bi-roz* is very tasty and has a superb nutty and earthy flavour. A garnish of water cress or alfalfa sprouts is agreeable and tops up its nutritional value.

Ingredients

170 g (6 oz) onion, peeled, finely chopped
560 g (1¼ lb) potatoes, washed and cut into 2 cm (¾ in) cubes
2–3 tbs extra-virgin olive oil
2 tbs double-concentrate tomato paste
200 g (7 oz) brown rice, rinsed once, drained
½ tsp allspice
½ tsp cinnamon
¼ tsp black pepper
850 ml (1½ pints) boiling water
1½ tsp salt or to taste

In a heavy-bottomed pan combine the onions and potatoes with oil, coating all their sides with the oil. Place the pan over medium–high heat, cover with a lid and cook for 2–3 minutes. Remove the lid, stir, reduce the heat to medium, add the tomato paste, rice, allspice, cinnamon and black pepper, stir gently for 1–2 minutes and add the water. Season with salt. Bring to the boil, cover and simmer for 35–40 minutes or until both potatoes and rice are soft. Check the water and add some if necessary.

Serve hot. Eat with Aubergines in Yoghurt.

Note: If using white rice, which is equally delicious, follow the recipe until you come to add the tomato paste, then add 500 ml (21 fl oz) of boiling water, season with the salt, bring to the boil, cover and simmer over medium heat for 15 minutes or until potatoes are tender. At this point add the rice, and check the water; if necessary add more. Season with the allspice, cinnamon and black pepper, stir, cover and simmer for 10 minutes longer or until rice is soft and water is absorbed. Turn the heat off and leave to stand covered for a minute or two, allowing the flavours to mellow.

Rice and Chick-Peas
Roz bedfine

This wholesome and inexpensive mixture of chick-peas and brown rice speaks for itself. From time out of mind, *roz bedfine* has enriched the Lebanese menu, mainly in the mountains where *burghol*, being more readily available, was used instead of rice. *Roz bedfine* was one of the dishes that gave villagers energy to work in the field. People knew by instinct and experience what science has now confirmed, that whole grains are an excellent source of complex carbohydrates and fibre. *Roz bedfine* is a typical case in point. Moreover, it is cholesterol-free, and when cooked with rice it is also gluten-free.

Ingredients

1½ tbs extra-virgin olive oil
200 g (7 oz) onion, peeled and roughly sliced
115 g (4 oz) dried chick-peas (soaked overnight), drained half pre-cooked
½ tsp cinnamon
¼ tsp allspice
¼ tsp white pepper
1.2 l (45 fl oz) hot water
200 g (7 oz) brown rice, rinsed once and drained
1½ tsp ground caraway seeds
1½ tsp salt or to taste

Set a pan over medium–high heat, combine the oil and onions then toss to coat onions thoroughly with oil. Sauté until soft (about 2–3 minutes), stirring constantly. Reduce heat to medium, drain the chick-peas and add to cook with the onions for 6 minutes longer, stirring occasionally. Season with the cinnamon, allspice and white pepper, stir and add the water, bring to the boil, cover and simmer for about 50 minutes. Add the brown rice, cover and simmer over low heat 40 minutes longer or until rice and chick-peas are tender and water has been absorbed. 5 minutes before the end of cooking season with caraway and salt, stir once and cover to finish the cooking time.

Serve hot. If desired, top with watercress and eat with yoghurt.

Stuffed Vegetables
Khodar mehshiyeh

An assortment of vegetables, filled with a highly-seasoned mixture of earth essences, each releasing different nutrients and aromas; a medley that combines, traditionally, short-grain white rice or coarse *burghol* with juicy tomatoes, mint, onions and a large amount of parsley; lemon sharpens the taste and olive oil deepens it. The small amount

of water used and the cooking over a low flame produce an intense flavour.

The filling varies from one region to another according to custom. In some villages lentils are substituted for chick-peas, or both are omitted, as when stuffed grape leaves (*warak enab*) are prepared.

The dish is genuinely uncomplicated, although it needs a long time to prepare and to cook; but do not be put off, because you can do it in stages. *Khodar mehshiyeh* is filling, perfect for vegetarians and ideal as a part of a summer buffet.

Ingredients

3 tbs extra-virgin olive oil

1 large ripe tomato (about 170 g/6 oz), rinsed, sliced into 1¼ cm (½ in) rounds

50 g (2 oz) chick-peas, soaked overnight, rinsed, drained, pre-cooked for 50 minutes in cold water (about 575 ml/20 fl oz)

125 g (4½ oz) brown rice, rinsed once, pre-cooked over low heat for 13 minutes in 200 ml water (about 7 fl oz) and ½ tsp salt

225 g (8 oz) ripe tomatoes, rinsed, finely chopped

125 g (4½ oz) onion, peeled, finely chopped

half a bunch or more of parsley (about 125 g/4½ oz), stems cut off, chopped medium–fine, rinsed and drained

15 g (½ oz) mint leaves, rinsed, finely chopped

4–5 tbs lemon juice

1 tbs pomegranate syrup (optional)

½ tsp allspice

½ tsp cinnamon

¼ tsp freshly milled black pepper

1½ tsp salt or to taste

4 small aubergines, about 6–7 cm (2½–3 in) long

4 small courgettes, about 6–7 cm (2½–3 in) long

4 medium–small sweet peppers

300 ml (10 fl oz) water

In a pan large enough to hold the vegetables in one layer, put 1 tbs of the oil, spread the sliced tomatoes over it in a layer and keep aside for later use.

In a mixing bowl combine the chick-peas, rice, chopped tomatoes, onions, parsley and mint. Add the lemon, pomegranate syrup, if used, and remaining oil, season with the allspice, cinnamon, black pepper and ¾ tsp of salt. Mix well and reserve this mixture.

Then cut across the tops of the aubergines, courgettes and peppers, reserving the tops of the peppers. With a corer gently scoop out the pulp from the aubergines and courgettes, leaving a shell about ⅓ cm (⅛ in) all the way round. Make sure not to puncture otherwise it will burst open during the cooking. Core and remove seeds of peppers, rinse all vegetables including the pepper tops and drain upside down in a colander.

From the reserved mixture fill the aubergines and courgettes loosely, leaving room for the rice to swell; fill the peppers to the top, cover with their tops and arrange over the reserved tomatoes in the pan, leaning slightly to the side so that the liquid penetrates to the inside of the vegetables while cooking. Add the water and the remaining salt, bring to boil over high heat, reduce heat to medium–low. Cover tightly and simmer for 1 hour or until rice and chick-peas are soft. After 50 minutes check the water level and taste the filling from inside the peppers with some of the resulting liquid. Make sure the salt and lemon juice are adequate; if not add a little to the liquid. Cool for at least two hours, then transfer gently to a serving dish.

Eat with yoghurt and bread if desired.

Note: You can vary the colours of the peppers for a more exotic look.

Stuffed Swiss Chard
Silk bi-zeit

One of the most favoured dishes among the Lebanese, although it needs patience to prepare. My recipe differs from the traditional one because I include brown instead of white rice in the filling. Brown rice takes longer to cook, so it is pre-cooked for a short time. This is a good recipe to accustom a wary family to brown rice, because its presence is not conspicuous. *Silk bi-zeit* is ideal for a buffet on warm days or eaten as a main meal any day. For a nourishing meal eat with a raw vegetable salad and a piece of white cheese.

Ingredients

4 tbs extra-virgin olive oil

250 g (8½ oz) potato, unpeeled, washed, gently scrubbed and sliced

75 g (2½ oz) chick-peas, soaked overnight, drained, cooked in water to cover by 3–4 cm (1½ in) for 50 minutes and drained again

140 g (5 oz) short grain brown rice, pre-cooked in 200 ml (7 fl oz) water and ½ tsp salt for 12 minutes or until water is absorbed

350 g (12 oz) ripe tomatoes, rinsed, finely chopped

1 bunch of parsley (about 200 g/7 oz with stems on), stems cut off, chopped (yielding about 100 g/3½ oz), rinsed, drained

a large handful of mint leaves, rinsed, drained and chopped

150 g (5½ oz) onion, peeled and finely chopped

4 tbs lemon juice

½ tsp allspice

½ tsp cinnamon

¼ tsp black pepper

2 tsp salt or to taste

1 kg (2 lb 4 oz) Swiss chard leaves, rinsed, white ribs cut off, reserved
1 tomato (about 85 g/3 oz) rinsed, cut into $1\frac{1}{4}$ cm ($\frac{1}{2}$ in) slices

To a medium-sized thick-bottomed pan, add 1 tbs of the oil, cover with a layer of the sliced potato; reserve for later.

Next prepare the filling: in a mixing bowl add the chick-peas, brown rice, tomatoes, parsley, mint, onions and lemon juice. Season with the allspice, cinnamon, black pepper and 1½ tsp of the salt. Add 2½ tbs of the oil and combine this mixture thoroughly. Then place the Swiss chard, in batches, into a pan filled with boiling salted water; leave for a minute or until soft and pliable. Remove from water and drain in a colander.

Take one leaf at a time and place over a working surface with raised rib facing up, trim or smooth by pressing it down with your finger. At the rib end place about 2 tbs of the filling, depending on the size of the leaf, and roll up into a long, fat cigar (remember to stir the filling from time to time to coat the ingredients in the bowl with the juices). Repeat with remaining leaves and filling. Over the oil and potatoes in the reserved pan place 3–4 of the white ribs and over them arrange the stuffed Swiss chard, seam down; top with the sliced tomatoes, add the remaining oil and the left-over juices from the mixing bowl. Season with remaining salt and barely cover with boiling water (about 200 ml/7 fl oz). Place over high heat, bring to the boil, cover and simmer over medium–low heat for 1 hour.

Cool for at least two hours before serving. Arrange on a dish with the reduced liquid, which contains many of the vitamins; eat with bread and yoghurt.

Note: The remaining reserved Swiss chard ribs can be prepared as in Lemony Lentil Soup; or as the variety *tahini* sauce. Stuffed vine leaves can be prepared in the same way, but do not add chick-peas, and tuck the sides of the leaves before you finish rolling them up.

Thyme bread (*mankoushi bi-zaatar*)

Bread

No fork, no spoon but also no fingers. Traditionally thin slices of bread were used to convey food from plate to mouth. Bread remains not an accompaniment but an essential part of any Lebanese meal. It is hard to imagine eating a plate of *hoummos* or *foul* without it, and when bread is not needed, as in *tabbouleh*, it is replaced by the *burghol* that is an ingredient of that salad. We do not know whether the consumption of bread in Lebanon dates back as far as in the Egypt of the Pharaohs, but Lebanon was, during the millennia before Christ, under the influence of the Pharaohs, who made use of its timbers and quarries, if not of its soil, when fighting the people of Mesopotamia. It is not unreasonable to assume that bread was also part of the exchange.

Bread
Khoubz

The flat Arabic loaves (pitta) are nowadays readily available in many parts of the Western world. As this was not the case a few years ago, I used to bring some with me from Lebanon each time I returned from a visit home, not simply as a treat, but because some of our meals taste better with that kind of bread—*shawarma*, *moujaddara*, *falafel* and *kafta*, for instance.

Of course bread bought in this country is perfectly acceptable but if you have the time to experiment and make your own you will obtain a better flavour. For this bread I follow the traditional method using ordinary yeast, but feel free to use fresh or easy-blend; the only difference is that I add honey for flavour and colour.

Ingredients

$1^{1}/_{2}$ tsp active dry yeast
3 tbs lukewarm water
450 g (1 lb) wholewheat flour
$1^{1}/_{4}$ tsp salt

$^1/_2$–$^3/_4$ tsp honey (optional)
250 ml (8 fl oz) lukewarm water or as necessary

Dissolve the yeast in 3 tbs lukewarm water, stir and leave to stand for 10 minutes or until froth appears on the surface. Meanwhile combine the flour and salt, add the yeasty water; dissolve the honey (if used) in lukewarm water and gradually mix it into the flour until firm. Turn dough on to a lightly floured working surface and knead for 10 minutes or until dough is smooth and elastic. Return to the bowl, cover with a plastic wrap and leave in a warm, draught-free place to rise for 2–3 hours.

When dough has nearly doubled in size, deflate by punching it down in the centre to release the air, knead lightly and form into balls. Place balls 5 cm (2 in) apart, cover and leave in a warm place to rest for a short time (about 10–15 minutes). Remove balls and dip each one lightly in flour, flatten a little with your hand and, with a rolling pin, roll into a circle on a lightly floured surface $^1/_3$–$^1/_2$ cm ($^1/_8$–$^1/_4$ in) thick and 12–13 cm (5 in) in diameter. Cover with clean cloth; repeat with others and leave to rest, covered, in a warm place for another 10 minutes.

Pre-heat the oven to high (230° C/450° F/gas mark 8). Place a baking sheet on the lower rack in the oven. Gently transfer the bread circles to the hot sheet and leave to puff up (about 3–4 minutes) and remove. Repeat with all the remaining bread circles; allow to cool then store them in polythene bags. Refrigerate. Reheat before using.

Thyme Bread

Mankoushi bi-zaatar

Mankoushi is a flat round loaf of bread dough topped with a richly flavoured, home-prepared *zaatar* mixture (*see below*) and cooked at a nearby bakery. *Mankoushi* is a much-loved breakfast for the Lebanese; they eat it anywhere, in their homes, on foot or on the road. If you take a stroll in the streets of Beirut early in the morning you will be inebriated by the smell of *mankoushi*, coming hot from the wood-fire oven, and will probably find the taste of this crusty, moist thyme bread irresistible too.

Mankoushi needs a little time and patience. *Bouchées manakish* (plural of *mankoushi*) are ideal with cocktails.

Ingredients

For the dough
275 g (9$^1/_2$ oz) unbleached white flour
$^3/_4$ tsp salt
1 tsp easy-blend or quick-action dried yeast
1 tbs extra-virgin olive oil
$^1/_2$ tsp honey (optional)

150 ml (5 fl oz) lukewarm water

For the topping
5 tbs thyme mixture (*zaatar*)
8 tbs extra-virgin olive oil
1 small onion (about 50 g/2 oz), preferably white, peeled, very finely chopped

Sift the flour and salt into a large bowl. Add the yeast, then rub the oil well into the flour. Dissolve the honey in the water and add gradually to form at first a sticky dough. Turn it on to a lightly floured working surface and knead until dough is smooth, shiny and elastic (about 8 minutes). Form into a ball and return to the bowl, cover with a damp cloth or plastic wrap and leave to rise in a warm, draught-free place for about 2 hours. Remove from the bowl and place on a lightly floured surface. Knead briefly, divide into 6–8 equal parts, form each into a ball and leave to rest for 8 minutes. Roll each ball lightly in flour, coating all sides to prevent sticking.

With your hand flatten each ball, then roll out with a rolling pin into a circle $\frac{1}{3}$ cm ($\frac{1}{8}$ in) thick and 12–13 cm (5 in) in diameter. Repeat with remaining dough balls. Cover with a clean cloth and leave to rest in a warm, draught-free place for 5–10 minutes.

Meanwhile mix thyme with oil and onions if used (they give more flavour). While the bread circles are resting, set a lightly oiled, heavy-bottomed skillet over medium heat; at the same time pre-heat the grill to use later.

Using your fingers, flute and raise the edges by successive pinches all around each bread circle and gently remove to place inside the skillet. Spread on the surface about 1 tbs of thyme mixture. With a fork prick all over the surface to prevent it from puffing up and forming large bubbles. Leave to cook undisturbed for 1 minute or a little more, until the base is golden brown and edges are relatively dry. Check by lifting the side; if the base is golden and dry remove with a spatula and place on a baking sheet. Every time you finish one or two circles, grease the skillet with an oil-damped piece of cotton wool. Repeat with remaining circles until all are ready.

Place the baking sheet under the grill and while keeping an eye on it cook the thyme bread until the top is golden (about 1–2 minutes depending on the heat of your grill).

Serve and eat sandwiched with fresh mint and, if desired, spring onions.

Chilli Bread
Mankoushi bi-har

This is a speciality of the Shouf Mountains and, more particularly, of the Druse people. It is amazing, particularly in view of the small size of Lebanon, how recipes from one area can be unknown or find little favour in others. Mankoushi bi-har is one such.

For the dough and preparation, I follow the recipe for Thyme Bread (*mankoushi bi-zaatar*), except that for this dough I prefer wholemeal flour, or white

Spinach triangles (*fatayer bi-sabanekh*)

and wholemeal flour in equal quantities. Remember that wholemeal requires more water.

Ingredients

For the dough
Prepare dough as in Thyme Bread using wholemeal flour

For the topping
2 onions (about 175 g/6½ oz), peeled, very finely chopped, or puréed in a food processor
1 small red chilli, de-seeded, rinsed and very finely chopped (optional)
¼ tsp cayenne pepper or to taste
1¼ tsp salt
4 tbs *kishk*
5 tbs extra-virgin olive oil
4 tbs lemon juice
4 tbs sesame seeds, preferably toasted
4–5 tbs good quality tomato ketchup
50 g (2 oz) coarsely crushed walnuts (optional)

Combine the onions with the chilli peppers (if used), cayenne pepper, salt, kishk, oil, lemon juice, sesame seeds, tomato ketchup and walnuts, if used, in a bowl.

Spread the bread circle with 2 tbs, or as necessary, of the chilli mixture and prepare as for Thyme Bread.

Serve and eat sandwiched with lots of fresh mint.

Spinach Triangles
Fatayer bi-sabanekh

A nutritious Lebanese speciality and one of my favourites, made of a dough that is kneaded with olive oil, producing a very tasty pastry to encase a delicious blend of flavourful, fresh ingredients.

Spinach Triangles make an attractive accompaniment to grilled dishes and are handy when unexpected guests appear; so make a large amount, cook and, when cool, freeze them. Defrost and reheat.

Ingredients

For the dough
250 g (8½ oz) wholemeal or unbleached white flour

$\frac{1}{2}$ tsp salt

$2\frac{1}{2}$ tbs extra-virgin olive oil

125 ml (4 fl oz) lukewarm water

For the filling

225 g (8 oz) spinach leaves

$1\frac{1}{4}$ tsp salt

90 g (3 oz) onion, peeled and finely chopped

$\frac{1}{4}$ tsp black pepper

2 tbs pomegranate seeds (optional)

60 g (2 oz) pine-nuts

3–4 tbs lemon juice

3–4 tbs extra-virgin olive oil

$\frac{1}{4}$ tsp cayenne pepper

1 tbs *sumak*

Put the flour and salt into a large bowl, add the oil and rub into flour. Gradually add the water. Work the dough until it is firm, then transfer to a clean surface and knead for 5 minutes or until smooth and elastic. Form dough into a ball and put in a bowl, cover with a cloth and leave to rest for $\frac{1}{2}$–1 hour in a warm place.

In the meantime remove tough stems from spinach leaves, wash several times in cold water and drain well. Sprinkle 1 tsp of salt all over the spinach and rub until spinach reduces in size. Squeeze excess water, chop finely and place in a bowl. Rub the onions with the remaining salt and black pepper and combine with the spinach in the bowl. Add the pomegranate seeds, if used, the pine-nuts, lemon juice, oil, cayenne pepper and *sumak*. Combine well and reserve spinach mixture.

Knead the dough for a minute and divide into 2 equal parts. Take one part at a time and over a lightly floured surface roll into circles $\frac{1}{3}$ cm ($\frac{1}{8}$ in) thick. Cut out circles with a 4 cm ($1\frac{1}{2}$ in) pastry-cutter. Spoon about 1 tbs or more of spinach mixture into the centre of each circle. Bring up the three sides of the pastry to the centre, at the same time pinch the edges firmly to seal in the filling, forming a triangle with three pronounced edges. Repeat with the remaining circles until all (about 20) are ready. Pre-heat the oven to 200° C (400° F/gas mark 6), place on an oiled baking sheet, brush with oil and bake for 20 minutes or until golden and crisp. Serve warm or at room temperature.

Variation: Sorrel is said to have been used in Pharaonic times. The leaves are rich in potassium, vitamins A and C and sulphur, and it makes a good alternative to spinach. It has a pleasant, sharp, lemony taste. You need to use a small amount (about 140–170 g/5–6 oz), and $1\frac{1}{2}$ tbs lemon juice; omit both cayenne pepper and pomegranate seeds.

You can also use purslane or wild chicory; remember to taste the filling and adjust seasonings.

Turnovers Filled with Meat
Sambousek bi-lahm

Delicious, crisp turnovers filled with different delightful mixtures to suit everyone's taste; they appear constantly with a *mezze* or at a large buffet.

Traditionally the dough that encases the meat filling is made with flour rubbed in clarified butter, which produces a soft texture and adds richness and succulence to the flavour. In my recipe I add some butter along with olive oil to cut down somewhat on saturated fats. It also produces an excellent texture and taste.

Ingredients

For the dough
250 g (9 oz) unbleached white flour
½ tsp salt
30 g (1 oz) softened butter
2 tbs extra-virgin olive oil
125 ml (4 fl oz) water

For the filling
1 tbs extra-virgin olive oil
30 g (1 oz) pine-nuts
1 onion (about 120 g/4 oz) peeled and finely chopped
170 g (6 oz) lean ground meat (preferably lamb)
½ tsp allspice
½ tsp cinnamon
¼ tsp black pepper
½ tsp salt or to taste
1 tbs *sumak* (optional)
a handful of parsley leaves, rinsed, drained and finely chopped

Sift the flour and salt into a bowl, add the butter and oil and work them into flour with fingertips. Add the water gradually; when dough is firm enough, transfer to a clean, lightly floured surface and knead for 6–8 minutes. Form into a ball, place in a polythene bag and refrigerate for ½–1 hour.

Meanwhile prepare the filling. Put the oil in a heavy frying pan over medium–high heat; when oil is hot but not smoking sauté the pine-nuts until golden in colour and remove with a slotted spoon.

To the oil remaining in the pan add the onions, stirring constantly for a minute. Add the meat to the onions and cook until lightly browned (about 4 minutes), making sure no traces of blood remain, stirring and breaking any lumps of meat with the back or side of a wooden spoon. Season with the allspice, cinnamon, black pepper and salt. Stir well and turn off the heat. Add the *sumak* (if used) and parsley, stir and reserve meat mixture for a while.

Remove dough and divide into two equal parts. Take one part of the dough, coat both sides lightly with flour, and roll out with a rolling pin into a circle $\frac{1}{3}$ cm ($\frac{1}{8}$ in) thick . Using a 6 cm (2½ in) pastry-cutter, place 1 heaped teaspoonful of filling (or more) in the centre of each circle; fold the pastry over the filling and pinch the edges to seal. Hold sambousek on the extremity of your open hand and with the knuckle of your thumb form a notch, knocking the pastry edge inwards, forming half a pleat. A simpler method is to fold the pastry over the filling and press with a fork around the edge.

Deep-fry in olive oil over medium heat, until golden brown and crisp, or bake. Pre-heat the oven to 200° C (400° F/gas mark 6), brush turnovers lightly with oil or butter, place on an oiled baking sheet and bake for 15–20 minutes or until golden. Makes about 2 dozen.

Eat with *baba-ghannouj*.

Variation 1: Combine the filling ingredients mentioned above but do not cook. Add 1 finely chopped tomato and 2 tbs *tahini* and mix, then spread uncooked mixture over dough circles and do not fold. Cook in a hot oven until nicely browned.

Variation 2:
200 g (7 oz) white cheese (preferably fetta)
1 egg yolk
a large handful of parsley leaves, rinsed, chopped and drained
a pinch of white pepper

Mash the cheese and mix with egg yolk, parsley and white pepper. Prepare as for *Sambousek bi-lahm*.

Soups

Soups are quick to prepare, easily digested, nourishing, substantial, economical and warming. I grew up drinking a soup of one kind or another nearly every night, especially in the cold winter months between November and March.

Soups are equally suitable as a first or a main course. Served in elegant bowls and garnished with fresh herbs, they look attractive and can be prepared ahead of time and reheated. They can be prepared in an infinite variety of ways and can be very wholesome when they contain such foods as brown rice, beans, potatoes and vegetables. They are energizing, kind to the system and give gastronomic satisfaction.

In my soup recipes I have omitted frying with butter, since the ingredients used are naturally rich in taste. This means also that the soups are suitable for slimmers as part of a calorie-controlled diet.

These aromatic soups are delicious accompanied by a home-baked bread, dishes of olives and radishes or a salad rich in vitamin C. They also supply energy and mental stamina that encourages a feeling of well-being. In fact, since ancient times soups have rightly been used as a remedy for ailments.

Chicken Soup with Rice and Parsley
Shorba djaj bi-roz wa bakdouness

A delicious version of chicken soup flavoured with fresh parsley, which imparts a deep and delicate taste. It is nutritious and low in fat, thus perfect as part of a calorie-controlled diet, but is also pleasantly satisfying.

Ingredients

1 kg (2 lb 4 oz) free-range chicken, skinned, cut into 4 or 6 pieces
1.56 l (56 fl oz) water
1 onion (about 85 g/3 oz), peeled
bouquet garni: 1 bay leaf, 4 cardamoms, 5 whole black peppercorns, 1 large cinnamon stick

85 g (3 oz) brown rice
28 g (1 oz) parsley, finely chopped, rinsed, drained
1¹⁄₂ tsp salt or to taste

Remove skin and excess fat from the chicken and clean as in introduction to the section on Poultry. Place in a stew-pot with the water over high heat, skim the foam from the surface of the water and bring to the boil. Add the onion, bouquet garni and rice. Reduce the heat to medium, cover and simmer for 55–60 minutes or until chicken is tender. Just a few minutes before the end of the cooking time, add the parsley, season with salt, taste and adjust the seasonings, cover and finish cooking. Remove from heat, place in a large serving bowl. Serve immediately with a dish of lemon wedges. A few drops of lemon will give the soup a delicious taste.

If you like, before you add the parsley, remove the chicken from its broth, place on a plate, debone and cut chicken into bite-sized pieces. Discard the bones. Return chicken pieces to the pot, add the parsley and the salt and finish the cooking time.

Note: If using white rice, add it to the chicken after 40 minutes, allowing 15 minutes to simmer.

Chicken Soup with Vegetables

Shorba djaj maa al-khodar

A delectable soup known for its medicinal properties since ancient times. I myself have experienced its beneficial effects and recent research has found a substance in chicken joints that may alleviate arthritic pains. The dish is easy to make, substantial and quite economical, and it makes an excellent one-course meal accompanied by home-baked bread and a side dish of green olives.

Ingredients

1 kg (2 lb 4 oz) free-range chicken, skinned, trimmed of excess fat
1.75 l (60 fl oz) water
bouquet garni: 1 cinnamon stick, 1 bay leaf, 4 cardamoms, 5 whole black peppercorns
1 onion (about 115 g/4 oz), peeled and finely chopped
55 g (2 oz) brown rice, rinsed once, drained
1 large carrot, peeled and finely diced
1 large courgette, finely diced
115 g (4 oz) green beans, rinsed and finely diced
1 potato, gently scraped, rinsed, cut into 2¹⁄₂ cm (1 in) cubes
1 tomato (about 115 g/4 oz), rinsed, finely chopped
55 g (2 oz) small cauliflower florets, rinsed

115 g (4 oz) fresh peas, podded
1½ tsp salt or to taste
¼ tsp black pepper
28 g (1 oz) parsley, rinsed and finely chopped

Clean chicken and place with the water in a large pot over high heat; skim the foam from the surface of the water and bring to the boil. Add the bouquet garni, onions and rice, cover and simmer for 40 minutes. Then add the carrot, courgette, green beans, potato, tomato, cauliflower florets and peas. Season with the salt and black pepper. Cover and simmer for 10–15 minutes longer. Add the parsley and cook for a further 3 minutes.

Remove from heat and serve hot with lemon wedges. Even the smallest amount of lemon juice will greatly enhance the flavour. Before adding the parsley you can remove and debone the chicken then cut into small pieces and return to the pan.

Lemony Lentil Soup

Adas bi-hamud

A hearty and substantial soup that sparkles with healthful ingredients, rich in B vitamins, minerals and fibre. Unlike the authentic method, this recipe does not require you to sauté the onions, garlic or coriander. Omitting frying whenever it is possible to do so without substantially changing the flavour is a wise healthy option. *Adas bi-hamud* has a special and regular place on most tables during the holy month of Ramadan.

Ingredients

225 g (8 oz) green lentils, picked over and rinsed
1.1 l (40 fl oz) water
1 onion (about 140 g/5 oz), peeled and finely chopped
potatoes (about 255 g/9 oz), rinsed, gently scraped, cut into 2½ cm (1 in) cubes
5–6 leaves of bunch silver beet, rinsed, chopped
½ tbs extra-virgin olive oil
a few sprigs of coriander (about 55 g/2 oz), roots cut off, rinsed and finely chopped
4 cloves of garlic, peeled and finely crushed
1¼ tsp salt or to taste
¼ tsp black pepper
4 tbs lemon juice
1 wholemeal pitta bread or 2 slices of wholemeal bread, cut in small squares, well toasted

In a large pot combine the lentils and water. Bring to the boil over high heat. Add the onions, potatoes, silver beet and oil, return to the boil, reduce the heat to medium, cover

Dried pea soup (*shorba al-bazela*)

and simmer for 10 minutes. Add the coriander and garlic, season with the salt and black pepper, stir, bring again to the boil, cover and simmer over medium–low heat for 15 minutes longer or until lentils are soft.

Remove from heat, stir in the lemon juice and serve in a large soup bowl accompanied by toasted bread, if desired, tossed just before serving in olive oil for extra taste.

Creamy Lentil Soup
Crema shorba al-adas

A hearty soup, rich in B vitamins, minerals and fibre. Eat with wholemeal bread and some cheese to obtain a good balance of nutrients and include foods rich in Vitamin C, such as tomatoes and peppers, to enhance the body's ability to absorb the iron in lentils.

Ingredients

225 g (8 oz) lentils, picked over and rinsed
1.1 l (40 fl oz) water
1 onion (about 85 g/3 oz), peeled and finely chopped
1 carrot, peeled
2 wholemeal pittas (or other bread) cut into 2½ cm (1 in) squares
¼ tsp cinnamon
a pinch of black pepper
¼ tsp allspice
1 tsp salt or to taste
a large handful of parsley, rinsed and finely chopped

In a pot combine the lentils and water. Bring to the boil over high heat, add the onions and carrot. Reduce the heat to medium–low, cover and simmer for 25–30 minutes or until lentils are soft.

Meanwhile, spread the bread squares over a shallow pan and bake in the oven until they become hard, golden and crunchy. Turn the oven heat off and allow ten minutes or more before removing the bread squares.

Place lentils and their liquid in a food processor and blend until creamy. Return to the same pan, season with cinnamon, black pepper, allspice and salt, stir well, cover and simmer for 5–8 minutes longer.

Serve hot garnished with parsley. If desired, toss the bread in 2 tbs extra-virgin olive oil just before serving.

Thick Red Lentil Soup
Shorba al-adas al-ahmar

This soup is delicious, healthy, utterly satisfying and quick to prepare. Traditionally short-grain white rice is used. To provide more nourishment, brown rice is used, which I think marries well with lentil. A good quantity of onions are sautéed in olive oil until golden brown and that contributes greatly to the flavour of the soup.

Ingredients

225 g (8 oz) split red lentils, rinsed once and drained
1 l (35 fl oz) water
About 85 g (3 oz) brown rice,
    pre-cooked in 200 ml (7 fl oz) water over low heat until soft
3 tbs olive oil
1 onion (about 140 g/5 oz) peeled,
    thinly sliced in half-moon shapes
1 tsp sugar (optional)
1 tsp cumin
$1^1/_4$ tsp salt, or to taste
1 tbs parsley, rinsed and finely chopped (optional)

In a heavy-bottomed pan combine the lentils and water. Bring to the boil, cover partially and simmer for 5 minutes over medium heat. Add the pre-cooked rice and if necessary add more hot water (but remember it is a thick soup). Cover and simmer for 8 minutes longer.

Meanwhile set a frying-pan over medium–high heat. Add the oil; when oil is hot but not smoking add the onions. Sauté for about 2 minutes, sprinkle the sugar evenly over them, reduce the heat and cook, stirring constantly, until they have a nice golden brown colour (but do not burn them). Add the onions to the lentils and allow to simmer with the lentils and rice for 1 minute. Finally season with the salt and cumin.

Remove from heat, serve immediately in separate bowls. If desired garnish with chopped parsley.

Note: You can use short grain white rice, which does not require pre-cooking.

Soup with Meat
Shorba al-ima

A very flavourful and unusual soup. It is healthful and filling.

Traditionally the cubed lamb, mini-meatballs and onions are fried in butter before simmering in the liquid. In my recipe I omit frying any of these ingredients to avoid including more saturated fat, for the liquid is already enriched from the meat that produces a delicious stock. The soup requires 15 minutes' preparation and is really delicious.

Ingredients

225 g (8 oz) meat from the leg of lamb,
    cut into 2½ cm (1 in) pieces
1.5 l (52 fl oz) water
bouquet garni: 1 bay leaf, 1 cinnamon stick,
    4 cardamoms, 5 whole black peppercorns
1 onion (about 85 g/3 oz), peeled and finely chopped
2 tsp salt or to taste
1–1½ tsp double-concentrate tomato paste
225 g (8 oz) lean ground meat (preferably lamb)
¼ tsp cinnamon
¼ tsp black pepper
¼ tsp allspice
285 g (10 oz) tomato, rinsed and finely chopped
about 50 g (2 oz) short-grain
    white rice, rinsed once and drained
50 g (2 oz) parsley leaves, rinsed and finely chopped

Trim all extra fat from lamb pieces; place in a soup-pot with the water over high heat. Skim the foam from the surface and bring to the boil, add bouquet garni and onion, bring again to the boil and reduce heat to medium. Season with half the amount of salt and add the tomato paste, cover and simmer until meat is tender but not very soft (about 40 minutes).

Meanwhile combine the ground meat with the cinnamon, black pepper, allspice and ½ tsp of the remaining salt. From this mixture make 36 mini-meatballs, rolling each portion with your fingers to form a cherry-sized mini-ball. Place on an ungreased, hot oven sheet and broil under a hot grill, 10 cm (4 in) from the heat, for 5 minutes or until meatballs are nicely browned (no need to turn them, they will cook on all sides). Remove from heat and add to the lamb which has already cooked for 40 minutes. Add the tomatoes and rice, bring to the boil, cover and simmer over medium heat for 12–15 minutes or until rice is soft. Finally and just 1–2 minutes before the end of the cooking time add the remaining salt and parsley and allow to simmer for 2 minutes longer, remove from heat and leave to stand covered for a minute or two.

    Serve hot in a soup bowl with a dish of lemon pieces. A few drops of lemon juice added to the soup enhance the flavour greatly.

Note: If using brown rice, add 15 minutes after skimming the foam from the surface of the water.

Peasant Soup
Shorba al-fallah

This soup is based on nature's wealth of fresh herbs and vegetables. Traditionally it is made with rice, onions, tomatoes, butter and spices. In my version I add green beans, carrots and fresh parsley, to top up the nutritional value, enrich the taste and give a better texture. Peasant Soup is flavourful and easy to make. Use your imagination to add as many vegetables as are on hand.

Ingredients

1.5 l (50 fl oz) water
1 onion (about 85 g/3 oz) peeled finely chopped
170 g (6 oz) tomatoes, rinsed and finely chopped
1 tsp double concentrate tomato paste
1¼ tsp salt or to taste
½ tsp extra-virgin olive oil
85 g (3 oz) brown rice, rinsed once and drained
50 g (2 oz) green beans, rinsed and diced
1 large carrot, peeled and diced
1 clove of garlic, peeled and finely diced
¼ tsp cinnamon
a pinch of black pepper
15 g (½ oz) parsley rinsed and finely chopped (optional)

In a pan combine the water, onions, tomatoes and tomato paste, salt and olive oil. Bring to the boil add the rice, boil again, reduce the heat to medium, cover and simmer for 20 minutes. Add the green beans, carrots, garlic, cinnamon and black pepper. Cover and simmer for 10–15 minutes longer or until rice is soft. Finally add the parsley, if used, cover and simmer 3 minutes longer. Remove from heat and let it stand covered for 1 minute, taste and adjust the seasonings.

    Serve hot in a large bowl or in individual bowls, with a plate of lemon wedges; a few drops of lemon juice will lift the taste of the soup greatly. Eat with home-made wholemeal bread.

Bean Soup
Shorba al-fasoulia

A sustaining and comforting winter soup, which contains meat, adding a rich taste to the stock. Although this soup is not as well known as *adas bi-hamud*, I believe it should be on the menu more often, especially in the cold season. You may also experiment with it, for instance by dropping into it a little broken-up vermicelli just before serving. Children are sure to like this soup.

Ingredients

225 g (8 oz) meat, preferably from the leg of lamb, cut into 2½ cm (1 in) cubes
1 or 2 bones, rinsed and trimmed of excess fat (optional)
1.5 l (50 fl oz) water
1 onion (about 85 g/3 oz), peeled and finely chopped
1 cinnamon stick
1 bay leaf
1¼ tsp salt
115 g (4 oz) oz butter beans, soaked for 6 hours, or any other white beans (check soaking time on packet), drained and rinsed
1 leek, rinsed and chopped
1 carrot, peeled and diced
170 g (6 oz) ripe tomatoes, rinsed and finely chopped
¼ tsp black pepper
2 tbs parsley, rinsed and finely chopped

Place the meat, bones (if used) and water in a large pot over high heat, skim the foam from the surface of the water and bring to the boil. Add the onions, cinnamon stick, bay leaf and salt. Cover and simmer over medium–low heat for 30 minutes or until meat is tender. Meanwhile cook the beans in a separate pan with 575 ml (20 fl oz) water over high heat, skim the foam from the surface, bring to the boil, then cook over medium–low heat for about 20 minutes or until tender. Drain and add, along with the leek, carrot and tomatoes, to the meat in the pan. Season with black pepper, cover and simmer for 12–15 minutes longer, taste and adjust the seasonings if necessary. A few minutes before the end of the cooking time add the parsley.

Serve hot.

Dried Pea Soup

Shorba al-bazela

A beautiful, bright-green soup that is very tasty, rich in fibre, B vitamins and iron. It is a fine soup and can be served as a first course at dinner, accompanied with home-prepared wholemeal bread. *Fromage frais* is not a traditional addition, but I recommend it to enrich the flavour.

Ingredients

200 g (7 oz) dried split peas
1–1.1 l (35–40 fl oz) water
100 g (3½ oz) onion, peeled and chopped
1 large leek (about 140 g/5 oz), rinsed well and chopped
1¼ tsp salt or to taste
3 tbs fromage frais (optional)

Rinse the peas once, drain and place with clear water in a pot. Bring to the boil, add the onion, leek and salt, bring to a second boil, cover and simmer over medium heat for 45 minutes. Remove from heat and gently place in a blender, blend until peas are smooth and creamy. Return to the pot, place over a moderately low heat, add the *fromage frais* if used, stir round once or twice and heat for 2 minutes or so, but do not let it boil.

Remove from heat, garnish with 1 tbs finely chopped parsley, and serve hot with toasted wholemeal bread.

Tomato Soup

Shorba al-banadoura

This savoury and aromatic soup bursts with distinctive flavours. It is energizing and quite substantial owing to the addition of rice and potatoes. For best results use ripe tomatoes, which produce a beautiful colour and an appetizing taste. Traditionally the soup contains meat that is cooked in the liquid to create a rich broth; meat is omitted in my recipe. To make up for the protein serve it with some cheese or with a mixed bean salad. This soup is perfect for vegetarians.

Ingredients

900 g (8 oz) ripe red tomatoes, peeled and chopped
1 l (35 fl oz) water
1 chilli pepper, de-seeded, rinsed and very finely chopped
    (or a pinch of cayenne pepper)

$1\frac{1}{2}$ tsp salt or to taste
1 large potato, rinsed gently, scraped, cut into cubes $2\frac{1}{2}$ cm (1 in) or less
50 g (2 oz) rice, preferably brown basmati
a pinch of white pepper
1 tbs yoghurt or fromage frais (optional)
1 tbs parsley, rinsed and finely chopped

In a stew-pot combine the tomatoes, water, chilli or cayenne pepper and salt. Bring to the boil. Cover and simmer over medium–low heat for 20 minutes. Remove from heat and gently pour into a blender. Process until the tomato mixture is smooth and creamy, then strain through a fine sieve over the same stew pot. Bring to the boil, add the potatoes and the rice, cover and simmer for about 20 minutes or until potato and rice are soft. Season with white pepper and stir in the yoghurt or fromage frais, if used, to give a sweetness and improve the flavour.

Serve hot garnished with parsley.

Fish

In 1915 Amin al-Rihani, a great Lebanese writer and contemporary of Kahlil Gibran wrote *Zanbakat al-Ghor* (Lily of the Valley), in which one of the characters said, 'Fish is the most digestible and nutritious meal.'

Long before that the Hebrews had attributed another virtue to fish, which they called '*dag*', a word denoting fecundity. Fish is also mentioned several times in the Gospels; there is nothing astonishing in that, for most of Jesus's disciples were fishermen and it was from the fishing nets that he called them (Mark 1:16-20). According to the Gospels Jesus ate a piece of broiled fish with his disciples after his resurrection (Luke 24:42-43).

In the early Christian era, especially during periods of persecution, fish symbolized Christ in depictions. A mosaic representing fishes found in a house in Pompeii clearly has the same connotation. Fish has too a special status in the holy Quran, the sacred book of Islam; while the destruction of all, except noxious, animals is forbidden during the pilgrimage, fishing in the sea is permitted (s 5: 97).

Remarkably enough, the Church allowed the eating of fish on the two days of the week, Wednesday and Friday, when meat was forbidden. That was of course before the rule was eased and finally abandoned, possibly because fish became as expensive as meat.

Fish is highly valued nearly everywhere for other reasons, notably its delicate flesh and an adaptability to various ways of cooking. Still, not everyone has shared that view, as instanced by an old French saying, *'La sauce fait manger le poisson* ('Sauce helps the fish go down').

In my experience many fishes, such as sea bass, sea bream and red mullet are not only health giving, but also taste wonderful grilled, baked or fried. The sauces in my fish recipes complement the dishes, to make them more imaginative and to satisfy the Lebanese palate, which likes variety.

The Lebanese are great lovers of fish, not surprisingly since the sea stretches along Lebanon's entire length, some 220 kilometres from Nahr al-Kabir in the North to Ras Nakura in the South. Historic towns are scattered along Lebanon's coast: Tripoli (the Crusaders' fortress and then a Mamluk stronghold), Byblos (the world's oldest town still inhabited), Beirut (basically Ottoman, then a cosmopolitan city), Sidon (the oldest fishing port in history) and Tyre (famous for its desperate resistance to Alexander the Great). Phoenicians, Greeks, Romans, Byzantines, Arabs, Crusaders, Ottomans and French have occupied these settlements in turn and left an imprint on the culture and on the way of life, and certainly on the culinary traditions. It is no wonder that legends and myths are legion. According to one account, George, a soldier under the Roman Emperor Diocletian, slayed a sea dragon near the mouth of Beirut River, an ancient fishermen's haunt; the Crusaders spread his legend in Europe and he became the patron saint of England in the 14th century.

From ancient times up to the present fishing methods have probably remained the same. Fishermen leave with their small boats in the middle of the night and the faint glow of their lanterns sprinkles light on the dark blue waters, as though reflecting the stars in the clear sky. Meanwhile, restaurateurs await their return hoping to pick up the favourite fish in Lebanon, the red mullet (*sultan ibrahim*) and thus meet the demands of their innumerable customers.

As health awareness has grown so the nutritional value of fish has been increasingly recognized. Fish provides a good mixture of lightness, taste and nourishment. It is low in fat and high in the polyunsaturates that protect arteries from damage; it is an excellent source of protein and iodine, is easily digestible and has a significant amount of essential amino acids.

In the Levant basin of the Mediterranean as many as 324 species are listed, of which 177 were reported from the coastal waters of Lebanon. I will name those most commonly used in cooking.

Red mullet (*sultan ibrahim*) is the most sought-after and the most expensive of the fishes. In Lebanon small ones are preferred, which are deep-fried until crisp and served hot. This fish has a distinctive and wonderful flavour and looks marvellous when served in quantity on a large platter covered with fried pitta bread and accompanied by lots of lemon wedges and a bowl of *tahini*. In restaurants the *sultan ibrahim* platter is brought to the table after the *mezze* and served as a main dish.

Then comes the sea bass (*lukos*), which is also a delicacy with its firm flesh and subtle flavour. *Lukos* grows quite large and it is served as a main dish, either seasoned with herbs and baked, or served cold as Chilli Fish (*samaka harra*) as part of a buffet.

Then comes the sea bream (*farride*), which can be as big as 4 kg (8 lbs). It has a good taste and costs much less than sea bass, which it can replace in *samaka harra*. Small specimens of around 14 cm (5–6 in) are deep-fried and served as a main dish accompanied by fried pitta bread and wedges of lemon.

Next are certain tiny fishes: the reddish-gold red mullet babies (*sultan ibrahim bizri*); the light silver-grey whitebait (*samak bizri*); and the garfish babies, similar to sardines but light in colour. All these tiny fishes are served hot or warm, mostly as a starter, and washed down with *arak*, the favourite native alcoholic drink.

Tuna, called *balamida*, is a silvery-blue. The flesh is firm, strong in flavour and dry. My mother used it in *tagen* so that its dryness would be camouflaged by adding *tahini* and onions.

Among other fishes seen on Lebanese tables is sturgeon (*samakat al-hafsh*) which is considered in Lebanon inferior to sea bass (*lukos*). It has a meaty white flesh and could be used for Fish with Rice and Cumin (*sayadieh*) or Chilli Fish (*samaka harra*). Stickleback, known as *samakat al-shok* in Beirut and *ikais* in the north, has a dark silver-grey colour for the male and a light silver grey for the female. One has to be careful in handling this fish for the fins are slightly poisonous. Nonetheless it is a good fish for frying. Fishermen catch rabbitfish, or spine-foot (*samakat al-zalak*), attracting it with a lilac leaf. It is a good fish for grilling, juicy and mildly flavoured. Eel (*hankliss*) is another tasty fish, mostly fried. Sea animals and sea shells, such as calamari (*al-kalam*), squid (*sabideg*), octopus (*akhtabout*), lobster (*karakand*) and shrimps are eaten in Lebanon but they are scarce and are mostly prepared following Western recipes.

There was a time when Lebanese people could not imagine eating anything but fresh fish. Frozen fish was scorned. Hard times have changed that. Still, whenever possible, the Lebanese favour fresh fish, which is recognizable by the bright and bulging eyes, the reddish gills, the firm flesh and an unadulterated odour. Frozen fish, once thawed, should not be refrozen.

Never overcook fish otherwise it will lose its moistness and flavour. If you can, get your fishmonger to scale the fish and cut its fins. If not, grasp the tail firmly, and with a sharp knife remove the scales as well as the fins. Always rub the fish with a piece of lemon to remove any rank fish odour, then wash it under cold running water and keep it in the coolest place in your refrigerator until it is ready to be cooked. If it is very fresh it should keep for two days but it is always best to cook it the day of purchase. Remember the Spanish proverb that says, 'Guests and fish stink on the third day.'

The fish recipes chosen for this book taste delicious and are aesthetically attractive.

Quanto plura parasti,
Tanto plura cupis
(*The more you get, the more you want*)
Horace, *Epistles*

Fried Red Mullet
Sultan ibrahim mikli

Sultan is a title of honour that indicates the preeminence of red mullet among fishes.

During a recent visit to Beirut I was taken for lunch to an unpretentious restaurant located in the outskirts of Byblos. The restaurant, which is built on rocks alongside the sea, turned out to serve good, simple food. What I really wanted to do was to chat to the owner, who is a real fisherman. He was not very talkative and I could barely extract any information.

He advised my host to have the fresh yield of the day, which was red mullet and sea bream. In a matter of seconds our table was laid with a *mezze* consisting of nearly a dozen wonderful and varied dishes, which was followed by the most glorious platter of *sultan ibrahim* served covered with fried golden-coloured pitta breads, accompanied by a dish of lemon wedges and a bowl of *tahini*.

Ingredients

4 red mullets (about 675–900 g/1 lb 8 oz-2 lb), gutted and scaled
1½ tsp salt
enough flour to dip fish in
olive oil for deep-frying

Wash mullet with cold water, pat dry with kitchen paper. Sprinkle salt inside and on the outer surface of the fish and dip in flour. Shake off excess.

In a frying-pan big enough to take 4 mullets heat the oil until it is hot but not smoking (about 190° C/375° F). Immerse and fry the mullet for about 3–4 minutes on each side or until crispy.

Serve hot or warm with fried pitta bread, a bowl of *tahini* sauce and lots of lemon wedges. If desired, eat with fried potatoes.

Fish with Rice and Cumin
Sayadieh

Sayadieh is a word derived from sayad (fisherman). This is a delicious dish favoured by the locals of Tripoli in the North of Lebanon, although it is also eaten all along the coast. In restaurants it is served once a week as a plat du jour, normally on Fridays, and in homes on special occasions or for honoured guests.

Although the recipe is elaborate, if followed correctly and patiently it is rewarding.

Sayadieh is usually prepared with sea bass but any other fleshy white fish will do, as long as it has a head to be used in the stock to add a richer flavour. Otherwise you have to use a stock cube, which is very much second best.

Cumin in this recipe blends well with the remaining ingredients, heightening the flavour without dominating it.

Ingredients

For the fish
1 sea bass (about 900 g/2 lb) with head, gutted, scaled, cut into large steaks and rinsed

1 onion (about 50 g/2 oz) peeled

1.1–1.3 l (40–48 fl oz) water

Bouquet garni (1 large cinnamon stick, 2 bay leaves, 4–6 cardamoms, 6–8 black peppercorns, 1 parsley sprig)

1$^{1}/_{2}$–1$^{3}/_{4}$ tsp salt or to taste

For the rice

150–175 ml (5–6 fl oz) olive oil

300–350 g (10–12 oz) onion, peeled and thinly sliced into half-moon shapes

200 g (7 oz) rice

1 tsp salt or to taste

$^{1}/_{2}$–$^{3}/_{4}$ tsp ground cumin

a heaped $^{1}/_{4}$ tsp ground cinnamon

$^{1}/_{2}$ tsp ground white pepper

30 g (1 oz) pine nuts (or more) sautéed in a little oil until golden in colour

30 g (1 oz) flaked almonds (or more) sautéed in a little oil until golden in colour

For the sauce

2–3 tbs lemon juice

a pinch of cinnamon

Place the fish head and onion in a large saucepan, cover with water, set over medium–high heat; skim the scum from the surface. Bring to the boil, add bouquet garni, fish steaks, season with salt and return to the boil. Reduce the heat to medium, cover and simmer for a mere 8–9 minutes, otherwise the fish will fall apart.

From the saucepan remove fish steaks with a slotted spatula, leaving fish head and bouquet garni to simmer covered for 6–8 minutes longer over low heat. As soon as the fish steaks are cool enough to handle, remove the flesh, barely cover with stock to keep it moist. Return the bones and skin to simmer with the fish head in the saucepan; this will enrich the stock.

In another saucepan heat the oil until hot but not smoking, add the onions and fry over moderately high heat for 2–3 minutes. Reduce the heat to medium and continue fry-ing until onions are brown in colour but not burned, about 12–15 minutes longer. This will enhance the taste and give the rice an exquisite chestnut colour. When onions are browned pour off excess oil and return to heat; strain the fish stock over them through a sieve, discarding bouquet garni, fish head and bones.

Bring to the boil over high heat, reduce heat to low, cover and simmer for 30 minutes or until onions are soft enough to filter. When onions are soft remove and strain through a sieve set over a bowl, pressing the onions down with the back of a spoon. Make sure all the onions are pressed—the taste of the rice depends a lot on them.

Stir the resulting stock, measure 450 ml (15 fl oz), pour into a saucepan and set over high heat. Add the rice, stir and bring to the boil. Reduce the heat to low, season with salt, cover and simmer for about 10 minutes or until rice is soft. About 3 minutes before the end of the cooking time, season with the cumin, cinnamon and white pepper (they need short cooking to retain their strong flavour) stir gently, cover and finish cooking.

In the meantime to make the sauce, measure 300 ml (10 fl oz) from the same stock, combine with the lemon juice in a small saucepan and simmer for a few minutes over medium heat; season with cinnamon and reserve.

Turn the heat off and leave the rice to stand covered for a minute or two, allowing the flavours to blend and the rice to fluff.

To serve, reheat the fish for a few seconds. In the meantime spread the rice over a warm serving dish, cover with fish steaks and garnish with pine-nuts and almonds.

Serve with the reserved sauce in a bowl, spooning over as much as desired.

Fish with Tahini

Tagen al-samak

Tagen al-samak is nourishing and extremely satisfying. It consists of fish steaks, onions and *tahini* (sesame paste). It is served cold as part of a *mezze*, or hot as a main dish accompanied with a dish of rice. In Lebanon thrifty housewives used the left-overs of any baked fish to make tagen. This recipe does not bind you to one kind of fish. Tuna, for instance, blends well with *tahini,* which moistens its dryness. Sea bass is favoured traditionally; haddock is also a good fish to use.

For this recipe cod and tuna are equally acceptable.

Ingredients

4 cod fillets, about 115–125 g (4–4$^{1}/_{2}$ oz), skinned and boned
1$^{1}/_{2}$ tsp salt or to taste
$^{1}/_{4}$ tsp black pepper or to taste
flour to dust fish
4 tbs extra-virgin olive oil
150 g (5$^{1}/_{2}$ oz) onions, peeled, thinly sliced into half-moon shapes
150 ml (5 fl oz) white *tahini*
75 ml (3 fl oz) lemon juice
150 ml (5 fl oz) water
2 tbs chopped parsley, rinsed and drained

Wash the fish with cold water, pat dry, sprinkle with the salt and black pepper and dip in flour, shaking off excess. Leave in a cool place to absorb its seasonings.

Meanwhile over moderately high heat in a medium-sized, heavy-bottomed, non-stick frying pan, heat 3 tbs oil. Add the onions and cook, stirring frequently, for about 2 minutes. Reduce to medium heat and cook the onions until golden in colour. Remove onions from pan with a slotted spoon allowing oil to drip back into pan; spread onions evenly in a baking dish.

Return frying pan over medium heat; add the remaining 1 tbs oil and when oil is hot add the fish pieces and cook for about 2–3 minutes on each side. With a spatula remove from pan and place over onions in the baking dish.

In a bowl put the *tahini* and lemon juice and whisk (at first it will thicken); add the water gradually until it forms a very thin liquid like single cream (make sure *tahini* does not stick to the base of the bowl). If necessary add a little more water.

Pour this sauce all over fish and onions in the baking dish. Sprinkle with parsley and bake in a pre-heated oven (180° C/350° F/gas mark 4) for about 20 minutes or until the top is pale brown.

Serve hot with Vermicelli Rice and an Oriental Salad or at room temperature with wholemeal pitta bread. A plate of fresh radishes makes a pleasant accompaniment.

Hot or Chilli Fish
Samaka harra

A simple and highly nourishing recipe to prepare, providing great nourishment. *Samaka harra* is a favourite of the coastal people in Lebanon, especially the inhabitants of Tripoli in the north, where the dish originated. It is a meal also appreciated by my non-Lebanese friends.

After baking the fish (usually sea bass, *miskar* or dogfish), removing and discarding the bones, the fish is reconstituted and served whole, entirely covered by a cream-like sauce with a tangy, nutty and spicy flavour.

Ingredients

1 sea bass or hake (about 900 g/2 lb), gutted and scaled
³/₄ tsp salt or to taste
¹/₄ tsp black pepper or to taste
¹/₄ tsp cinnamon or to taste
1 clove garlic, peeled and crushed
2 stems of coriander with leaves, rinsed and drained
1 slice lemon (with skin) cut into 6 pieces
1¹/₂–2 tbs extra-virgin olive oil

For the sauce
5 tbs *tahini*
6 tbs lemon juice
6–7 tbs water
4–6 large cloves garlic, peeled and finely chopped
1¹/₂ tbs olive oil,

1 red chilli pepper, rinsed,
   de-seeded and finely chopped
a handful coriander, tough ends discarded,
   rinsed, chopped and drained
$\frac{1}{4}$ tsp ground chilli pepper
56–84 g (2–3 oz) pine-nuts, finely chopped
56–84 g (2–3 oz) walnuts, finely chopped
$\frac{1}{2}$ tsp salt

Wash fish with cold water, pat dry. Score 2 diagonal cuts on each side. Sprinkle with salt and black pepper. Rub its cavity only with cinnamon and garlic, then fill it with coriander and lemon, place in a baking dish and smear oil over all sides of fish. Leave aside for 5 minutes (or longer) to allow fish to absorb its seasonings.

Meanwhile prepare the sauce. In a medium saucepan, whisk *tahini*, lemon juice and water to form a smooth, thin liquid. Reserve until further use.

In a frying-pan over moderately low heat sauté the garlic in oil for a few seconds, but do not brown it, otherwise it will be bitter. To the garlic in the frying-pan add the chilli pepper, coriander, and ground chilli; stir once and add the reserved *tahini* sauce. Cook for about 2–3 minutes, stirring frequently, then add the pine-nuts, walnuts and salt. Stir for a few seconds and remove from heat; reserve this mixture.

Meanwhile pre-heat the grill and put the fish under to cook for about 5–7 minutes or until the skin flakes. Remove from heat and place on a serving platter. Cool for about a minute and carefully skin, leaving the head. Spread the reserved *tahini* mixture all over fish except head.

Serve warm or at room temperature. Hot or Chilli Fish, accompanied by the traditional *kibbeh* and *tabbouleh*, is good for parties.

Fish Kibbeh
Kibbet al-samak

This exceptional recipe is another favourite of mine. It is said that *kibbet al-samak* was originally prepared during Lent by the inhabitants of Lebanon's coastal towns. It is so tasty that very soon it was adopted enthusiastically by most Lebanese.

Burghol (cracked wheat) and meaty white fish are its basic ingredients. The dish is prepared along the same lines as the national dish *kibbeh*. The intense flavour of coriander, orange rind and saffron give it a unique and distinctive aroma.

Traditionally sturgeon or sea bass, both white and meaty fishes, are used to prepare this dish. I use cod because it is not only inexpensive but also versatile enough to blend successfully with the other ingredients.

Kibbet al-samak is ideal for parties and has the advantage that it can be prepared in advance.

Fish with rice and cumin (*sayadieh*)

Ingredients

125 ml (4 fl oz) extra-virgin olive oil

400 g (14 oz) onion, peeled thinly sliced into half moon shapes

$\frac{1}{2}$ tsp saffron threads, ground gently in mortar and pestle

$\frac{1}{4}$ tsp turmeric

$\frac{1}{4}$ tsp white pepper

$\frac{1}{2}$ tsp salt

For the dough

1 onion (about 85 g/3 oz), peeled

$\frac{1}{4}$–$\frac{1}{2}$ tsp orange rind

$\frac{1}{4}$ tsp black pepper

$\frac{1}{4}$ tsp cinnamon

$\frac{3}{4}$ tsp salt

170 g (6 oz) fine *burghol*, rinsed and well drained

3–4 tbs flour

550 g (1$\frac{1}{4}$ lb 4 oz) cod fillets, skinned, boned and cut into chunks

6–8 sprigs coriander, tough ends discarded, rinsed and patted dry

75 ml (3 fl oz) extra-virgin olive oil

In a frying-pan over medium–high heat, add the oil and heat until hot but not smoking. Add the onions, cook for 2 minutes, reduce heat to moderate and continue cooking until onions are golden-brown in colour, stirring frequently. Add the saffron, turmeric, white pepper and salt and stir well.

Remove the pan from heat. Spoon the onion mixture evenly over the base of a baking dish. Leave aside for later use.

To prepare the dough:

Grate or grind the onion and orange rind until smooth, place in a bowl and rub in the black pepper, cinnamon and salt. Squeeze excess water from the *burghol* and rub well with the onions. Reserve *burghol* mixture.

Rub fish with flour to rid it of rank fish odour and shake off excess.

In a blender add alternately fish chunks and coriander, blending until uniform in consistency. Add the reserved *burghol* mixture gradually and blend for a few more seconds. Remove the resulting moist dough from the blender. Shape into a ball.

Take a small portion at a time of the fish dough and flatten over the onion mixture in the baking dish, dipping hands in flour because the dough is sticky.

Cover this layer with oil and cut into a criss-cross pattern right down to the onions, allowing the oil to seep through.

Put the baking dish in a pre-heated oven (180° C/350° F/gas mark 4) and bake for 30 minutes or until the top is nicely browned. Remove from the oven, pour out excess oil and allow to cool slightly.

With a small palate knife remove the lozenges of *kibbeh* following the criss-cross pattern. Place them in a serving dish with the onions facing upwards.

Serve warm or cold with Onion tagen. Cabbage Salad is a further nutritious accompaniment.

Baked Fish
Samak meshwi

This is a simple way of preparing fish. In Lebanon until the 1950s, before people had ovens in their homes and when each area had its baker, fish was wrapped in newspaper and sent to the local bakery to be cooked. When the fish was ready it was unwrapped, skinned and served warm or cold, the latter being convenient for buffets, served with the classical bowl of *tahini* and a separate dish of lemon wedges.

Ingredients

1 sea bass, hake or sea bream (about 900 g/2 lb), gutted and scaled
1 tsp salt, or to taste
$\frac{1}{4}$ tsp black pepper or to taste
$\frac{1}{4}$ tsp nutmeg
$\frac{1}{4}$ tsp cinnamon
2 slices lemon (with peel), cut in half
110 g (4 oz) onion, peeled and sliced
2 stems of coriander or parsley with the leaves on, rinsed and patted dry
2–3 tbs extra-virgin olive oil

Wash the fish with cold water and pat dry. Score 2 diagonal cuts on each side. Sprinkle with the salt and pepper inside and out. Rub its cavity with the nutmeg and cinnamon, and fill it with the lemon slices, onion slices and coriander or parsley. Place in a baking dish. Smear the oil all over the fish's sides and bake in a pre-heated oven (180° C/350° F/gas mark 4) for about 20 minutes. Do not overcook, or it will become dry.

When the fish is ready, remove from the oven and place it on a serving dish. Serve immediately with a separate dish of lemon wedges and a bowl of *tarator bi-bakdouness* (*tahini* sauce with parsley).

Fried Whitebait
Samak bizri mikli

Traditionally *samak bizri* is dipped in flour and deep-fried in olive oil until crisp. It is served hot with lemon wedges as an appetizer and may be accompanied with a bowl of

tahini sauce. Lebanese also enjoy sipping *arak* with *samak bizri*.

Samak bizri are tiny fishes which have not been gutted and may taste bitter. To avoid this my mother gave me two tips. One is to soak the fish for half an hour in lots of lemon juice mixed with a little water. The other is to soak it in milk for the same length of time, drain it, pat it dry, dip it in flour, and fry it in hot oil until golden in colour. I recommend the latter method which, in my opinion, renders the fish more delicious and lighter.

A third tip was given to me by a woman fishmonger who presides over a stall in the amazing Marche Forville of Cannes in the South of France. She told me to soak the fishes in beer for 15 minutes and to fry them in hot oil until crisp. I tried it and indeed it worked wonderfully.

Ingredients

450 g (1 lb) of whitebait
300 ml (10 fl oz) milk
flour
olive oil for deep-frying
salt to taste
lemon wedges

In a bowl soak the whitebait in milk for about 40 minutes in a cool place, then drain off the milk. Pat the fishes dry and dip in flour, gently shaking off any excess.

In a frying-pan heat the oil until hot but not smoking (about 190° C/375° F) and fry whitebait a little at a time, shaking pan gently while cooking to prevent the fish from sticking. Cook until crispy and golden in colour.

Remove from pan and drain on kitchen paper. Arrange on a serving dish, sprinkle with a little salt. Serve hot with lemon wedges. If desired accompany with *tahini* sauce.

Fish with Dry Thyme
Samak bi-zaatar

Samak bi-zaatar is one of my favourite fish recipes. The stuffing is made of vegetables and herbs, adding more richness to the fish flavour.

Zaatar (thyme) one of the ingredients, is a popular herb all over Lebanon, mainly used to top *manakish*; it blends well with the green and chilli peppers, garlic and oil, giving this dish a distinctive and succulent flavour without overpowering the taste of the fish. *Zaatar* is believed by the Lebanese to stimulate the brain. A present of *zaatar* is highly valued among Lebanese expatriates.

This dish has an irresistible aroma and is a delight even for those who are watching their diet.

Fish with almonds (*samak bi-loz*)

Ingredients

1 sea bass (about 900 g/2 lb) or any other firm-fleshed white fish, gutted and scaled
1 tsp salt, or to taste
$^1/_4$ tsp black pepper or to taste
a pinch of white pepper
2–3 tbs extra-virgin olive oil
1 small green pepper, rinsed, de-seeded and finely chopped
1 chilli pepper, rinsed, de-seeded and finely chopped
3 cloves of garlic, peeled and crushed
3 tsp *zaatar* (dry thyme without sesame seeds and *sumak*)
2 tbs lemon juice.

Wash fish with cold water, pat dry. Score it with 2 or 3 diagonal cuts on both sides and rub it with the salt, black and white peppers inside and out.

Place the fish in a baking dish and with 1 tbs olive oil, oil it well all over. Let it stand for 5 minutes in a cool place to absorb its seasonings.

Meanwhile, combine green and chilli peppers, garlic, *zaatar*, lemon and the remaining oil and stir well 2 or 3 times. Scoop out more than half the mixture and stuff the cavity of the fish. Spread the remaining mixture evenly over all sides of the sea bass, except head.

In a pre-heated oven (150–80° C/350–75° F/gas mark 4–5) bake the fish for 20 minutes, making sure not to overcook it, to keep it moist and tender.

When the fish is ready, remove from the oven and place carefully on a hot serving dish. Arrange around it some fresh thyme and lemon wedges. Serve immediately with a mixture of vegetables.

Fish with Rice
Samak bi-roz

This succulent, saffron-scented fish rice recipe is nourishing, filling and easy to prepare.

Traditionally *samak bi-roz* is prepared with sea bass or any other good quality and meaty fish. My choice is monkfish, which I came to like after I settled in England. It has a firm texture that holds well while cooking, it cooks quickly and has a delicious subtle taste.

Saffron is said to have been known as early as Solomon's time and travelled everywhere with Phoenician traders. Because ground saffron loses its flavour when stored for a long time, I have used saffron threads, which give a wonderful aroma and a beautiful yellow colour. If you do not like saffron, turmeric is a good substitute; it has little taste but also gives the dish a yellow colour.

Samak bi-roz is a delight and a good introduction to a healthier diet for people who hitherto have not particularly liked fish.

Ingredients

2 tbs extra-virgin olive oil

100 g (3½ oz) onion peeled and sliced thinly into half moon shapes

½ tsp saffron threads (ground gentlywith a mortar and pestle)

500 ml (16 fl oz) water

675 g (1 lb 8 oz) monkfish, cut into 2½ cm (1 in) pieces

200 g (7 oz) white rice (preferably basmati)

1½ tsp salt, or to taste

¼ tsp white pepper

15 ml (½ oz) pine-nuts, toasted in lightly oiled,
    heavy-bottomed pan until golden in colour

30 ml (1 oz) almond flakes, toasted in lightly oiled,
    heavy-bottomed pan until golden in colour

In a saucepan, heat the oil. Add the onions, sauté for about 2–3 minutes, stirring frequently, until onions become tender and pale in colour and lose their strong smell. Add the saffron and the water and bring to the boil. Add fish pieces, return to boil. Add the rice, stir and return to the boil, then reduce heat to medium–low. Season with salt and pepper. Cover and simmer for 8–10 minutes. The smell from the pot is exquisite.

Remove from heat but keep pan covered for about 2 minutes, allowing the flavours to blend. While hot, spread over a serving dish and garnish with toasted pine-nuts and almonds. Eat with a seasonal salad.

Prawns
Koraidis

Along the Lebanese shores small prawns are found in limited quantities and for a short season (summer). Traditionally prawns are not prepared elaborately, but are simply boiled or fried. Their small size renders them unsuitable for grilling. Some years ago, under the combined influence of East and West, prawns started to be served either in curry or *à la provençale*.

This recipe was prepared in my kitchen by my friend Yankit So, the eminent writer of Chinese cookbooks. The prawns were marinaded in the Chinese style, then fried the Lebanese way in olive oil, garlic and lemon juice. The result was much more interesting than if they had merely been fried.

Ingredients

12 large raw prawns (450 g/1 lb) in their shells

½ tsp salt

1 tsp cornflour
1 tbs egg white, beaten lightly
3–4 tbs extra-virgin olive oil
1–2 large cloves of garlic
3 tbs lemon juice

Shell the prawns: hold each between the fingers; using a pointed knife slit along the back, removing and discarding the black vein, if any.

To marinade the prawns, place them in a mixing bowl, add the salt and stir in one direction for about 2 seconds. Add the cornflour and the egg white. Stir again as above. Cover and refrigerate for 2–4 hours. This will make the prawns crisper in texture. Just before frying them, separate the prawns.

In a frying-pan heat the oil until really hot, add the prawns to the oil and fry for about 20 seconds, then add the garlic, stirring all the time, and continue this operation for about $^1/_2$ minute or until they become pinkish in colour, curling up at the same time. At this point add the lemon juice, stir once, remove from heat and serve, spooning over the juices in the frying-pan.

Fish with Almonds
Samak bi-loz

Samak bi-loz makes a luxury lunch or dinner. Because it is practical and easy to make, however, it is useful for entertaining or as a treat for oneself.

This recipe is the reflect of the influence of French cuisine on ours.

Originally trout was used, but trout was never abundant in Lebanon's rivers until farming was introduced in the 1960s. Since then Trout with Almonds has been served in restaurants near trout farms, such as Sad al Karoun in the western Bekaa valley or Chtoura on the road to Damascus.

In my recipe I use Dover Sole, which is as succulent as Lebanon's trout.

Ingredients

2 tbs extra-virgin olive oil
4 tbs almond flakes
2 Dover soles, about 900 g (2 lb), filleted (8 fillets)
15 g ($^1/_2$ oz) unsalted butter
$^3/_4$ tsp salt, or to taste
1 tbs lemon juice (optional)

In a large, heavy-bottomed non-stick frying-pan heat the oil until hot but not smoking. Add the almond flakes and fry until golden in colour. Remove with a slotted spoon, allowing the oil, to drip back into the frying-pan and reserve.

Wash the fish fillets with cold water and pat dry. To the oil remaining in the frying-pan add the butter and heat over moderately high heat. When oil and butter are hot, add the fish fillets and fry for about 2–3 minutes, reducing heat to moderate and turning them over once. Season with the salt. Sprinkle the reserved almonds over the fish fillets, continuing to heat for a few more seconds. Finally, add the lemon juice if used.

Remove the fillets with the almonds from the frying-pan. Place on a serving dish or on separate dishes. Serve immediately. Eat with Rocket Salad.

Fish Stew
Yakhnet al-samak

This is a wholesome stew, providing a good combination of flavourful ingredients. Cumin, *sumak* and coriander, traditional Lebanese and Middle Eastern spices and herbs, give the stew its consistency and character.

This dish is not served in Lebanese restaurants and seldom in homes, which is strange as it is fairly inexpensive and quite energizing.

Owing to the richness of the ingredients I have skipped the frying of the fish and the onions; instead the fish is simmered gently in its own juices.

Ingredients

1 sea bass or St Peters (Tilapia) or any firm white fish (about 900 g/2 lb),
    gutted and scaled
350 ml (12 fl oz) water
bouquet garni: 1 large cinnamon bark, 4 cardamoms,
    6 black peppercorns, 1 bay leaf
140–170 g (5–6 oz) onion, peeled and chopped
115 g (4 oz) tomatoes, rinsed and chopped
1 green pepper, de-seeded, rinsed and diced
a handful of coriander, roots cut off, rinsed and chopped
1 red chilli pepper, rinsed and finely diced
1 clove of garlic, peeled and finely chopped
1 tsp salt, or to taste
1 tsp *sumak* (optional)
$^1/_2$ tsp cumin
2 tbs lemon juice

Wash the fish with cold water. With a sharp knife cut through skin and bones to make 2–3 thick pieces to fit in your pan; leave the fish head, which gives an intense flavour to the liquid.

Cover the fish with cold water. Add bouquet garni and put the saucepan over a moderately high heat; skim the foam off and bring to the boil. Reduce to moderate heat and add the onions, tomatoes, green pepper, coriander, chilli pepper and garlic. Stir. Season with the salt, sumak and cumin. Return to the boil. Cover and simmer for 10–12 minutes allowing all the different vegetables, herbs and seasonings to be absorbed, producing a delicious flavour and a good consistency.

Just one minute before the end of the cooking time add the lemon juice to give a mild, tangy zest to the flavour.

Remove the pan from heat, gently remove all fish pieces and head. Scoop out fish meat, return to stew to keep it hot, discarding the bones, skin and head.

Serve the stew in a bowl. Eat with *Roz al-samak*.

Red Mullet in Tomato Sauce

Sultan ibrahim bi-banadoura

This recipe is another variation for red mullet; it requires short preparation and is quite common in France and Italy.

Red mullet is found in many waters but the Mediterranean variety is deemed the best. In this recipe the combination of fresh and canned tomatoes gives a deep red colour to the dish and brings out its full succulent flavour.

In Lebanon the tomato sauce is also used as a base for shrimps. At the end of cooking a few drops of lemon juice are added to heighten the taste. This dish is always served with rice.

In this recipe I grill the red mullet instead of frying, in order to cut down on fat without losing any of the flavour.

Ingredients

1 tbs extra-virgin olive oil
55–75 g (2–2$\frac{1}{2}$ oz) onions, peeled and chopped
250 ml (8 fl oz) water
1–1$\frac{1}{2}$ tsp flour
1 chilli pepper, rinsed, de-seeded, finely chopped
$\frac{1}{4}$ tsp cayenne pepper or to taste
115 g (4 oz) tomatoes, peeled and chopped
450–500 g (1 can) chopped, peeled tomatoes
1 tsp salt or to taste
a pinch of white pepper
$\frac{1}{4}$ tsp sugar
4 red mullets

In a saucepan combine the oil, onions, water, flour, chilli and cayenne peppers, fresh and canned tomatoes, salt, white pepper and sugar. Bring to the boil over high heat, reduce heat to moderate, cover and simmer this tomato mixture for 20 minutes.

Meanwhile pre-heat the grill; wash the red mullet with cold water and pat dry. Score fish with two diagonal cuts on both sides. Sprinkle salt all over, including cavity. Place fish on a slightly oiled baking sheet and cook under the grill about 2–3 minutes each side, or until crispy.

Remove fish from grill and add to simmer with the tomato mixture for 5 minutes longer.

Serve hot on separate dishes covered with the sauce, along with *Roz al-samak* and a seasonal side salad.

Poultry

Until a few decades ago chickens were highly valued and raised particularly for eggs. Older chickens were sacrificed for the cauldron, to make a meal for a festive occasion or an eminent visitor. After childbirth, a mother used to be fed for 40 days on the traditional chicken soup or stuffed chicken until all her strength was regained. The belief that chicken soup is invigorating and curative is an old one. It is said that centuries ago Maimonides, the Jewish philosopher and scholar, treated Saladin's son for asthma with chicken soup.

When battery rearing of chickens became customary in the 1960s the quality dropped but so did the price, with the result that chicken was cheaper than meat and it became popular. Various recipes then evolved, for chicken is versatile and adopts the flavours derived from the spices, aromatic herbs or vegetables of any given recipe.

Recently health has been demonstrated to be closely linked with diet; certain foods strengthen the immune system and protect the body from degenerative diseases. Chicken has regained favour as a good source of protein with a low fat content.

The following recipes are simple, designed for four or five people. They are enjoyable to experiment with, delicious to eat, and most of all constitute good nourishment. The chicken in these recipes is combined with rice, spices, aromatic herbs, vegetables, pine-nuts or almonds, or again baked, grilled, simmered or sautéed. All the dishes are prepared with a small quantity of olive oil, unlike the traditional way which uses *samneh*, giving nevertheless an exquisite earthy flavour.

Some recipes are elaborate and suitable for special occasions, others are quick to put together for simple, everyday dinners, with the great advantage that they can be prepared ahead of time.

Chickens carry harmful bacteria, which thorough cooking destroys. Freshly cooked chicken can be kept in the refrigerator for up to 2 or 3 days.

To clean the chicken remove all visible fat around the neck and tail, remove giblets from the cavity, sprinkle the chicken generously with salt and rub inside and out with half a lemon to rid it of rank odour. Next wash the chicken inside and out with cold water, pulling and discarding all bloody bits. Remember to wash your hands, surfaces and utensils with hot soapy water after every preparation with raw chicken and before handling or

Chicken kebab (*djaj bi-shish meshwi*)

touching other ingredients. Proceed with the cooking.

The secret of good cooking lies in buying good quality produce, preparing all the ingredients needed beforehand, and tasting and checking the food half-way through cooking so you can adjust the seasonings and liquid.

Free-range chickens are generally best because they are allowed to rear freely and are fed on natural food; I also use corn-fed chicken, which I find very tasty, and which has a distinct yellow colour derived from the corn. Nowadays both varieties are widely available and for our convenience they are sold in individual parts. Some of my recipes call for pieces of chicken. I mostly use the white meat, but if you wish you can select the dark meat or mix the two.

In most of the recipes the skin is removed to cut down on fat; in roasting, however, the skin and fat protect the flesh from drying.

Turkey Stuffed with Rice

Habash mehshi bi-roz

Chicken form the major part of Lebanon's livestock. Turkey, on the other hand, is rather alien to Lebanese cuisine, except that it is enjoyed during the festive seasons of Christmas and the New Year. However, turkey is not a recent addition to the Lebanese table, but was imported into Lebanon from Cyprus at least as long ago as the 19th century.

Turkey with Rice is filled with a highly flavoured stuffing, which adds a lot of flavour to the meat. The bird is cooked covered with yoghurt to keep it moist and give it a nice golden-brown colour.

Turkey is nourishing and low in fat. This dish, which is entirely different from the turkey prepared in the West, is very tasty. For a change present it to your family and friends next Christmas.

Ingredients

For the rice
2–3 tbs extra-virgin olive oil
450 g (1 lb) lean ground meat (preferably lamb)
1 apple, peeled, cored and very finely chopped
550 g (1 lb 4 oz) rice
2 tsp cinnamon
2 tsp allspice
$\frac{1}{2}$ tsp black pepper
$\frac{1}{2}$ tsp nutmeg
$\frac{1}{4}$ tsp ground cloves
16 chestnuts without the skin
1.66 l (56 fl oz) water or preferably chicken stock (for stock see

Chicken Rice with Ground Meat recipe)
2 tsp salt or to taste

For the garnish
olive oil for frying
85 g (3 oz) blanched almonds
85 g (3 oz) pine nuts
85 g (3 oz) pistachio nuts

For the turkey
a 4.5–5.4 kg (10–12 lb) turkey
lemon wedges
salt
black pepper
scant $\frac{1}{2}$ tsp white pepper
55 g (2 oz) unsalted butter, softened (optional)
yoghurt

Set a pan over medium heat, add and heat the oil, add the meat and sauté until it changes in colour and cooks through (about 5–6 minutes). Add the apple, stir for a minute longer, then add the rice, cinnamon, allspice, black pepper, nutmeg and ground clove. Stir for 1 or 2 minutes to bring out their flavour. Add the chestnuts and water or chicken stock, season with salt, bring to the boil, reduce heat to medium–low and cook until rice is soft and water has been absorbed (about 10–12 minutes).

Meanwhile heat the oil in a frying-pan and sauté the almonds until golden-brown in colour; remove and drain on kitchen paper. Add the pine-nuts to the oil in the pan, sauté until golden in colour, remove and drain. Finally add the pistachio nuts, sauté until lightly browned and drain on kitchen paper. Reserve all the nuts.

Pre-heat the oven to 200° C (400° F/gas mark 6). Rub the turkey with a lemon wedge and some salt to remove impurities; rinse under running cold water and pat dry with kitchen paper. Sprinkle the turkey inside and out with the salt and black and white peppers. Gently loosen the turkey breast skin and fill with butter, if used. Loosely stuff the cavity and neck with some of the cooked rice, sew all openings and truss. Spread the turkey all over with yoghurt and place, breast down, on a rack over a roasting-pan. Roast for 30 minutes, then reduce heat to 180° C (350° F/gas mark 4) and cook through (about 2$\frac{1}{2}$ hours), turning the bird over for the last half hour to brown. To check whether it is done, prick the knee joint of the thigh: if it is, the juices should run clear. Transfer to a large hot serving dish, re-heat the remaining rice and pile around it, garnish rice with reserved nuts and serve with a large salad.

Note: If desired, after filling the turkey, sprinkle the remaining rice with 3 tbs rose water. Reheat rice before serving.

Stuffed Chicken
Djaj mehshi

A divine, rich winter dish, this old-time, classic recipe was considered a delicacy in the Lebanese cuisine when chicken was rare and very special. Nowadays it has become more accessible and is made throughout the country for festive occasions or Sunday lunches. It is time-consuming to prepare, especially for those who have never come across this kind of cooking, but it is worth the trouble and quite straightforward if you follow the recipe carefully.

The chicken is stuffed with a delicious blend of rice, ground meat, spices, a generous amount of nuts and a splash of the fragrant rose water, which my mother advised me to add. Then the stuffed bird is browned in olive oil, which is renowned for its health giving properties, although traditionally a home-made fat, *samneh*, was used instead. Then water is added, a cinnamon bark and a clove-studded onion, and all are left to simmer over a low flame, allowing the flavours to blend and harmonize to produce a succulent, rich broth. Half-way through cooking the chicken, a handful of rice and another of parsley are added to the liquid, so that from one recipe you derive both a delightful soup and a full chicken dish.

Ingredients

45 ml (3–4 tbs) extra-virgin olive oil
28 g (1 oz) whole blanched almonds or almond flakes
28 g (1 oz) pine-nuts
225 g (8 oz) ground meat, preferably lamb
200 g (7 oz) white rice (preferably basmati)
$\frac{1}{2}$ tsp cinnamon
$\frac{1}{2}$ tsp allspice
$\frac{1}{4}$ tsp black pepper
$\frac{1}{5}$ tsp ground clove
$1\frac{1}{2}$ tsp salt or to taste
2 tbs rose water
1.6 kg (3 lb 8 oz) chicken with skin on
2.1 l (70 fl oz) water
1 onion (about 115 g/4 oz), peeled and studded with 6 whole cloves
1 large cinnamon bark
1 bay leaf
28 g (1 oz) short grain rice (known as pudding rice)
28 g (1 oz) chopped parsley, rinsed, drained

In a saucepan heat half the amount of oil over moderately high heat until hot but not smoking. Add the almonds, stirring constantly for a few seconds or until the colour starts

Lebanese couscous (*moghrabiyeh*)

to change slightly to pale yellow. Add the pine-nuts and continue stirring until both nuts are golden in colour; add the meat, stirring occasionally until it changes colour and cooks through (about 3 minutes). Add the rice, cinnamon, allspice, black pepper, ground cloves, and half the amount of salt; stir for 1 minute longer, gently to prevent rice from breaking. Turn heat off and stir in the rose water to combine with the rice mixture in the saucepan. Reserve for later use.

Meanwhile clean the chicken, as directed in the introduction to the Poultry section, and fill its cavity loosely with ¼ the amount of the reserved rice mixture (about 6 tbs), reserving the remaining rice. Sew all openings and tie the chicken with string.

In a large pot heat the remaining oil over moderately high heat until hot but not smoking. Sauté the chicken, turning gently until browned all over (about 10 minutes).

Discard excess oil from the pot and add the water, studded onion, cinnamon stick and bay leaf. Skim any foam from the surface of the water and bring to the boil. Reduce the heat to medium. Cover and simmer for 50 minutes or until chicken is tender.

Just 10 minutes before the end of the cooking time, measure 300 ml (10 fl oz) of the resulting broth and add to the remaining reserved rice in the saucepan; bring to the boil, then reduce heat to low. Cover and simmer for about 8–10 minutes or until rice is tender and broth is absorbed. Meanwhile add the pudding rice and parsley to the chicken broth in the pot, cover and simmer for 8–10 minutes.

To serve, discard the cinnamon stick and bay leaf. Transfer the chicken to the middle of a large serving dish, surround with rice from the saucepan and keep warm to eat after serving the broth as a soup.

Note: If almond flakes are used, remove them from saucepan before adding meat, otherwise they will break and disappear into the mixture.

Chicken Rice with Ground Meat

Djaj bi-roz wa-lahm mafroum

A classic, this popular Lebanese dish is tasty, economical and easy to prepare. It is very suitable as a main dish for dinner with friends or for a buffet to accompany other dishes. In this recipe, as in the others, I use skinless chicken; it cuts some of the fat intake, without altering its rich, succulent flavour.

Ingredients

1 corn-fed chicken (about 1.35 kg/3 lb), skinned and rinsed
1 onion (about 115 g/4 oz), peeled
1.5–1.75 l (50–60 fl oz) water
Bouquet garni: 1 large cinnamon stick, 4 cardamoms, 6 whole black peppercorns, 1 bay leaf

1½ tsp salt or to taste

2 tbs extra-virgin olive oil

25 g (1 oz) pine-nuts

25 g (1 oz) almond flakes

175 g (6 oz) lean ground meat (preferably lamb)

200 g (7 oz) rice (preferably basmati)

½ tsp cinnamon

½ tsp allspice

¼ tsp black pepper

¼ tsp nutmeg

450 ml (15 fl oz) chicken broth (from the liquid in which the chicken has been
   cooked)

Place the chicken, onion and water in a large pot over medium–high heat, skim the foam from the surface and bring to the boil. Add bouquet garni, reduce to medium heat, cover and simmer for about 50 minutes or until chicken is tender. 5 minutes before the end of the cooking time season with ½ tsp of the salt.

Meanwhile place a saucepan over medium–high heat. Add the oil; when oil is hot but not smoking add the pine-nuts. Cook, stirring constantly, until golden in colour, remove with a slotted spoon and reserve. Add the almonds to the same oil in the pan, sauté until golden in colour, remove with a slotted spoon and reserve. To the oil remaining in the pan add the meat and cook for about 3 minutes or until meat changes colour and is browned. Add the rice, season with the cinnamon, allspice, black pepper, nutmeg and finally the remaining salt; stir gently for a minute. Add the chicken broth, bring to the boil, cover, reduce to medium–low heat and simmer for 8–10 minutes or until broth is absorbed and rice is soft.

Meanwhile, remove chicken from pan and place on a plate. With your fingers pull out the chicken meat in medium-sized pieces, or carve, if preferred, discard the bones and keep the chicken pieces warm for later use.

When rice is ready arrange over a large dish, cover evenly with chicken pieces, garnish with the reserved pine nuts and almond flakes.

Serve immediately. Eat with Oriental Salad.

Note: This dish can be prepared without the ground meat.

Chicken with Yoghurt
Fattet djaj

Another favourite of mine, this fine, satisfying and succulent dish is made along the lines of the Chicken Rice recipe. The toasted bread, rice and chicken are layered in a deep serving dish, topped with the soothing sweetness of yoghurt and heightened by the mouthwatering taste of the sautéed coriander.

The delicate taste comes from the remarkable affinity between yoghurt, chicken, rice and coriander. Topped with fried nuts, the dish gains depth and richness in flavour and nutrients.

Ingredients

Chicken Rice with Ground Meat recipe, with or without meat
1 large clove of garlic, peeled and crushed
$^{1}/_{2}$ tsp salt or to taste
575 ml (20 fl oz) live yoghurt
olive oil for frying
30 g (1 oz) pine nuts,
30 g (1 oz) almond flakes (optional)
1 wholemeal pitta bread, cut into $^{1}/_{2}$ cm ($^{1}/_{4}$ in) squares
50 g (2 oz) coriander, rinsed, roughly chopped

Prepare the recipe of Chicken Rice with Ground Meat. Meanwhile in a salad bowl crush the garlic with the salt until smooth and creamy. Add the yoghurt and whisk, combining them well. Reserve for later.

In a skillet heat 2 tbs of the oil over moderately high heat; add the pine-nuts, stir constantly until golden in colour, then remove and drain on kitchen paper. To the same oil add the almond flakes if used, and cook until golden in colour; remove with a slotted spoon, allowing the oil to drip back into the pan. Drain on kitchen paper and reserve.

To the oil in the skillet, add enough oil to fry the bread. When the oil is hot add the bread squares in batches and fry until golden and crisp; remove with a slotted spoon, drain on kitchen paper and spread evenly in a deep serving dish. Reserve.

Reduce the quantity of oil remaining in the pan and sautée the coriander; remove and drain on kitchen paper.

Then remove the chicken from the pot, carve into bite-sized pieces and keep warm.

When rice is ready, arrange it evenly over the reserved bread, then cover with chicken pieces, top all over with the reserved yoghurt and finally garnish with the nuts and coriander.

Serve immediately with a seasonal salad.

Note: If preferred, toast the bread and nuts.

Chicken with Rice and Tomatoes
Djaj bi-roz wa-banadoura

The addition of fresh spices and ripe tomatoes to this delightful recipe makes it different from the previous chicken rice recipe, transforming the taste completely. The chicken, onion and garlic are browned in olive oil; the tomatoes follow with water. All are left to simmer gently until the meat is tender and the sauce is thickened to acquire a good consistency. Then the liquid, along with the vegetables, is forced through a sieve, producing a delicious sauce, in which the rice is left to simmer. The dish has a wonderful appetizing aroma and a succulent flavour.

Ingredients

550 g (1 lb 4 oz) cut-up chicken, mixture of dark and white meat, skinned and rinsed
$\frac{1}{2}$ tsp cinnamon
$\frac{1}{2}$ tsp black pepper
$\frac{1}{2}$ tsp allspice
$1\frac{1}{4}$ tsp salt, or to taste
3–4 tbs extra-virgin olive oil
30 g (1 oz) flaked almonds
onions (about 225 g/8 oz), peeled and sliced
6 cloves of garlic, peeled
Red ripe tomatoes (about 285 g/10 oz), chopped
1 tsp double-concentrate tomato paste
Bouquet garni: 1 cinnamon stick, 6 whole black peppercorns, 1 bay leaf, 4 cardamoms
1.1 l (40 fl oz) water
200 g (7 oz) white rice (preferably basmati) rinsed once and drained

Season the chicken pieces all over with the cinnamon, black pepper, allspice and salt and leave to stand. Meanwhile in a pot heat the oil over moderately high heat. When oil is hot but not smoking sauté the almonds until golden. With a slotted spoon, remove and reserve. Add the chicken pieces to the oil remaining in the pot and sauté to seal their juices for about 6 minutes or until nicely browned, turning them once. With a slotted spoon remove chicken pieces to a side dish. To the oil remaining in the pot add the onions and garlic, adding more oil if necessary. Sauté until lightly browned, stirring occasionally; add the tomatoes and tomato paste, stir well then return the browned chicken to the pot, add the bouquet garni and water. Bring to the boil over high heat, then reduce to medium, cover and simmer for 40 minutes or until chicken is tender.

When chicken is tender transfer to a plate, slice the chicken meat into medium-sized pieces, keep warm and discard the bones; discard the bouquet garni. Then strain the broth through a fine sieve, forcing the tomatoes, onions and garlic through with the back of a spoon. From the resulting sauce measure 250 ml (8 fl oz), thin with 150 ml (5 fl oz) water and place in a saucepan; bring to the boil over high heat, add the rice, bring to boil again, reduce heat to medium–low, cover and simmer for 8–10 minutes. Half-way through cooking taste the rice and adjust the seasonings if necessary. When rice is ready leave to stand covered for a few minutes to absorb the flavours.

Spread over a warm serving dish, arrange the chicken pieces all over, and garnish with almond flakes.

Chicken Rice and Vegetables
Djaj bi-roz al-khodar

An excellent family meal. Simple to make and delightful to eat, especially on a winter night after a long working day.

The chicken is cooked to produce a rich broth, then the rice, the cut-up vegetables, and the strong aromatic herb coriander are simmered in the resulting broth. This dish looks and is appetizing and has a wonderful texture. Garnish, if you like, with pine-nuts or flaked almonds.

The preparation for this dish can be done ahead of time.

Ingredients

1 free range chicken (about 1.35 kg/3 lbs), skinned and rinsed
1 onion (about 140 g/5 oz) peeled
1.5 l (50 fl oz) water
Bouquet garni: 1 large stick of cinnamon, 4 cardamom, 6 whole black peppercorns, 1
    bay leaf
1$\frac{1}{4}$ tsp salt, or to taste
1 tbs extra-virgin olive oil
1 onion (about 140 g/5 oz) peeled and chopped
1 clove of garlic, peeled and finely chopped
1 carrot (about 115 g/4 oz), peeled and finely diced
1 small green pepper (about 115 g/4 oz), de-seeded and finely diced
200 g (7 oz) rice, preferably basmati, rinsed once and drained
$\frac{1}{4}$ tsp cinnamon
$\frac{1}{4}$ tsp black pepper
about 200 g (7 oz) of ripe tomatoes, finely chopped
375 ml (12 fl oz) chicken cooking liquid
fresh or frozen peas (about 140 g/5 oz)
15 g ($\frac{1}{2}$ oz) coriander, coarsely chopped, rinsed

Place the chicken, whole onion and water in a pot over high heat, skim the foam from the surface and bring to the boil. Add the bouquet garni and reduce the heat to medium; cover and simmer for 45–55 minutes, or until chicken is tender. Five minutes before the end of the cooking time season with ¹/₂ tsp salt. From the chicken broth measure 375 ml (12 fl oz) of the cooking liquid, and reserve to cook the rice later.

In a saucepan heat the oil, add the onions and cook over medium heat until transparent and pale in colour, stirring occasionally (about 2 minutes). Add the garlic, stir for a few seconds, add the carrot, green pepper, rice, remaining salt, cinnamon and black pepper. Stir gently, add the tomatoes; keep stirring a few more seconds, add the reserved cooking liquid, bring to the boil, add the peas and coriander and bring to a second boil. Reduce heat to medium–low, cover and simmer for about 8–10 minutes or until rice is soft and broth is absorbed. While the rice is cooking transfer the chicken to a plate, carve the meat into serving pieces, discard the bones, and keep warm for later use.

When rice is ready turn the heat off and keep the saucepan covered for 2 minutes, allowing the flavours to blend and the rice to become fluffy.

Then spread over a serving dish, arrange the chicken pieces evenly all over the rice and serve immediately. Eat with a seasonal salad.

Note: If using brown rice add 450 ml (14 fl oz) of the chicken stock and cook for 30–40 minutes or until rice is soft and broth is absorbed.

Roasted Chicken

Djaj mohammar

For this recipe a chicken must be marinated for several hours or overnight with a blend of fresh spices, such as chillies, which boost the circulation and add a mild piquant flavour; garlic and onion, known since ancient times for their medicinal benefits in strengthening the immune system; and oil and vinegar, which add more zest, tenderize and give the chicken a beautiful reddish-brown colour. For a special meal serve with the appetizing Aubergine Dip.

Ingredients

1 tsp salt or to taste
¹/₂ tsp freshly-milled black pepper or to taste
1 free-range chicken with the skin (about 1.35 kg/3 lb), rinsed and patted dry
2 chilli peppers, de-seeded and rinsed
2 cloves of garlic, peeled
1 onion (about 115 g/4 oz), peeled
1 tbs organic cider vinegar
1 tbs extra virgin olive oil

Salt and pepper the chicken and leave aside in a glass container for later use. In a blender place the chillies, garlic, onions, vinegar and oil; purée until smooth and creamy. Pour this purée all over the chicken, including the cavity. Cover and refrigerate overnight. One hour before roasting the chicken remove from refrigerator, allowing it to reach room temperature. Pre-heat the oven to 200° C/400° F/gas mark 6, and place the chicken on a roasting rack to roast for 20 minutes. Reduce the oven temperature to 190° C/375° F/gas mark 5 and continue roasting for 60 minutes longer, basting the chicken every 30 minutes. Towards the end of roasting prick the chicken near the thigh to make sure that the juices run clear, which indicates that the chicken is cooked. Remove from oven and transfer to a serving dish. Let it stand five minutes, then carve and eat with a seasonal salad.

Spiced Chicken
Shawarma djaj

The Lebanese like to indulge in very tasty food. *Shawarma djaj* is one such dish although its reputation is less than that of the great meat shawarma. Chicken *shawarma* is unfamiliar to many Lebanese and to my knowledge it is not served in restaurants.

Ingredients

4 boneless chicken breasts with skin on, rinsed and patted dry
2 cloves of garlic, peeled and crushed
125 ml (4 fl oz) lemon juice
1$\frac{1}{2}$ tbs extra-virgin olive oil
1 tsp cider vinegar (optional)
2 bay leaves, each broken in half
1 cinnamon stick, broken into quarters
1$\frac{1}{4}$ tsp salt
$\frac{1}{4}$ tsp ground cloves
2 tsp ground cardamom
$\frac{1}{4}$ tsp cinnamon
$\frac{1}{4}$ tsp white pepper
pinch nutmeg
about 2 *miskee* (Arabic gum) pieces ground gently with a little salt

In a glass bowl combine the chicken, garlic, lemon juice, oil, vinegar, bay leaves, cinnamon stick, salt, cloves, ground cardamom, cinnamon, white pepper, nutmeg and *miskee*, toss thoroughly and refrigerate covered overnight.

Remove the chicken half an hour before baking. Meanwhile pre-heat the oven to 200° C (400° F/gas mark 6). Place the chicken, with the marinade juices, in the oven and bake for 30 minutes. During baking turn the chicken once or twice with a spoon to coat evenly with the juices.

Remove the chicken, allow to cool enough to handle and carve over a wooden board into thin strips. Pre-heat the grill and return the chicken to the same baking pan; mix chicken with the pan juices and finish it off under a hot grill for about 2–5 minutes or until the surface of the chicken strips are golden, turning them once and making sure it does not dry.

Remove the chicken strips and place inside pitta bread pockets to keep warm. Eat with *tahini* sauce, pickles and fried potatoes.

Chicken with Potato
Djaj bi-batata

My daughter Nour's favourite recipe, which has the advantage of being prepared very quickly. The unpeeled potatoes absorb the flavours of the chicken, spices, lemon juice and oil as they cook. The flavour is dense and earth and the aroma succulent. Eat with an Oriental Salad for a very health-giving meal.

Ingredients

4 free-range, skinless chicken breasts (about 800 g/1 lb 12 oz)
2 unpeeled potatoes, rinsed and cut into 1 in pieces
1 onion (about 170 g/6 oz), peeled, sliced
3 cloves of garlic, peeled, crushed
1$\frac{1}{2}$ tsp salt or to taste
$\frac{1}{2}$ tsp cinnamon
$\frac{1}{4}$ tsp black pepper, or to taste
$\frac{1}{2}$ tsp allspice
3–4 tbs lemon juice
2–3 tbs extra-virgin olive oil
125 ml (4 fl oz) water

Combine the chicken, potatoes, onions, garlic, salt, cinnamon, black pepper, allspice, lemon juice, oil and water in a baking dish; mix thoroughly to blend well. Marinate for 2 hours or more in a cool place. Then allow to reach room temperature before baking.

Pre-heat the oven to 200° C/400° F/gas mark 6. Bake for 30 minutes. Reduce oven temperature to 190° C/375° F/gas mark 5 and bake for a further 50 minutes or until chicken and potatoes are nicely browned. For the last 20 minutes turn the chicken and potatoes to brown on the other side.

Serve hot. Eat with Oriental Salad and, if desired, *baba ghannouj*.

Chicken Kebab
Djaj bi-shish meshwi

Another meal made simple. Chicken breasts are cut into 1¼ cm (½ in) cubes (or you can buy them already diced), then left in a marinade that consists of lemon juice, olive oil, garlic and spices. Eat this dish with fattoush or aubergine dip for a very nutritious meal. Chicken Kebab can also make an excellent sandwich, especially in a pitta bread pocket, filled with salad.

Ingredients

450 g (1 lb) free range chicken breasts, cut into 1 cm (½ in) cubes
1 clove of garlic, peeled and crushed
¾ tsp salt
¼ tsp cinnamon
¼ tsp black pepper
¼ tsp allspice
2 tbs extra-virgin olive oil
3 tbs lemon juice

In a glass container combine the chicken, garlic, salt, cinnamon, black pepper, allspice, oil and lemon juice, mix well and marinate for 3–6 hours in the refrigerator. Thirty minutes before grilling remove from fridge, allowing it to reach room temperature. Pre-heat the grill. Place chicken on skewers over an oven sheet and cook until browned (6–8 minutes), turning skewers and basting with the marinade to keep moist.

Remove from heat, placing chicken inside the pocket of a large pitta bread. Serve hot and, if desired, eat with *hoummos* and Oriental Salad.

Chicken with Peppers
Djaj bi-falaifle

Colourful, with a subtle flavour, this dish is quick to assemble and can be prepared ahead of time. Chicken is so versatile that the taste is transformed according to the added ingredients. This dish is a good example; a combination of fresh green, red and yellow peppers, ripe tomatoes and onions, all sliced to cover the chicken, which is sprinkled with spices and baked in the oven so that the meat absorbs the vegetable juices. In this recipe I use water, but to enrich the flavour you can substitute any left-over chicken broth.

Ingredients

4 free-range skinless breasts of chicken
  (about 550 g/1 lb 4 oz)
$^1/_2$ tsp allspice
$^1/_2$ tsp cinnamon
$^1/_2$ tsp black pepper or to taste
$1^1/_4$ tsp salt or to taste
2 cloves of garlic, peeled and finely crushed
1 onion (about 200 g/7 oz) peeled,
  cut across into $^1/_2$ cm ($^1/_4$ in) rings
1 green, 1 red, 1 yellow pepper (about 170 g/6 oz each),
  de-seeded, cut across into $^1/_2$ cm ($^1/_4$ in) rings
2 large ripe tomatoes (about 450 g/1 lb),
  cut across into $^1/_2$ cm ($^1/_4$ in) rings
2–3 tbs olive oil
200 ml (7 fl oz) water,
  or chicken stock, if available

Place the chicken in an ungreased deep baking dish; sprinkle evenly with the allspice, cinnamon, black pepper and half the amount of salt. Add the garlic and mix with the chicken. Next, layer the onion rings, green, red and yellow peppers evenly over the chicken; top with the tomatoes. Drizzle the oil and water or chicken stock all over and sprinkle with the remaining salt.

Bake uncovered in a pre-heated oven at 200° C (400° F/gas mark 6) for 20 minutes. Reduce oven temperature to 190° C (375° F/gas mark 5) and bake for a further 1 hour, basting twice during cooking.

When ready, remove from oven and serve immediately, if desired, with Fried Potatoes.

Chicken and Basil
Djaj bi-habak

This is one of the easiest recipes to prepare. Basil was planted in huge pots on our veranda and was within easy reach of my mother while she was cooking. Basil's scent, which is soothing and invigorating, is at its highest in the early mornings and at sunset. Basil aids digestion and is said to turn cooks into poets.

The chicken is left to simmer in its juices with the basil on a low flame. This dish is very low in fat and a very good recipe for people who are short of time.

Ingredients

450 g (1 lb) free range, skinless chicken breasts, cut into 2$\frac{1}{2}$ cm (1 in) pieces
1 large clove of garlic, peeled and crushed
1 onion (about 170 g/6 oz) peeled and thinly sliced
1 tsp extra-virgin olive oil
45 g (1$\frac{1}{2}$ oz) basil leaves coarsely chopped, rinsed
$\frac{1}{2}$ tsp salt or to taste
$\frac{1}{4}$ tsp black pepper
a pinch of white pepper

Place the chicken, garlic, onion, olive oil and half the amount of basil in a medium-sized pot over moderately high heat. Cook for about 3 minutes. Reduce the heat to low, cover and simmer, allowing the chicken to cook in the juices for about 15 minutes. Add the remaining basil, salt, black pepper and white pepper. Cover and simmer for 3–5 minutes. Towards the end of cooking turn the heat up to moderately high and cook until the juice is reduced to less than half and the chicken is slightly golden in colour. Remove from heat and serve on a platter. Eat with Peppers Moussaka.

Chicken with Thyme
Djaj bi-zaatar

Another delicious way of preparing chicken. Diced chicken is sautéed along with the aromatic herb *zaatar* (thyme) that elevates the taste greatly and satisfies the palate.

It makes a magnificent main meal accompanied by fried potatoes and Aubergine Dip.

Ingredients

4 free-range skinless chicken breasts (about 675 g/1 lb 12 oz)
$\frac{1}{2}$ tsp cinnamon
$\frac{1}{4}$ tsp black pepper
$\frac{1}{2}$ tsp salt or to taste
2$\frac{1}{2}$–3 tbs extra-virgin olive oil
1 onion (about 8 oz), peeled and chopped
1 clove of garlic, peeled and crushed
2 tsp *zaatar*
350 ml (11 fl oz) water

Sprinkle and rub all sides of chicken with the cinnamon, black pepper and salt. Keep aside for later use.

In a large deep skillet heat the oil; when oil is hot but not smoking, add the chicken breasts and cook for 6–8 minutes, turning once, when browned on both sides transfer to a plate with a slotted spoon, allowing the oil to drip back into the pan. Reserve. Add the onions to the remaining oil in the skillet; reduce heat to medium and cook until pale golden in colour (about 2 minutes). Add the garlic, cook for a few seconds and add the zaatar, stir once, return the browned chicken to the skillet and finally add the water. Bring to the boil, cover and simmer over moderate heat for 10 minutes. Reduce heat to moderately low and continue cooking for 25 minutes longer or until chicken is tender and the liquid has reduced and thickened. When ready transfer the chicken immediately to a serving platter with the remaining juices spooned over.

Eat on its own or with *fattoush* and fried potatoes.

Chicken with Almonds
Djaj bi-loz

Quick, interesting and pleasing to the palate. While the chicken, almonds and spices are simmered, their flavours merge together to produce a sweet, rich-tasting dish with a nutty texture, a beautiful deep gold colour and a moist meat.

Chicken and almonds constitutes one of the many recipes in a medieval Arabic treatise on food entitled *Kitab al-wusla-il al-habib.*

This is a good dish to make for simple entertaining and I suggest eating it with a selection of fried vegetables such as aubergines and potatoes.

Ingredients

4 free-range skinless chicken breasts (about 800 g/1 lb 12 oz)
700 ml (25 fl oz)) water
1 large cinnamon stick
2 tbs extra-virgin olive oil
210 g (7½ oz) onion, peeled and chopped
1 large clove of garlic, peeled and crushed
1¼ tsp flour
30 g (1 oz) almond flakes
½ tsp cinnamon
a pinch of black pepper
½ tsp salt

Place the chicken in a medium-sized pot over moderately high heat. Add the water and the cinnamon stick, skim off the scum from the surface, bring to the boil, reduce heat to medium, cover and simmer for 20 minutes.

Meanwhile in a frying pan heat the oil and sauté the onion until golden in colour. Add the garlic and stir constantly for a few seconds, then add the flour, almonds, cinnamon, black pepper and salt; keep stirring for 1 minute longer, add this mixture to cook along with the chicken for 30 minutes longer or until the chicken is tender.

When ready transfer to a deep serving dish, spooning the juices over the chicken. Serve immediately with a seasonal salad or, if desired, with fried potatoes.

Meat

When the 19th century was drawing to a close, a number of the inhabitants of Lebanon escaped increasingly harsh Ottoman rule and found refuge in Egypt. There, they materially contributed to the Arab renaissance in the fields of literature and journalism. If their intellectual contribution was welcomed in their adopted home, one of their culinary habits was not, namely the preparation of *kibbeh*. I was told by one of my great-uncles that whenever a Lebanese family expressed an interest in renting lodgings, the Egyptian landlord invariably stipulated that the use of a mortar for pounding meat was not to be allowed on the premises. Fortunately the restrictive and vexatious terms of autocratic Egyptian landlords did not stop the flow of immigrants from Bilad al-sham (the name given to the area of the Ottoman Empire that now comprises Lebanon, Syria and Jordan), nor was the literary renaissance compromised by such inconvenience. Who knows, mortars left idle along the Nile may have contributed to the invention of the Moulinex meat-grinding machine nowadays used by most Lebanese town dwellers when they prepare *kibbeh* and other recipes that include minced meat. Yet in the boroughs and villages of the mountains, *kibbeh* is still prepared the traditional way, as I was able to see for myself in Becharre, a large borough perched high in the mountains at the foot of the Cedars of Lebanon.

Becharre was the home of the great American-Lebanese author and poet Kahlil Gibran, the site of his mausoleum and a charming museum of memorabilia and paintings. After a dutiful visit to both I was the guest, for lunch, of the most hospitable people. Part of the feast was *kibbeh nayyeh*, prepared in front of us. A thin, nervous woman, her hair tidily covered by a scarf, sat on a low wooden stool in front of a large mortar made of stone. With a sizeable wooden pestle she started pounding raw meat. After a while she added cracked wheat, onions and spices, and resumed her rhythmic pounding.

The *kibbeh*, prepared with goat meat, was delicious. In other parts of the country and in towns lamb meat is used instead.

Lebanon has no proper grazing grounds and only meagre livestock. Goats are found in the heights, mainly in the north of the country, whereas lambs and cows are scarce and mostly imported.

Before distances became unimportant, and frozen meat shipped from Australia and

New Zealand became readily available, the Lebanese did not rely on meat for their daily diet. Whenever they ate local meat it had to be prepared in an elaborate way to make it more edible. In the process they made a delicacy of their concoctions. Lamb was used parsimoniously for some stews, or cooked in salt in quantity and stored as a preserve (*kawarma*) for the winter season. Beef steaks were almost unknown. In spite of the poor quality of meat, or maybe because of it, the culinary imagination of the Lebanese knew no limits. Like *kibbeh*, *kafta* is a culinary triumph, and there are dozens of recipes in which meat is not the main ingredient, but is used to lift the taste, to thicken the sauce and to provide protein.

Raw Kibbeh

Kibbeh nayyeh

A traditional and very popular dish all over the country. *Kibbeh* is a particular speciality in the northern mountainous region of Lebanon and in the town of Zahle. In the southern part of the country, *kibbeh* is prepared with a little difference, in that a few fresh basil leaves and a little marjoram are pounded with the onion and the spices to form a smooth paste, after which they are mixed with the meat and the cracked wheat. Both versions are delicious, although each region claims to offer the best.

The secret of good *kibbeh* is good-quality meat, which should be perfectly trimmed of all fat and gristle and then freshly and finely ground.

Concern about the dangers of eating raw meat obviously makes one uneasy about eating raw *kibbeh*. On the other hand, when the thinly sliced meat is pounded in a stone mortar with a heavy pestle, it seems to me that the long and repeated beats generate enough heat to half-cook the meat.

Ingredients

1 onion (about 75 g/2$^{1}/_{2}$ oz), peeled
$^{1}/_{2}$ tsp salt or to taste
$^{1}/_{4}$ tsp black pepper
$^{1}/_{4}$ tsp cinnamon
$^{1}/_{4}$ tsp white pepper
150 g (5$^{1}/_{2}$ oz) fine *burghol*, rinsed and drained
450 g (1 lb) ground meat, preferably from a leg of lamb
125 ml (4 fl oz) iced water

In a food processor blend the onion until smooth and creamy (if necessary add a very small amount of water). Remove, place in a bowl, sprinkle and rub the onion with the salt, black pepper, cinnamon and white pepper. Rinse *burghol*, drain, squeeze out excess water and add to the seasoned onion and combine thoroughly. Add the meat and work

Baked kafta (*kafta saynieh*)

this mixture. Add as much of the iced water as is necessary (not all) to achieve a smooth paste with a good consistency. Continue kneading until *kibbeh* mixture blends well together.

Taste and adjust the seasoning. Then over a serving dish spread and smooth the *kibbeh* mixture; drizzle generously with extra olive oil and decorate with fresh mint.

Eat accompanied with white or spring onions and bread (preferably pitta).

Variation: Along with the onion, blend in some sweet red pepper (about 115 g/4 oz) and about 8–10 fresh mint leaves.

Baked Kibbeh
Kibbeh bi-sayniyeh

This is one of my favourite versions of *kibbeh*, and it reminds me of relaxed family gatherings over Sunday lunches.

Kibbeh is baked traditionally with a liberal amount of olive oil and topped with large dots of *samneh*, which gives it a rich, fine flavour and protects the *kibbeh* from drying out in the oven. To cut down on saturated fat, however, I bake the *kibbeh* in olive oil then, when it is cooked, I remove it from the oven while the oil is still bubbling and pour out and discard more than half the oil. I guarantee that *kibbeh* so treated is just as nutritious and tasty.

Traditionally *kibbeh* is served as a main course or as part of a buffet and, in restaurants, as a plat du jour. It is bulky and satisfying. A soothing salad of yoghurt and cucumber complements the hot *kibbeh* nicely. My daughter Nour finds *kibbeh* equally delicious straight out of the fridge.

Ingredients

For the stuffing
2–3 tbs extra-virgin olive oil
30 g (1 oz) pine-nuts
1 large onion (about 285 g/10 oz), peeled and finely chopped
150 g (5 oz) lean minced meat, preferably lamb
$^3/_4$ tsp cinnamon
$^1/_2$ tsp salt or to taste
$^1/_4$ tsp black pepper

For the kibbeh dough
1 onion (about 100 g/3$^1/_2$ oz), peeled
1$^1/_4$ tsp salt or to taste
$^1/_2$ tsp allspice

¹/₂ tsp cinnamon
¹/₂ tsp black pepper
285 g (10 oz) fine *burghol*, rinsed and drained
450 g (1 lb) lean ground meat, preferably lamb
75–120 ml (3–4 fl oz) extra-virgin olive oil

In a heavy-bottomed frying-pan heat the oil until hot but not smoking; add the pine-nuts, sauté, stirring constantly, until golden in colour, remove with a slotted spoon allowing the oil to drip back into the pan. Reserve. Add the onions, sauté over medium–high heat until soft and pale in colour (about 2 minutes), add the meat to the onions, cook until meat changes colour and is lightly browned, return the reserved pine nuts to the frying-pan, season with the cinnamon, salt and black pepper. Stir well and remove filling from heat; reserve.

Heat the oven to 190° C (375° F/gas mark 5), grease a baking dish (26 x 26 cm/10½ x 10½ in) with 1 tbs of oil; reserve.

Meanwhile proceed with the preparation of *kibbeh* dough. In a food processor blend the onion until it forms a creamy paste. Remove from blender and place in a large bowl, sprinkle and mix with the salt, allspice, cinnamon, and black pepper. Squeeze excess water from the *burghol*, add to the onions and mix thoroughly until the *burghol* has absorbed all the seasonings. Add the meat and work the mixture, adding cold water as necessary (about 2–3 tbs or more) to achieve a smooth *kibbeh* paste with a good consistency. Continue kneading until *kibbeh* mixture blends well (if necessary blend in a food processor for a few seconds). Take small portions of *kibbeh* mixture at a time and flatten thinly over the lightly oiled baking dish to a uniform thickness, less than ½ cm (¼ in) thick.

Spread the reserved filling over evenly, cover with a slightly thicker layer of the remaining *kibbeh* mixture, moistening hand with cold water as necessary, press down and smooth the *kibbeh*. Drizzle the oil all over and quickly run a thin-pointed knife around the edge of the baking dish. Then cut through, dividing *kibbeh* into 4 or 8 portions (similar to pizza slices), allowing the oil to seep down between sides and middle of *kibbeh*; to decorate make a criss-cross pattern on the surface of each portion.

Bake in a hot oven for 40 minutes or until *kibbeh* is nicely browned. Remove from oven and while the oil is still bubbling carefully pour off excess oil. Arrange on a platter; eat with Yoghurt Cucumber Salad or Oriental Salad.

Fried Kibbeh
Kibbeh mikli

Some skill is needed to make an oval-shaped *kibbeh,* but do not be put off because a little experience makes it quite easy. *Kibbeh* shells are stuffed and, when fried, blend with the aromatic filling to give a crisp crunchy texture and a tasty flavour. *Kibbeh mikli* are perfect as appetizers or as a first course.

Ingredients

Prepare the *kibbeh* dough as in *Kibbeh sayniyeh*

For the stuffing
4 tbs extra-virgin olive oil
45 g (1$^{1}/_{2}$ oz) pine nuts
1 onion (about 225 g/8 oz), peeled and finely chopped
170–225 g (7–8 oz) lean ground meat, preferably lamb
$^{1}/_{2}$ tsp cinnamon
1 tsp salt or to taste
1 tbs lemon juice (optional)
oil for deep-frying

Moisten hands with cold water, take a small portion of *kibbeh* dough and roll each portion between the palms of the hands to form a ball. Hold the ball in one hand and with the index finger of the other poke a hole in the centre of the *kibbeh* ball, work around the inside with your finger until you have a very thin shell.

Fill *kibbeh* shells with 1½ tbs of the meat mixture (or less, depending on the size of the shells), gently reshape and smooth to enclose the filling into an oval shape, moistening fingers as necessary with cold water to smooth the surface of *kibbeh* shells); place on a side dish and repeat with others until all are completed.

In a deep-frying pan heat the oil until hot but not smoking, about 190° C (375° F). Fry *kibbeh* until they are golden-brown on all sides. Remove and drain on kitchen papers. Serve warm with lemon wedges, *baba ghannouj* or *hoummos.*

Variation: Pre-heat oven to 220° C (425° F/gas mark 7), lightly brush *kibbeh* shells with oil, place on an oven sheet and bake until nicely browned (about 10–15 minutes).

Kibbeh in Yoghurt
Kibbeh labanieh

Nutritious, filling and one of the most sought after dishes. *kibbeh labanieh* is formed from the soothing yoghurt and the small oval shaped *kibbeh*. The *kibbeh* shells can be left empty or filled in various ways. One filling consists of finely chopped onions and coriander, sautéed in olive oil and enhanced with cinnamon and black pepper. Another is made of meat and pine nuts as in the stuffing for Fried *Kibbeh*. For more fragrance, while *kibbeh* is simmering in the yoghurt, garlic and coriander, or garlic and crushed dried mint, are thrown in to dissolve in the yoghurt, bringing about a perfume no other herb can surpass.

Ingredients

(Prepare the *kibbeh* dough as in *Kibbeh arnabie*)
575 ml (20 fl oz) strained yoghurt
1 free range egg (yolk and white)
1 tsp salt or to taste
2–3 cloves of garlic, peeled and crushed
$\frac{1}{2}$ tbs dried crushed mint, or a large handful of coriander, ends trimmed, rinsed and
    finely chopped

Prepare the *kibbeh* dough, moisten hands with cold water, take a small portion of *kibbeh* and roll each portion between the palms of your hands to form an oval-shaped ball. Hold the ball in one hand and with the index finger of the other poke a hole in the centre of each ball and gently but firmly work around the inside with your finger, smooth and reshape until it forms a small slightly thick shell about 4 cm (1½ in) long. Repeat until all *kibbeh* shells are completed.

Pierce both pointed ends of *kibbeh* shells and put them into boiling salted water to simmer for 5–7 minutes, drain and reserve.

Meanwhile place the yoghurt in a bowl. With a fork, beat the egg and, using a wooden spoon, combine the beaten egg thoroughly with yoghurt and strain through a sieve over a stainless steel saucepan. Cook over medium heat and bring to the boil, stirring all the time with a wooden spoon and in the same direction, otherwise the yoghurt will curdle. Add the reserved *kibbeh*, keep stirring gently and bring to the boil again. Season with salt, reduce the heat to very low and cook uncovered for 3 minutes. Meanwhile set a frying-pan over medium–high heat and sauté in oil the garlic and mint or coriander. Stir them into the yoghurt and finish cooking.

Transfer to a serving bowl and eat immediately with Vermicelli Rice.

Kibbeh in Tahini Sauce
Kibbeh arnabie

Kibbeh arnabie is normally prepared when Seville oranges are in season (winter). Being a seasonal dish and time-consuming to prepare, it is deemed as a treat. Indeed, it has proud place on many tables on Sundays, especially in the coastal towns where citrus fruits grow. There are devotees of *kibbeh arnabie* and of *mouloukhiyeh*, and they argue about the superiority of their respective favourite.

Preparation of this dish is easier if you make it in stages. Whenever you make *kibbeh sayniyeh* set aside some of the dough. Shape *kibbeh* shells, keep whole, pierce each shell from both ends with a toothpick, drop them in salted boiling water for ten minutes. Remove with a slotted spoon, cool and freeze until needed.

Ingedients

285 g (10 oz) meat from leg of lamb, cut into pieces 2½ cm (1 in) thick
1–2 bones from lamb knuckle end (optional)
2 tsp salt or to taste
1.1 l (40 fl oz) water
255 g (9 oz) onion, peeled and roughly sliced
2 cinnamon sticks
100 g (3½ oz) chick-peas, soaked overnight, rinsed, drained, pre-cooked

For the kibbeh
1 small onion (about 85 g/3 oz), peeled
a generous ¼ tsp cinnamon
a generous ¼ tsp allspice
a generous ¼ tsp black pepper
1 tsp salt
140 g (5 oz) *burghol*, rinsed and drained
225 (8 oz) ground meat, preferably lamb

For the tahini *sauce*
250 ml (8 fl oz) light or white *tahini*
125 ml (4 fl oz) each of the juices of clementine and orange
250 ml (8 fl oz) seville orange juice (if not in season, lemon juice)

Combine the meat, bones, if used, salt and water in a pan. Place over high heat and skim any foam from the surface of the water. Add the onions and cinnamon stick, cover and simmer over medium–low heat for 60 minutes or until meat is tender. 15 minutes before the end of the cooking time, drain and add the cooked chick-peas and finish cooking this meat mixture.

Meanwhile, to make *kibbeh* process the onion in a blender until creamy, remove and mix with the cinnamon, allspice, black pepper and salt. Squeeze excess water from *burghol* and rub with the seasoned onions, incorporate the meat and knead, add a little iced water to give the dough a smooth texture. From this dough shape *kibbeh* shells 4 cm (1½ in) long, following instructions as described in *kibbeh mikli*, except that the shells should be thicker.

Pierce each *kibbeh* shell lightly with a toothpick from both ends, drop them in boiling salted water and cook for 5–8 minutes, drain and reserve.

To prepare the sauce:
Add the clementine, orange and seville orange (or lemon) juices to the *tahini,* and whisk to form a thin, cream-like sauce. Add this *tahini* sauce, and the reserved *kibbeh.* to the meat mixture and its reduced stock (350 ml/12 fl oz). Stir constantly until it boils, reduce heat to medium–low, and leave to simmer for 8–10 minutes. Remove from heat, discard bones and cinnamon sticks and transfer into a serving bowl.

Serve immediately with Vermicelli Rice and radishes.

Mother's Milk
Laban ommoh

The name of the dish is a reference to its goodness and digestibility. Patience is needed with the yoghurt, which needs to be stirred constantly until it boils to prevent it from curdling and separating.

In this recipe I have used lamb, but veal is equally good. The meat is cooked in the liquid until soft and nearly falling apart, and the liquid is reduced, after which the yoghurt is added. The dish is an earthy yet delicate.

Ingredients

850 ml (28 fl oz) water
450 g (1 lb) meat from a leg of lamb cut into 2H cm (1 in) cubes
1 large cinnamon stick
2 large onions (about 450 g/1 lb), peeled and sliced
1 tsp salt or to taste
1 free range egg (yolk and white)
700 ml (25 fl oz) live yoghurt
2 cloves of garlic, peeled and crushed
H tsp dried mint

In a pot combine the water, meat and cinnamon stick. Bring to the boil, skimming any foam from the surface of the water, and add the onions and salt. Cover and simmer over

medium–low heat until meat is soft and liquid has reduced by more than half.

Meanwhile beat the egg with a fork, combine with the yoghurt then strain through a sieve over a saucepan; set over medium heat, stirring with a wooden spoon in the same direction all the time, otherwise the yoghurt will curdle. Bring just to a boil, add the soft meat, onions and their reduced liquid (should be about 60–75 ml/2–3 fl oz) while still stirring in the same direction. Add the garlic, bring to the boil and simmer uncovered on low heat for 3 minutes. Discard cinnamon stick and sprinkle with the dried mint.

Serve hot. Eat with rice.

Stuffed Grape Leaves
Warak enab

Warak enab is one of the most popular dishes in the Levant. It has travelled to the West and is for sale ready-cooked in many supermarkets and Middle Eastern specialty shops.

Grape leaves are green in colour, with a wonderful lemony flavour, which contributes to the taste of the dish, especially when they are fresh. They are wrapped artistically to form finger-like shapes. Grape leaves have been used to wrap food since ancient times and the practice is referred to in the writings of the Greeks and Persians.

Fresh grape leaves when in season are available for sale in Middle Eastern specialty shops. They need blanching in boiling water for a few seconds; when canned they need a longer time, which also helps to rid them of the salt.

The following recipe is quite rich since slices of shoulder of lamb are layered between the stuffed grape leaves. White rice is used in the filling, but brown rice can be a healthy option and marries well, I think, with the flavour of the grape leaf. But remember that brown rice has to be half-cooked before combining it with the other filling ingredients.

Ingredients

100 g (3½ oz) short grain white rice
225 g (8 oz) ground meat, preferably from leg of lamb
6 tbs hot water
3 cloves of garlic, peeled and finely crushed
¼ tsp cinnamon
¼ tsp allspice
¼ tsp black pepper
1½ tsp salt or to taste
4 lamb cutlets (optional)
1 tbs extra-virgin olive oil
115 g (4 oz) grape leaves (about 30 leaves)
450 ml (15 fl oz) water or enough to barely cover
5–7 tbs lemon juice

Meatballs in tomato sauce (*daoud pasha*)

In a bowl combine the rice, meat, water, garlic, cinnamon, allspice, black pepper and half the amount of salt; mix thoroughly, reserve meat mixture.

In a medium-sized pot fry the lamb cutlets in oil until browned on both sides. Then proceed with the preparation of the grape leaves. Trim off the stem of each leaf and, if fresh, blanch in batches of 6 for a few seconds in boiling water. Remove them carefully to prevent breaking and drain in a colander. On a clean surface place one leaf at a time, stem end towards you with shiny side facing down. Near stem end place and spread evenly 1½ tsp of the reserved meat mixture, roll once then fold in both sides of the leaf over the filling, continue to roll firmly into an elongated roll shape, about 5 cm (2 in) long, depending on the size of the leaf. Repeat with the remaining leaves and meat mixture. Arrange the stuffed grape leaves over lamb cutlets in the pan, packing tightly one next to the other. Season with the remaining salt, pour the water over and place a small dish on top to prevent the grape leaves from opening while cooking.

Place this pan over high heat, bring to the boil, reduce heat to medium. Cover and simmer for about 10 minutes, then reduce heat to medium–low, cover and simmer for another hour and 20 minutes or until leaves are tender (to check remove one leaf and taste). 10 minutes before the end of cooking add the lemon juice and cover.

When cooking time is over, remove pot from heat and carefully press with your fingers on the plate and empty the reduced liquor over a bowl to ease unmoulding. Unmould into a serving dish.

Serve immediately with the liquor spooned over. Eat with yoghurt.

Note: Brown rice harmonizes well with grape leaves but remember to cook it beforehand.

Stuffed Cabbage
Malfouf mehshi

An attractive and homely delight, prepared with one of the oldest vegetables. Cabbages prompted the interest of ancient philosophers and poets. Pythagoras, the Greek philosopher and mathematician of the 6th century BC, recommended it for its curative properties, and the poet Horace was fond of it.

Malfouf mehshi is prepared with cabbage leaves wrapped around a succulent mixture of ground meat, rice and spices. Diverging from the classical method, in my recipe I opt for brown rice instead of white, for it is superior in nutrients. I find also that it marries superbly with the cabbage. Stuffed Cabbage is served hot on its own as a main dish or accompanied by a bowl of yoghurt and wholemeal pitta bread.

Ingredients

1 white or green cabbage (about 900 g/2 lbs)

For the stuffing
115 g (4 oz) brown rice, pre-cooked in 225 ml (6½ fl oz) water over low heat until
    water is absorbed
285 g (10 oz) ground meat, preferably lamb, leg or shoulder
½ tsp cinnamon
½ tsp allspice
¼ tsp black pepper
1¼ tsp salt or to taste
4 tbs water
½ tbs olive oil
12 cloves of garlic, peeled
10 g (a little under ½ oz) butter
1–1½ tsp crushed dried mint
6 tbs lemon juice

Cut out and discard the core of the cabbage, then gently remove the leaves one at a time; put them in a pan with just enough boiling water to cover and let them stand for a few minutes until limp and easily pliable. Drain.

Meanwhile in a bowl combine thoroughly the rice, meat, cinnamon, allspice, black pepper, half the amount of salt and the water. Leave this meat mixture aside.

Over a clean surface place several cabbage leaves, thick vein side up. Trim the thick vein or flatten with your thumb. Place about 1 tbs of meat mixture, or as necessary, at stem end of each leaf. Roll around the mixture; repeat with all leaves until completed. Reserve.

Over medium–high heat set a pan, add the oil, heat until hot but not smoking; add 8 of the garlic cloves and stir until golden brown (about 1 minute). Remove pan from heat and place the reserved cabbage rolls, seam side down, placing garlic at intervals between rolls. Pour enough water to cover cabbage rolls by 2½ cm (1 in), season with the remaining salt, bring to the boil, reduce heat to medium, cover and simmer for 30 minutes. Meanwhile crush the remaining garlic until smooth and sauté in butter for a few seconds over medium heat. Add the mint, stir for a few seconds more, and add, along with the lemon juice, to the cabbage rolls. Cover and reduce heat to medium–low and cook for 30 minutes longer.

Serve hot with plain yoghurt and pitta bread.

Sheikh al-mehshi

A pleasant variation on cooking the aubergine, the star of vegetables. An anecdotical story is told in praise of the aubergine. During the aubergine season, a wife was tradition-ally expected to know all the unlimited number of dishes that can be prepared with aubergines. If her husband came home after a long day asking what was for dinner and the answer was, 'I did not know what to prepare today,' the wife could expect trouble and, eventually, divorce.

This recipe is subtle, with an interesting taste. The aubergines are filled with a classic Lebanese mixture, then left to bake undisturbed.

Ingredients

8 medium small aubergines (about 550 g/1$\frac{1}{4}$ lbs)
4 tbs extra-virgin olive oil
15 g ($\frac{1}{2}$ oz) pine-nuts
1 onion (about 115 g/4 oz), peeled, finely chopped
125 g (4 oz) ground meat
1 tomato (about 85 g/3 oz), rinsed and finely chopped
1 tsp salt, or to taste
$\frac{1}{4}$ tsp allspice
$\frac{1}{4}$ tsp black pepper
a pinch of cinnamon
a pinch of white pepper
300–350 ml (10–12 fl oz) boiling water
2 tbs double-concentrate tomato paste
1 tbs lemon juice

Trim the green cap of the aubergines, leaving half the stem intact. Peel them lengthwise. Set a medium-sized frying-pan over medium heat, add the oil; when oil is hot but not smoking, add the aubergines 4 at a time and cook until lightly browned and soft. Remove with a slotted spoon, allowing the oil to drip back into the pan; reserve. To the oil in the pan add the pine-nuts, sauté until golden in colour, stirring constantly; quickly add the onions, stirring for a few seconds, add the meat and cook until browned (about 5–6 min-utes), add the tomatoes and stir, season with half the amount of salt, add the allspice, black pepper, cinnamon and white pepper, stir for one second and remove mixture from heat and allow to cool slightly.

Next, cut a deep slit along one side of each reserved aubergine and with your fingers or a spoon, fill the aubergine and place in a deep baking dish. In a small glass bowl combine the water, remaining salt, tomato paste and lemon juice; stir and pour all over the aubergines.

Bake for 30–35 minutes in a pre-heated oven at 190° C (375° F/gas mark 5).

Serve immediately with Vermicelli Rice.

Okra stew (*yakhnet al-bamieh*)

Stuffed Aubergines
Batinjan mehshi

A familiar and simple Mediterranean speciality, made with fine ingredients. The aubergines are hollowed to leave a thin shell to encase the mixture of rice, meat, tomatoes and spices. The dish bubbles over a low flame until all the flavours are awakened and the beautiful orangey-red liquid is thickened. This is an enchanting and satisfying dish, if skilfully prepared, especially when served along with the cooling yoghurt.

Ingredients

85 g (3 oz) white rice
115 g (4 oz) ground meat
1 clove of garlic, peeled and crushed (optional)
1 ripe tomato (about 115 g/4 oz) rinsed, finely chopped
$^1/_4$ tsp allspice
$^1/_4$ tsp cinnamon
$^1/_4$ tsp black pepper
1 tsp salt or to taste
300–350 ml (10–12 fl oz) water
1 tsp butter
8 small aubergines, about 7–8 cm (3 in) long
2 tbs double-concentrate tomato paste

In a glass bowl combine the rice, meat, garlic, tomato, allspice, cinnamon, black pepper, half the amount of salt, 2 tbs water, and butter. Leave the mixture aside for later use.

Over a hard board place the aubergines, press each one and roll under the palm of your hand until soft; that will make them easier to hollow out. Next cut across the top of each aubergine and hollow the inside, leaving a very thin shell. Fill with the reserved mixture. Repeat with all the aubergines and place in a pot, combine the remaining water with tomato paste and pour over the aubergines. Season with the remaining salt and bring to the boil over moderately high heat. Reduce heat to medium–low. Cover and simmer gently for 25–30 minutes.

Serve hot. Eat with yoghurt and pitta bread.

Stuffed Artichokes
Ardichowki mehshi

A delicacy with elegance, fresh stuffed artichokes are time-consuming to prepare, but the result is worthwhile.

In Lebanon stuffed artichokes are served as part of the home cuisine, and in some restaurants as a *plat du jour*. The combination of ground meat, onions, pine-nuts and spices is browned, then stuffed into the artichoke hearts, which are simmered gently in water and lemon juice. Fresh artichokes are available in many outlets the whole year and good frozen or canned brands can be bought at supermarkets.

I use fresh artichokes, which have more flavour. The artichoke leaves are cut off and the choke is scraped out. If preferred, steaming or boiling are good alternatives, for the leaves will not be wasted and the base is also used.

Ingredients

8 fresh artichokes
half a lemon
1½–2 tbs extra-virgin olive oil
30 g (1 oz) pine-nuts
85 g (3 oz) onion, finely chopped
170 g (6 oz) ground meat, preferably lamb
¼ tsp cinnamon
½ tsp allspice
¾ tsp salt
200 ml (7 fl oz) hot water
1 tsp flour
2–3 tbs lemon juice

To prepare the artichokes, cut off the stem close to the base and snap all the leaves one by one until you reach the base. With a sharp knife gently scoop out the choke and discard, then trim the tough skin around the base and quickly rub with lemon to prevent discolouration.

In a frying-pan over medium–high heat, heat the oil until hot but not smoking; add the artichokes 4 at a time and sauté for 1–2 minutes, coating all sides with the oil. With a slotted spoon remove to a plate and reserve.

To the remaining oil add the pine-nuts and sauté, stirring constantly, until pale golden in colour. Quickly add the onions and stir well to prevent the pine-nuts from turning darker in colour. Add the meat, keep stirring until onions and meat are browned (about 5 minutes). Add the cinnamon, half the amount of allspice and the salt, stir and turn off the heat.

Next with a spoon fill the reserved artichoke hearts with the meat mixture, pressing in as much as possible. Place in one layer in a medium-sized pot and carefully pour the water over the artichokes. Dilute the flour with the lemon juice and add to the water in the pot; season with the remaining allspice. Bring to the boil over medium heat, reduce heat to medium–low, cover and simmer for 20 minutes.

When ready transfer artichoke hearts to a serving dish, spooning the liquid over. Eat with Vermicelli Rice and a seasonal salad.

Stuffed Potatoes
Batata mehshi

In this dish the potato is half-emptied at the centre, which is then filled with a mixture of fine meat, pine-nuts and spices to make a nutritious and tasty main course.

Traditionally the potatoes are peeled, then sautéed in butter, but we now know that more than half the nutrients of the food are just under the skin, so I leave the potatoes unpeeled. I also avoid frying because both the potato and the meat mixture are rich enough to need no additions. You can of course follow the traditional way, if you like.

Ingredients

4 large potatoes (about 700 g/1 lb 10 oz)
1½ tbs extra-virgin olive oil
15 g (H oz) pine-nuts
1 onion (about 50 g/2 oz), peeled and finely chopped
170 g (6 oz) ground meat, preferably lamb
½ tsp allspice
¼ tsp black pepper
¼ tsp cinnamon
1 tsp salt or to taste
1 tbs lemon juice
2 tbs double-concentrate tomato paste
1½ tsp flour
500 ml (16 fl oz) boiled water

Wash the potatoes several times and scrub the skin gently. Cut across the top of the potato; reserve caps. With a corer or a knife, scoop out the inside of each potato, leaving thick potato walls all round. Set aside for later use.

In a frying-pan heat the oil, add the pine-nuts and sauté until golden in colour; remove and reserve. To the same oil in the pan add the onions, sauté for 1 minute over medium–high heat, add the meat and cook with the onions until the meat changes colour (about 3 minutes); return pine-nuts to the same pan, season with the allspice, black pepper, cinnamon, half the amount of salt and the lemon juice. Stir and remove this mixture from heat.

Next fill each potato shell with the meat mixture, pressing it down well. Arrange upright in a pot. Cover with the potato caps. Dissolve the tomato paste and flour in a little water and pour over the potato along with the remaining water, season with remaining salt and bring to the boil. Reduce heat to medium, cook for about 40 minutes or until potatoes are soft.

Serve hot with rice.

Chick-peas with yoghurt and minced meat (*fattet al-houmnos bi-laban*)

Stuffed Courgettes
Koussa mehshi

One of the infinite number of ways of preparing the versatile courgette. When the French poet Lamartine visited the Emir of Lebanon, Bashir al-Shehabi, in 1832, *koussa mehshi* was one of the dishes offered to him. The poet liked it and wrote in his journal, '*Courges semblables à nos courgettes. C'est le mets le plus savoureux, en effet, que l'on puisse manger dans tout l'Orient* (*This is the most succulent dish that one could eat in the whole orient*).'

Ingredients

8 small courgettes, about 6–7 cm (3 in) long
1 tbs extra-virgin olive oil
1 onion (about 115 g/4 oz), peeled and sliced
1 large ripe tomato (about 200 g/7 oz), rinsed and finely chopped
85 g (3 oz) lean ground meat, preferably lamb
45 g (1½ oz) rice, rinsed once and drained
½ tsp allspice
½ tsp cinnamon
½ tsp black pepper
1 tsp salt or to taste
450 ml (15 fl oz) water
2 tbs tomato concentrate

With a knife cut across the top of each courgette and trim the other end. Gently scoop out the inside of each courgette, scraping gently to prevent puncturing the skin (otherwise it will burst open during the cooking) and leaving a shell with equal thickness all around. Set aside and reserve the pulp.

In a stew-pot heat the oil, add the onions, sauté for 2–3 minutes, add the tomatoes and the reserved courgette pulp; reserve this vegetable mixture.

In a bowl combine the meat and rice, season with the allspice, black pepper, cinnamon, half the amount of salt and 2 tbs water. Fill the reserved courgette shells loosely and arrange on top of the reserved vegetable mixture. Add the water and tomato concentrate and season with remaining salt. Bring to the boil over high heat, reduce heat to medium–low, cover and simmer for 40–50 minutes or until rice is soft and flavours are blended.

Transfer to a deep serving dish and eat with yoghurt and wholemeal pitta bread.

Koussa kablama

A humble and homely dish for lunch or dinner. The baby courgettes are sautéed with a little olive oil until golden-brown and the skin is slightly wrinkled. The courgettes are filled with a generous amount of the fine mixture of ground meat and pine-nuts, after which they simmer over a gentle flame.

Ingredients

2 tbs extra-virgin olive oil
8 courgettes, about 6–7 cm (3 in) long, both ends trimmed, rinsed
15 g (½ oz) pine nuts
1 small onion (50 g/2 oz) peeled and finely chopped
85 g (3 oz) ground meat
¼ tsp allspice
¼ tsp cinnamon
¼ tsp black pepper
¾ tsp salt, or to taste
2 tbs double-concentrate tomato paste
300 ml (10 fl oz) water
3 tbs lemon juice
a pinch of white pepper

In a heavy-bottomed frying-pan heat the oil; when hot add the courgettes, fry until skin is browned and wrinkled. Remove to a side dish with a slotted spoon allowing the oil to drip back into the pan; reserve. Add the pine-nuts to the same oil in the pan, stir constantly until golden in colour. Remove and reserve. To the same oil in the pan add the onions, stir for a minute, add the meat and cook together with the onions until meat changes colour (about 3–4 minutes). Season with the allspice, cinnamon, black pepper and half the amount of salt; return the reserved pine nuts, stir and remove from heat, reserve the meat mixture for later use.

With a knife or a spoon make a deep lengthwise cut in each reserved courgette, making sure not to puncture the other side. With the back of a spoon remove some of the pulp of courgette, fill the hollow with reserved meat mixture and place in a pot. Dissolve the tomato purée with the water and pour gently over the filled courgettes, season with the remaining salt, add the lemon juice and white pepper, bring to the boil, reduce to medium heat, cover and simmer for 20 minutes.

Remove from heat, arrange courgettes over a platter, spooning the sauce over them. Eat with Vermicelli Rice.

Courgettes in Yoghurt
Koussa bi-laban

This meal was and still is a favourite of mine. Apart from its enjoyable taste, it brings to mind memories of a happy childhood... Our family was a huge one, with a huge appetite. Each member ate at least six of these courgettes at a sitting. This meant, as I now realize, that my mother had to prepare at least 60 courgettes. She had help, nonetheless she never relinquished control of her kitchen.

Ingredients

8 small courgettes about 6–7 cm (3 in)
75 g (2$\frac{1}{2}$ oz) lean ground meat, preferably lamb
30 g (1 oz) short-grain white rice
3–4 tbs water
$\frac{1}{4}$ tsp cinnamon
$\frac{1}{4}$ tsp black pepper
$\frac{1}{4}$ tsp allspice
1$\frac{1}{4}$ tsp salt or to taste
550 ml (18 fl oz) yoghurt
1 free-range egg (yolk and white)

Cut across the tops of the courgettes, trim the other end and hollow the inside of each courgette, leaving a shell of equal thickness all around, scraping the pulp gently to prevent puncturing the skin. Reserve.

In a small bowl combine meat, rice and water with cinnamon, black pepper, allspice and ½ tsp of the salt. From this mixture fill the reserved courgettes and gently drop them into salted boiling water or, preferably, meat stock to cover by 4½ cm (1½ in). Cook over medium–low heat for about 40 minutes or until tender.

Meanwhile place the yoghurt in a bowl, beat the egg and combine thoroughly with yoghurt using a wooden spoon; strain through a sieve over a saucepan. Stir all the time in the same direction (otherwise it will curdle), cook over moderate heat until it boils. Reduce heat to low, gently drop the cooked courgettes into the yoghurt sauce, sprinkle with the mint; cook for 3–4 minutes, transfer to a serving bowl and serve immediately.

Note: Remember if using brown rice to half-cook it before adding it to the other ingredients.

Fried Meat Patties
Kafta mikli

A popular Middle Eastern version of the hamburger, made of ground meat combined in abundance with the richly-flavoured herb parsley, a blend of spices and, in some recipes, bound with egg. *Kafta* is easy to prepare and can be inexpensive.

This medley is the basis of numerous recipes cooked in a variety of ways. *Kafta* is excellent for frying, as below, or grilling; it is often accompanied by fried potatoes and *baba ghannouj*, which goes particularly well with it. *Kafta* also makes delicious sandwiches.

Ingredients

1 onion (about 115 g/4 oz), peeled and finely chopped
55 g (2 oz) parsley, rinsed and drained, stems cut off
450 g (1 lb) ground meat, preferably lamb
$\frac{1}{2}$ tsp cinnamon
$\frac{1}{4}$ tsp black pepper
$\frac{1}{4}$ tsp allspice
1 tsp salt or to taste
90–120 ml (3–4 fl oz) extra-virgin olive oil

Place the onion and parsley in a food processor and blend to a smooth consistency. Remove and mix thoroughly with meat; season with the cinnamon, black pepper and allspice and shape into a ball. From this mixture take a small portion at a time and flatten between the palms of the hands to form medium-sized patties (about 5 cm/2 in in diameter), moistening hands with water as necessary. Arrange *kafta* patties over a lightly floured dish; reserve for later use.

Heat the oil in a skillet over medium–high heat; when oil is hot but not smoking add the *kafta* patties and cook over medium heat until browned on both sides (about 6–8 minutes). Remove with a slotted spoon, drain on kitchen paper and arrange on a dish.

Serve with Oriental Salad and Aubergine Dip or *hoummos*.

Note: To cut back on frying, place the *kafta* patties over a lightly oiled oven sheed and grill on both sides until browned.

Meat with Burghol on Skewers
Kafta meshwi bi-burghol

Easy, filling and nourishing, especially when eaten with a mixed salad. *Kafta bi-burghol* can be even more delicious when tucked into a pitta bread pocket that has been spread with a generous amount of *baba ghannouj*.

Ingredients

100 g (3 oz) fine *burghol,* rinsed, drained
450 g (1 lb) finely ground meat
1 onion (about 50 g/2 oz) peeled, finely chopped
$\frac{1}{2}$ tsp cinnamon
$\frac{1}{4}$ tsp allspice
$\frac{1}{4}$ tsp black pepper
a handful of fresh mint, rinsed, drained and finely chopped

Squeeze *burghol* to remove excess water; place in a bowl and combine thoroughly with the meat, onion, cinnamon, black pepper, allspice, salt and mint. If desired place in a food processor and run the motor for a few seconds to achieve a smooth consistency.

Remove and divide the mixture into 10–12 portions. Set each portion on a skewer pressing the mixture gently and firmly over ¾ the length of the skewer.

Cook under a hot grill until browned on all sides (about 4 minutes) turning as necessary.

Remove from grill and place inside pitta bread pockets. Serve immediately and eat with *baba ghannouj*.

Baked Kafta
Kafta sayniyeh

Kafta sayniyeh, another homely and delicious dish, is easy to prepare and is baked with fresh vegetables to give an interesting flavour and a good presentation. Traditionally the potatoes and meat are both fried in oil; in this recipe frying is omitted with no noticeable change in the taste.

Ingredients

(Prepare *kafta* mixture as in Fried Meat Patties)
1 tbs extra-virgin olive oil
550 g (1 lb 4 oz) potatoes, washed, gently scrubbed and
   cut across into slices $\frac{1}{2}$ cm ($\frac{1}{4}$ in) thick
200 g (7 oz) onion, peeled, cut across in slices $\frac{1}{2}$ cm ($\frac{1}{4}$ in) thick

2 large ripe tomatoes (about 450 g/1 lb),
    rinsed and cut into rounds
³/₄ tsp salt or to taste
¹/₄ tsp freshly milled black pepper, or to taste
¹/₄ tsp cinnamon
¹/₄ tsp allspice
2 tbs double-concentrate tomato paste
400 ml (14 fl oz) boiled water or meat stock

Brush the oil over the inside of a deep baking dish. With moist hands spread and smooth *kafta* mixture to about ½ cm (¼ in) depth. Place under a hot grill and cook until lightly browned (about 4–5 minutes). Remove and spread on top of *kafta* the potatoes, then the onions, then the tomatoes. Combine the salt, black pepper, cinnamon, allspice and tomato paste with water, or stock if used, and pour all over the vegetables in the baking dish.

Bake covered on the lower middle rack of a pre-heated oven, temperature 190° C (375° F/gas mark 5). Baste twice with pan juices. Cook until potatoes are tender (about 1½ hours uncovering the baking dish for the last half hour.

Remove from oven and serve immediately with a seasonal salad.

Meatballs with Rice
Kafta bi-roz

Kafta bi-roz includes a good quantity of fresh vegetables along with meat and rice, and is thus both tasty and nutritious. It is easy to make, but requires time and patience. It is best to start with the sauce and then proceed with the other preparations.

Ingredients

For the sauce
1 tbs extra-virgin olive oil
1 onion (about 115 g/4 oz) peeled and chopped
4 cloves garlic, peeled and chopped
1 tbs flour
1 carrot peeled, diced
1 tomato (about 200 g/7 oz) chopped
2 tbs double-concentrate tomato paste
1 red chilli pepper, de-seeded and rinsed
850 ml (30 fl oz) water
³/₄ tsp salt
a pinch of white pepper
a pinch of nutmeg

For the kafta *mixture*
450 g (1 lb) ground meat
1 tbs flour
1 egg yolk
$^1\!/_2$ tsp salt
$^1\!/_2$ tsp cinnamon
$^1\!/_4$ tsp white pepper
a pinch of nutmeg
a pinch of allspice

For the rice
150 ml (5 fl oz) water
225 g (8 oz) rice, rinsed once and drained
$^3\!/_4$ tsp salt or to taste

To garnish
225 g (8 oz) fresh or frozen peas (steamed or boiled)
2 tbs parsley, rinsed, finely chopped (optional)

In a medium-sized pot heat the oil over moderately high heat; when hot but not smoking add the onions and sauté until lightly coloured. Add the garlic, reduce the heat to medium and keep stirring for a minute longer. Still stirring, add the flour, carrot, chopped tomatoes, tomato concentrate, chilli pepper and water; stir well and bring to the boil, reduce heat to medium–low, season with salt, white pepper and nutmeg, cover and simmer for 30 minutes. Remove from heat and strain twice through a fine sieve. From the resulting sauce measure 200 ml (7 fl oz) and reserve for later to cook the rice. Set remaining sauce aside.

Meanwhile make *kafta* mixture; combine the meat, flour, egg yolk, salt, cinnamon, white pepper, nutmeg and allspice. With your hands work the mixture until well blended. Divide the mixture into 34 pieces and roll each piece into a mini-ball.

Arrange them on an ungreased oven tray and place under a hot grill to cook until browned (no need to turn) about 5 minutes. Gently remove *kafta* mini-balls to a side dish while still hot, otherwise they will stick to the pan.

To the remaining sauce in the pot add the *kafta* mini-balls and bring to the boil over high heat, reduce heat to medium–low, cover and simmer for 10–15 minutes.

In the meantime combine the reserved 200 ml (7 fl oz) sauce and the 150 ml (5 fl oz) water in a saucepan, bring to the boil, add the rice, bring again to the boil, reduce heat to medium–low and season with salt. Cover and simmer about 8–10 minutes or until rice is soft.

To serve arrange the rice evenly on a serving dish, top with cooked peas and parsley, if used, and place the *kafta* balls in a separate bowl, spooning the sauce over them.

Eat mixed together.

Meatballs in Tomato Sauce
Daoud Pasha

Daoud Pasha was the first governor of Mount Lebanon appointed by the Ottomans with the approval of the Western powers, after the bloody war that opposed the Druzes and the Christian Maronites in 1860.

Daoud Pasha with rice was said to be a favourite of his. Traditionally its main ingredients, the onions and the mini-meatballs, are fried in a generous amount of *samneh*, after which the liquid, tomato paste and seasonings are added, and the dish is left to simmer over a low flame. I omit the frying of the onions and the meat, yet the meal retains its succulence while being lighter to digest.

Ingredients

For the meatballs
225 g (8 oz) lean ground meat
¼ tsp cinnamon
¼ tsp black pepper
a pinch of allspice
½ tsp salt

For the sauce
725–900 ml (26–32 fl oz) water
3 onions (about 250 g/9 oz), thinly sliced
3 tbs double-concentrate tomato paste
½ tsp salt or to taste
¼ tsp cinnamon
¼ tsp allspice
28 g (1 oz) pine nuts
1 tsp flour
1 tbs lemon juice

In a bowl combine the meat, cinnamon, black pepper, allspice and salt and mix thoroughly. From this mixture form mini-meatballs 2 cm (¾ in) in diameter. Arrange in one layer over an ungreased, hot oven sheet, 4 in away from heat, and brown nicely under a hot grill for about 4–5 minutes. Quickly remove meatballs to a dish, to prevent them from sticking, and reserve for later use.

To a pan add the water and the onions, bring to the boil, cover and simmer over medium heat for 10 minutes. When cooking time of onions is over add the tomato purée, salt, cinnamon, allspice, pine nuts, flour and reserved mini-meatballs, stir well, bring to the boil, cover and simmer over medium–low heat for about 25–30 minutes.

Remove from heat. Add the lemon juice and leave to stand covered for 1 minute so that the flavours blend.

Serve hot with Vermicelli Rice and a side salad.

Shawarma

A very popular Middle Eastern speciality. The meat and fat of the lamb are marinated for 12–24 hours, after which they are placed in alternate layers over a large skewer and placed in front of an upright heat to grill while the skewer is turning slowly. When the meat is browned, it is thinly sliced over a split Arabic or pitta bread to serve as a take-away or to eat in a restaurant. *Shawarma* is irresistible but it is very rich in saturated fats, which does not fit in with a healthy lifestyle. For this reason I use lean meat marinated in olive oil, a monounsaturate known to improve the balance of HDL. The meat is baked, then finished off under the grill which gives as nearly as possible the flavour of the real *shawarma*.

Shawarma is delicious, easy to prepare, and suitable for an exotic dinner or lunch or to add to the variety of a buffet.

Ingredients

675 g (1 lb 8 oz) meat (preferably from leg of lamb or beef fillet)
    sliced into $1/2$ cm ($1/4$ in) thick strips
a generous $1/2$ tsp cinnamon
$1/4$ tsp black pepper
a generous $1/2$ tsp allspice
$1/4$ tsp white pepper
$1/4$ tsp nutmeg
$1/4$ tsp ground cardamom
a pinch of ground cloves
2–3 pieces of *miskee* (Arabic gum) gently crushed with a little salt
4 tbs lemon juice
5 tbs organic cider vinegar
2 tbs extra-virgin olive oil
$1/2$ tsp salt or to taste
$1/4$–$1/2$ tsp orange zest
1 small tomato, rinsed and very finely chopped
1 small onion (about 55 g/2 oz), peeled and very finely grated

For the sauce
125 ml (4 fl oz) *tahini*
5–6 tbs lemon juice
5–6 tbs water or as necessary to thin the sauce
$1/4$ tsp salt or to taste

Place meat in a glass bowl. Season and rub on all sides with the cinnamon, black pepper, allspice, white pepper, nutmeg, ground cardamom and cloves. Add the *miskee*, toss with the lemon juice, vinegar, oil and salt; add the orange zest, tomato and onion, mix thoroughly and leave to marinate, covered, in the fridge for 12–18 hours, tossing 2–3 times in between.

Half an hour before cooking remove the meat and marinade from fridge and allow it to reach room temperature. Pre-heat oven to 190° C (375° F/gas mark 5) and arrange the meat mixture in one layer on a baking dish. Bake for about 30–40 minutes or until cooked through.

Meanwhile prepare *tahini* sauce; in a bowl whisk the *tahini* and the lemon juice. It will thicken at first. While whisking gradually add the water and salt; it should look like cream, neither too thin nor too thick. Taste and adjust the seasoning. Reserve.

Remove meat from oven and place under a hot grill, 4 in from the heat, for about 2–3 minutes or until nicely browned, turning once or twice. Split a large pitta bread, place the meat inside the pitta pocket and serve immediately.

Eat with *tahini* sauce or *hoummos* and, if desired, a dish of pickles and a dish of thinly sliced onions, tossed with 2 tsp of *sumak* and topped with a handful of coarsely chopped parsley leaves.

Lamb brochettes

Lahm meshwi

Lebanon is blessed with beautiful temperate weather that invites leisurely outdoor gatherings. Spring and early summer are particularly rich in the odours of flowers and the earth. At such times you can see people scattered all over the place, playing cards or preparing lunch. Lamb brochettes is one of the dishes they may be making.

The pieces of meat are pushed on to skewers to be grilled in a metal utensil over glowing hot charcoals until browned all over. Their smell, caught by the breeze, is hearty and mouthwatering.

Good-quality meat can be grilled, then seasoned with freshly ground black pepper and salt, with no need to marinate.

Ingredients

900 g (2 lb) lean meat, preferably from a leg of lamb, cut into $^3/_4$ cm ($1^1/_4$ in) pieces
1 tsp salt or to taste
$^1/_4$ tsp black pepper or to taste
$^1/_2$ tsp allspice
2 tbs lemon juice
2 tbs extra-virgin olive oil
225 g (8 oz) small or pearl onions, peeled

Place meat in a bowl, season and rub with the salt, black pepper and allspice. Add the lemon juice and oil, mix well and allow to marinate for a few hours in the refrigerator. Half an hour before grilling, remove the meat and let it reach room temperature.

Heat the grill, thread the meat pieces and onions alternately. Place the skewers over an oven sheet and grill, turning the skewers, until browned all over (about 6–8 minutes).

Remove from heat, place inside large pitta bread pocket. Serve immediately with Oriental Salad or *fattoush* and *baba ghannouj* or *hoummos*.

Meat in Vinegar
Lahm bi-khal

A hearty dish with a strong tasty flavour, reputedly a favourite of the Prophet Mohammad. Traditionally most Middle Eastern cooking uses *samneh* (butter) to fry the meat and vegetables before they are simmered in liquid. *Lahm bi-khal* is a rich and interesting combination of foods and it would be a pity to allow the oil to interfere with its delicacy, while adding unnecessary calories. For these reasons, and for simplicity, I leave out the oil, but without altering the fine, unique flavour.

It is served hot on a bed of rice as a main course. Brown rice is particularly good as the texture goes well with the consistency of the dish.

Ingredients

450 g (1 lb) meat from a leg of lamb, cut into $2\frac{1}{2}$ cm (1 in) cubes
1–2 bones from lamb knuckle end
575 ml (20 fl oz) water
225 g (8 oz) baby or pearl onions, peeled
1 cinnamon stick
10 cloves of garlic, peeled
$1\frac{1}{4}$ tsp salt or to taste
225 g (8 oz) aubergines, trimmed, rinsed, cut in $2\frac{1}{2}$ cm (1 in) cubes
225 g (8 oz) courgettes, trimmed, rinsed, cut in $2\frac{1}{2}$ cm (1 in) cubes
2–3 tbs organic cider vinegar
$\frac{1}{2}$ tbs flour
2 tsp mint
$\frac{1}{4}$ tsp cinnamon
$\frac{1}{4}$ tsp black pepper
$\frac{1}{4}$ tsp allspice

Cover the meat and bones with water, bring to the boil over medium–high heat, skimming the foam from the surface of the water. Add the onions, cinnamon stick, garlic and salt. Reduce heat to medium, cover and simmer about 40 minutes or until meat is tender.

Add the aubergines, courgettes, vinegar, flour and mint. Season with cinnamon, black pepper and allspice, bring to the boil. Cover and simmer for 15 minutes longer. Remove from heat, place in a bowl.

Eat with rice, preferably brown.

Jew's Mallow
Mouloukhiyeh

This recipe originated either in Aleppo or in Egypt; it then travelled to Lebanon, and in the process was adapted to the taste of the locals. The legend says that the Fatimid Egyptian Sultan, Hakim bi-Amr Allah, deified by the Druse faith, prohibited his congregation from eating *mouloukhiyeh*. Here there are two reasons for that prohibition. Some say that this was because of its reputed aphrodisiac qualities, others that the Sultan wished to punish his undisciplined people for improprieties. Whatever the reason, the result is that many Druses, and certainly the religious sheikhs, even now refrain from eating it.

The preparation is lengthy but it is worth trying for its rich aromatic taste and full nourishment. In season, when *mouloukhiyeh* comes in bunches, is the time to try the recipe, for the dried and frozen varieties are, to my taste, less appealing.

Ingredients

1 free-range skinless chicken (about 900–1350 g//2–3 pounds)
350 g (12 oz) meat from leg of lamb, cut into 3 cm
    (1¼ in) cubes, rinsed
2 bones from the knuckle end of lamb, rinsed
1¾ l (60 fl oz) water
1 onion, peeled
2 large cinnamon sticks
1½ tsp salt or to taste
3–4 bunches fresh *mouloukhiyeh*, leaves only (yielding about 450 g/16 oz),
    rinsed, patted dry
1 large onion (about 255 g/9 oz), peeled, very finely chopped
175 ml (6 fl oz) organic cider vinegar
2 medium pitta breads, toasted and broken into small pieces
1 bunch of coriander (about 125 g/4½ oz), roots cut off, rinsed,
    drained and finely chopped
8–10 garlic cloves, peeled and crushed
a heaped ¼ tsp cinnamon
a heaped ¼ tsp black pepper
3 tbs lemon juice

In a large pan combine the chicken, meat, bones and water, place over high heat, skim the foam from the surface and bring to the boil. Add the onion, cinnamon stick and salt, reduce heat to medium–low, cover and simmer for 50–60 minutes or until both chicken and meat are tender.

Meanwhile pack together small handfuls of *mouloukhiyeh* leaves and slice them very finely, or place in a food processor (make sure leaves are very dry) and run the motor on and off 7–8 times only, otherwise *mouloukhiyeh* will become too mushy (or use the food processor recently created to chop *mouloukhiyeh*). Reserve.

Then combine the onions and vinegar in a serving bowl. Place the bread in a serving dish and proceed with the last preparations.

Remove the chicken from the broth, de-bone and cut the meat into serving pieces; place on one side of a serving dish. Remove the meat from the broth and place next to chicken pieces. Remove the bones and discard, along with the cinnamon stick. Remove the onion, press through a fine sieve, and return to the broth. Add the coriander and garlic, bring to the boil, reduce heat to medium, cover and simmer for 5–6 minutes, then add the reserved *mouloukhiyeh*, season with cinnamon and black pepper, bring again to the boil and simmer for 2 minutes. Add the lemon juice, stir, taste. and adjust the seasonings.

Serve *mouloukhiyeh* in a soup bowl, a serving dish of plain cooked rice, the bowl of onion and vinegar and the toasted bread.

To eat, place in a soup plate about 2 tbs rice, top with a little chicken, some meat pieces and a little bread. Top with *mouloukhiyeh* then cover with onions and vinegar to taste and eat with a spoon.

Upside-Down Aubergines
Makloubet al-batinjan

An imaginative and delicious dish cherished by aubergine lovers and known throughout the Levant. *Makloubet* means upside-down; the dish, which is prepared in layers of meat, rice, and aubergine, is unmoulded after cooking as is done with cakes.

In this recipe, instead of cooking and layering the meat and rice separately as is normally done, I cook them both together for simplicity.

Ingredients

550–675 g (1 lb 4 oz-1 lb 8 oz) aubergine
salt
olive oil for baking and frying
30 g (1 oz) almond flakes
30 g (1 oz) pine-nuts
1 onion (about 3 oz) peeled and finely chopped
450 g (1 lb) ground meat

1 tsp salt
a heaped ¼ tsp black pepper
1 tsp allspice
1 tsp cinnamon
600 ml (21 fl oz) water or preferably meat stock
7 oz (200 g) long-grain brown rice, preferably basmati, rinsed once and drained
pinch of white pepper

Pare both ends of the aubergines but leave skin on, and rinse. Cut crosswise at 2½ cm (1 in) intervals, or into 2½ cm (1 in) cubes. Sprinkle lavishly with salt and let them stand in a colander for at least 40 minutes, to draw out their bitter juices and to minimize the absorption of oil. Rinse the aubergine slices and pat dry between kitchen papers. Oil well an oven sheet and from this oil coat both sides of the aubergine slices; arrange on the sheet then place under a hot grill and brown nicely on both sides. Reserve.

Heat 2 tbs of the oil in a frying-pan. Add the almond flakes, stir for 3–4 seconds only and add the pine-nuts, stirring constantly until both nuts are golden brown in colour; remove with a slotted spoon and arrange evenly over a small but deep baking dish and reserve. To the remaining oil in frying-pan add the onions and meat, sauté over high heat about 8–10 minutes or until browned, season with salt and black pepper and half each of the allspice and cinnamon. Add the rice and stir for a minute longer. Measure 500 ml (16 fl oz) water or meat stock, add to the rice. Bring to the boil, cover and simmer over medium–low heat for about 30–35 minutes or until water is absorbed. When this meat mixture is ready leave to stand covered for 2 minutes.

In the meantime arrange a layer of the reserved aubergines over the layer of nuts in the baking dish and line the wall of the dish with aubergines; inside this wall of aubergines layer alternately meat mixture and aubergines, repeating until you reach the top.

Then, with the remaining water, stir in the remaining allspice and cinnamon and add the white pepper. Pour all over the meat mixture, pre-heat the oven to 180° C (350° F/gas mark 4) and cook covered for 15–20 minutes. Remove from oven and leave to stand covered for 5 minutes.

Unmould on to a serving dish or serve straight from the baking dish. Eat with yoghurt.

Dervish's Beads

Masbahat al-derwich

The name of this recipe is somehow connected with the dervish's practice of incessantly repeating his prayers. *Masbahat al-derwich* is a homely dish, which I do not recall seeing on restaurant menus. Traditionally all the vegetables needed for the recipe, except for the tomatoes, are fried separately in butter, as is the meat. I have tried to recommend a simpler and healthier way.

Ingredients

285 g (10 oz) meat from leg of lamb, cut into 2½ cm (1 in) pieces
1.1 l (40 fl oz) water
2 tsp salt or to taste
1 onion (about 170 g/6 oz), peeled and sliced, or pearl onions, peeled
1 large cinnamon stick
1 aubergine (about 285 g/10 oz)
2 tbs extra-virgin olive oil
1 courgette (about 285 g/10 oz), rinsed, sliced ½ cm (¼ in) thick
2 potatoes (about 400 g/14 oz), washed, scrubbed and sliced ½ cm (¼ in) thick
450 g (1 lb) ripe tomatoes, rinsed, sliced ½ cm (¼ in) thick
1 tbs double-concentrate tomato paste
½ tsp allspice
½ tsp cinnamon
¼ tsp black pepper

Combine the meat, water and salt in a stew-pot over high heat; skim the scum from the surface and bring to the boil, add the onions or pearl onions and the cinnamon stick. Reduce heat to medium–low, cover and simmer for 40 minutes.

Meanwhile trim both ends of the aubergine, cut lengthwise into ½ cm (¼ in) slices, sprinkle lavishly with salt. Place in a colander, weighted down with a heavy dish. Leave for at least 40 minutes to drain off the bitter juices. Rinse, pat dry and reserve.

To a deep baking dish add 1 tbs of the oil and in successive layers spread the reserved aubergines, courgette slices, potatoes, cooked meat and onions, covering finally with the tomatoes. Measure 200 ml (7 fl oz) of the broth resulting from the meat, stir into it the tomato paste, allspice, cinnamon, black pepper and the remaining olive oil and pour all over the vegetables. Pre-heat the oven to 190° C (375° F/gas mark 5) and bake for 1¼ hours, or until the top is browned and the potatoes are soft.

Lebanese Couscous
Moghrabiyeh

Do not be misled by the name *moghrabiyeh*, which means 'Moroccan': this is a couscous with a difference, and has little to do with the many North African varieties. The origin could well have been North Africa but the taste and flavour of the Lebanese *moghrabiyeh* are very distinctive. *Moghrabiyeh* is very popular in Tripoli, the second largest town in Lebanon, and in the souks huge heaps of steamed semolina pellets on large copper trays are offered.

Ingredients

1 small free-range chicken (clean as in introduction to Poultry section)
225 g (8 oz) from a leg of lamb, cut into 4½ cm (1½ in) pieces
2 l (76 fl oz) water
2 cinnamon sticks
1–2 bay leaves
1½ tsp salt or to taste
85 g (3 oz) chick-peas, soaked overnight, rinsed and drained
12–14 baby or pearl onions, peeled
1 tsp cinnamon
1 tbs ground caraway seeds
3 tbs extra-virgin olive oil
225 g (8 oz) *moghrabiyeh* grains
30 g (1 oz) butter
450 ml (15 fl oz) stock from chicken and meat

In a large pan combine the chicken, meat and water over high heat. Skim the foam from the surface of the water and bring to the boil. Add the cinnamon sticks and 1¼ tsp salt. Reduce the heat to medium and cook for about 1¼ hours or until chicken and meat are tender (chicken cooks faster than red meat). Remove, de-bone, slice in large pieces and keep warm until serving. Continue to cook the meat until tender.

Meanwhile place the chick-peas in a saucepan and cover with water by 5 cm (2 in), skim off the foam and bring to the boil. Reduce the heat to moderately low, cover and simmer for 1½ hours, then add the onions and allow to simmer with the chick-peas for 30 minutes longer. 5 minutes before the end of cooking, season with ¼ tsp each of cinnamon and caraway and the remaining salt. Stir and reserve this chick-pea sauce.

To prepare *moghrabiyeh*:
To salted boiling water add 1 tbs oil. Drop in the *moghrabiyeh* grains and cook for 5–7 minutes, drain and rinse under running cold water; place in a colander and season with the remaining cinnamon and caraway, thoroughly coating the grains. Leave aside.

In a deep-frying pan melt the butter and add the remaining oil. Set over medium–high heat and when hot add the seasoned grains, reduce heat to low then stir them for about 3 minutes or more and, while stirring, gradually add the stock. Cover and simmer on low heat for about 10 minutes or until grains are tender and moist, not dry. Taste and adjust the seasonings.

Arrange the *moghrabiyeh* on a serving dish, spread the chicken pieces and some of the meat over them.

In a bowl ladle about 200 ml (7 fl oz) of the chicken and meat stock with remaining meat, and combine with the reserved chick-pea sauce.

Serve hot. Eat *moghrabiyeh* spooning over some of the chick-pea mixture.

Note: Save any left-over stock for use in other dishes.

Stuffed Meat Roast
Rosto madkouka mehshi

This splendidly delicious roast is one of my favourites. The finely pounded or minced meat is moulded into a baguette shape and wrapped around a tasty and nutritious mixture of carrots, fresh herbs, spices and pine-nuts. The rolled meat is then tied up with a string, browned all over in the olive oil and left to simmer in water until it reaches its utmost tenderness and flavour.

Ingredients

For the meat
450 g (1 lb) very lean minced meat, preferably from a leg of lamb
¼ tsp allspice
¼ tsp cinnamon
¼ tsp black pepper
¾ tsp salt or to taste

For the stuffing
1 carrot, peeled and very finely diced
handful of coriander or parsley, roots cut off, rinsed and finely chopped
2–3 cloves of garlic, peeled and finely diced
30 g (1 oz) pine-nuts, coarsely crushed
¼ tsp black pepper
¼ tsp allspice
¼ tsp cinnamon
½ tsp salt
1½ tbs olive oil for frying

For the stock
500 ml (16 fl oz) water
1 bay leaf
1 cinnamon stick
2 cloves
3 black peppercorns

In a bowl combine the meat, allspice, cinnamon, black pepper and the salt. Knead for a minute on a lightly floured surface.

Combine the carrot, coriander, garlic and pine-nuts, season with the black pepper, allspice, cinnamon and salt. Reserve this stuffing.

Flatten the meat into a long rectangular shape with a uniform thickness of about ½ cm (¼ in). Spread the reserved stuffing evenly over the end nearest to you. Starting with this end, roll up the meat, enclosing the mixture, packing it tightly and forming a log-shaped roll. In a medium-sized pot heat the oil over medium–high heat until hot but not smoking. Add the meat roll and brown on all sides.

Add the water gradually, then the bay leaf, cinnamon stick, cloves and peppercorns. Bring to the boil, cover and simmer over medium–low heat about 40-50 minutes. Remove the meat from pot and leave to stand for 10 minutes. To serve cut in 1 cm (½ in) slices with a sharp carving knife. Serve with the sauce spooned over.

Serve immediately with roasted potatoes, *baba ghannouj* and a seasonal salad.

Fried Liver
Kasbe mikli

Kasbe is one of the numerous appetizers, cold and hot, that come in a *mezze*. Small cubes of lamb's liver are served raw to be eaten with allspice (*b'harat*), onion and bread. They are also eaten grilled or fried. In my recipe I use either lamb's liver or calf's liver, which has a most delicate, delicious flavour. *Kasbe mikli* is quick to prepare, healthy and needs no planning ahead.

Ingredients

2 tbs extra-virgin olive oil
1 onion (about 200 g/7 oz) peeled, sliced thinly
4–5 cloves of garlic, peeled and cut across in half
450 g (1 lb) calf's or lamb's liver, cut in 2½ cm (1 in) cubes
½ tsp salt, or to taste
¼ tsp cinnamon
¼ tsp black pepper
¼ tsp allspice

125 ml (4 fl oz) water
3–4 tbs lemon juice

Heat the oil in a heavy-bottomed pan. Add the onion and the garlic and sauté until soft over medium heat (about 3 minutes). Add the liver and cook until nicely browned (about 5 minutes), season with salt, cinnamon, black pepper and allspice, add the water, bring to the boil, cover and simmer over medium heat so that the flavours blend (about 5 minutes). Remove the lid, add the lemon juice, cover and allow to cook for 1–2 minutes longer. Transfer to a dish.

Serve immediately. Eat with bread.

Roast Meat
Rosto

A delicious roast cooked in red wine, which gives a deep flavour and tenderness to the meat. The addition of red wine must be a legacy of the French, who ruled the country for nearly 25 years. It is very simple and can be made ahead of time. Roast meat can be served cold in a buffet. The left-overs make wonderful sandwiches tucked with lots of raw lettuce and tomatoes.

Ingredients

900 g (2 lb) eye of silverside or roasting meat
1½ tsp salt or to taste
½ tsp allspice
½ tsp cinnamon
¼ tsp black pepper
2 tbs olive oil
1 onion (about 8 oz) peeled and coarsely cut
1 carrot, peeled and coarsely cut
1 medium-sized potato washed, scrubbed and cut in half
6 cloves of garlic, peeled
200 ml (7 fl oz) red wine
170 ml (6 fl oz) water
1 large cinnamon stick
1 bay leaf
5 cloves

Season and rub the meat with the salt, allspice, cinnamon and black pepper, coating all sides. Leave aside.

In a heavy-bottomed pan heat the oil until hot but not smoking, add the meat and brown on all sides. Half-way through browning add the onion, carrot, potato and garlic and sauté along with the meat (about 8–10 minutes), then gradually add the wine, water, cinnamon stick, bay leaf and cloves. Bring to the boil, cover and simmer over medium heat for 15 minutes, then reduce heat to medium–low and simmer for 1¼–1½ hours.

Remove the meat and leave to stand for 5 minutes. Meanwhile discard the cinnamon stick, bay leaf, and cloves; strain the remaining liquid and vegetables through a fine sieve pressing the vegetables with the back of a spoon. Slice the meat into serving pieces, spooning some of the resulting sauce over.

Serve immediately; eat with a seasonal salad.

Stews

Stews are prepared in much the same way all over the Middle East; in Lebanon they come under the name *yakhne*. These simple peasant stews give all sorts of possibilities for using seasonal vegetables and provide good nutrition, comforting feelings of warmth and satisfaction.

In Lebanon stews can be cooked with or without meat. The meatless ones are called *tabikh bi-zeit* and are eaten at room temperature. Lately of course they have become very popular among vegetarians.

For my recipes I use the best quality meat, trim all excess fat and whenever possible boil rather than fry the meat. The vegetables are simmered in the liquid, not fried as in the traditional method. The cooking time is limited, to minimize loss of vitamins and minerals. These stews are nutritious and suitable for all ages.

Green Bean Stew
Yakhnet al-loubieh

This is one of the favourite stews eaten in Lebanese homes. The meat and bones enrich the stock and when the fresh vegetable is added the stew has a full-bodied flavour. When the onions are browned, the green beans are added and left until their flesh softens.

Ingredients

2 tbs olive oil
1 onion (about 115 g/4 oz) peeled, finely chopped
4–5 cloves of garlic, peeled and slivered
225 g (8 oz) meat from a leg of lamb, cut into 3 cm (1¼ in) pieces
450 g (1 lb) green beans, trimmed, rinsed and sliced into julienne
¼ tsp allspice
1 tsp salt
¼ tsp cinnamon

¼ tsp black pepper
1 tomato (about 170 g/6 oz), cut in 2½ cm (1 in) cubes
2 tbs tomato paste
400 ml (14 fl oz) water

Trim the ends of the beans, removing strings, if any, from each side. Reserve.

Set a pot over moderately high heat, add the oil; when oil is hot but not smoking add the onions, garlic and meat and cook until slightly browned (3–4 minutes), reduce heat to medium–low, add the reserved beans, allspice, salt, cinnamon and black pepper, cover and let them soften from the steam in the pot for about 10–15 minutes, turning beans twice in between, without disturbing the onions.

Add the tomatoes, tomato paste and water; bring to the boil over medium–high heat, reduce heat to medium–low, cover and simmer for 30–40 minutes to give them time to blend.

Serve hot with brown rice.

Okra Stew
Yakhnet al-bamieh

An excellent stew with a lemony flavour. Okra was cultivated by the Egyptians in the 12th century AD. When in season it appears frequently in the daily Lebanese home cuisine. The dish looks elegant since the okra is left complete except for trimming the tough, green cap. While you are trimming the cap, try not to puncture the pod, so keep the top in its pyramid shape. Before cooking the stew the okra is fried for a few minutes and, as in other stew recipes, it simmers gently to mellow and produce its own aromatic juices. In this recipe the okra is grilled, to cut back on the use of oil.

Ingredients

550 g (1 lb 4 oz) okra, rinsed
285 g (10 oz) meat from a leg of lamb
700 ml (25 fl oz) water
1½ tsp salt or to taste
3 cloves of garlic, peeled and crushed
a large handful of coriander, rinsed, drained and chopped
1 large ripe tomato (about 225 g/8 oz), cut in 2½ cm (1 in) slices
1½ tbs double-concentrate tomato paste
¼ tsp cinnamon
¼ tsp black pepper
¼ tsp allspice
2 tbs lemon juice

Trim the tops of the okra, being careful not to puncture the pods. Spread the okra over a tray and place under a pre-heated grill, 4 in from heat, for 2 minutes; remove from grill and reserve.

Set a pot over moderately high heat, add the meat and water, skim the scum from the surface of the water, bring to the boil, add the salt, cover and simmer over moderately low heat for 30 minutes or until meat is slightly soft.

Add the reserved okra, garlic, coriander, tomatoes and tomato paste. Season with the cinnamon, black pepper and allspice and simmer for 20–30 minutes longer. Towards the end of cooking taste and adjust seasonings, then add the lemon juice.

Serve hot with rice.

Cauliflower Stew
Yakhnet al-arnabit

Another simple stew as good as the others, and prepared similarly. It is a basic dish made of cauliflower florets, which contain a substance that may reduce the risk of cancer, particularly of the colon and stomach, the more so when eaten fresh. The florets are traditionally fried until brown before being cooked in the liquid with other ingredients. Although in my recipe I do not fry them, the meal keeps its rich taste, much of which is from the addition of fresh-scented herbs and spices. Ground meat is used instead of diced lamb, which I think marries well with the texture of the cauliflower florets.

This dish is a fine homely treat with a tantalizing aroma.

Ingredients

2 tbs extra-virgin olive oil
1 onion (about 140 g/5 oz), peeled and finely chopped
225 g (8 oz) ground meat
450–575 ml (15–20 fl oz) water
2 tbs double-concentrate tomato paste
675 g (1 lb 8 oz) cauliflower florets, rinsed
1 large carrot, peeled, cut into rounds
2–3 cloves of garlic, peeled and crushed
$\frac{1}{2}$ tsp cinnamon
$\frac{1}{4}$ tsp black pepper
$1\frac{1}{4}$ tsp salt or to taste
a few coriander sprigs (about 15–30 g/$\frac{1}{2}$–1 oz), roots cut off, rinsed and coarsely chopped
2–3 tbs lemon juice or to taste

Set a pot over moderately high heat, add the oil; when it is hot but not smoking add the onions. Stir for a few seconds and add the meat. Cook until brown, stirring occasionally (about 5 minutes); add the water and tomato paste and bring to the boil, add the cauli-flower florets, carrots, garlic, cinnamon, black pepper and salt. Cover and simmer over moderately low heat for about 20 minutes; half-way through cooking add the coriander and towards the end of cooking add the lemon juice.

Tomato Stew
Yakhnet al-banadoura

Tomatoes in Lebanon burst with flavour; they are abundant and delicious to eat uncooked, simply seasoned with salt, a splash of olive oil and some dried or fresh mint. No less tasty is this stew, which enhances the flavour of the tomatoes even more. I highly recommend it. To peel tomatoes drop them in boiled water for a few seconds or, if very ripe, with a sharp knife.

Ingredients

1$\frac{1}{2}$ tbs extra-virgin olive oil
1 onion (about 85 g/3 oz), peeled and finely chopped
4 cloves of garlic, peeled and finely chopped
450 g (1 lb) ground meat
30 g (1 oz) pine-nuts
675 g (1 lb 8 oz) ripe tomatoes, skinned, de-seeded and cut into 3 cm (1$\frac{1}{4}$ in) pieces
1 tbs double-concentrate tomato paste
1$\frac{1}{2}$ tsp salt or to taste
$\frac{1}{2}$ tsp cinnamon
$\frac{1}{4}$ tsp black pepper
$\frac{1}{4}$ tsp allspice
200 ml (7 fl oz) water
a handful of parsley leaves, rinsed and chopped

In a medium-sized pot heat the oil over medium–high heat. Add the onions, garlic and meat; sauté until lightly browned (about 6–8 minutes), breaking up any lumps with the edge of a wooden spoon. Add the pine-nuts, tomatoes and tomato paste, reduce the heat to medium and season with salt, cinnamon, black pepper and allspice. Add the water, bring to the boil, reduce heat to medium–low, cover and simmer for 20–30 minutes, allowing flavours to blend. 5 minutes before the end of cooking add the parsley.

Note: You can add one red chilli, whole, for a mildly piquant taste, or de-seeded and very finely chopped for a stronger one.

Jew's Mallow Stew
Yakhnet al-mouloukhiyeh

The plant *mouloukhiyeh* is popular and highly praised in the Levant and Egypt. Lebanese people prepare it and are proud to serve it, especially for lunch parties. It is also served in restaurants for Sunday lunch. Vegetarians can enjoy eating *mouloukhiyeh* by leaving out the meat.

For its preparation the leaves are pulled out of their stems, rinsed and left to drain well before being fried in generous amounts of butter with the freshest of herbs and spices that enrich the dish and give a particularly characteristic flavour.

Ingredients

450 g (1 lb) meat from leg of lamb, cut into 1 cm (½ in) pieces
2 bones from lamb knuckle end (optional)
1.1 l (40 fl oz) water
1 large cinnamon stick
1 tsp salt or to taste
2 tbs extra-virgin olive oil
1 onion (about 140 g/5 oz) peeled and finely chopped
9 cloves of garlic, peeled and crushed
½ tsp ground coriander
about ¾ bunch of coriander,
    roots cut off, rinsed and finely chopped
3–4 bunches of mouloukhiyeh leaves
    (yielding about 450 g/1 lb) whole or coarsely chopped
¼ tsp cinnamon
¼ tsp black pepper
¼ tsp allspice
a few lemon wedges

In a pan combine the meat, the bones if used and water and place over high heat. Skim the foam from the surface and bring to the boil. Add the cinnamon stick and salt. Reduce the heat to medium–low, cover and simmer for 40–50 minutes or until meat is soft.

Meanwhile set a frying pan over medium–high heat, add the oil; when oil is hot add the onions and sauté until pale in colour (about 1–2 minutes). Add the garlic, ground and fresh coriander and stir for 1 minute longer. Remove this mixture and add to the meat in the pan, along with *mouloukhiyeh* leaves. Season with the cinnamon, black pepper and allspice, cover and simmer over medium heat for 10–15 minutes longer. Taste and adjust the seasonings.

Serve, squeezing lemon juice on top to taste, but be careful as a little bit goes a long way.

Courgette Stew
Yakhnet al-koussa

Courgettes are versatile and appear in many recipes; they can be stuffed, cooked along with yoghurt, sliced for stew or diced to be added to soups. Whichever way they are prepared they add a pleasant and delicate flavour to the dish. This stew is a favourite of mine, prepared meatless or with meat. If meat is used I add tomato paste; if not I accentuate more the dried mint, to enrich its sauce.

Accompanied by rice it makes a wonderful family meal.

Ingredients

450 g (1 lb) meat from a leg of lamb, cut into 2½ cm (1 in) pieces
350–400 ml (12–14 fl oz) water
1 large onion (about 225 g/8 oz), peeled and sliced into half-moon shapes
½ tbs extra-virgin olive oil
1 large ripe tomato (about 225 g/8 oz) rinsed and quartered
1 tbs double-concentrate tomato paste
1 tsp salt or to taste
450 g (1 lb) courgettes, both ends trimmed and cut into quarters
¼ tsp allspice
¼ tsp cinnamon
¼ tsp black pepper
1 tsp dried mint (optional)

In a pan combine the meat and water over high heat, skim any scum from the surface of the water, and bring to the boil. Add the onions, oil, tomato, tomato purée and salt, bring back to the boil, cover and simmer for 20–25 minutes. After that add the courgettes. Season with the allspice, cinnamon, black pepper and mint. Bring to the boil, cover and simmer for 20 minutes longer.

Serve hot with Vermicelli Rice.

Artichoke Stew
Yakhnet al ardichowki

This stew is a harmonious combination of textures and flavours. Traditionally the meat and onions are browned in oil, then cooked thoroughly with the fresh vegetables in their juices. To make the dish more substantial I add potatoes, which, in my opinion, marry well with the artichokes. Remember to taste to adjust seasoning. This is a healthy home-cooking recipe characterized by its earthy flavour.

Ingredients

8 artichokes, base only
　　(to prepare see Artichoke Salad recipe)
225 g (8 oz) meat from leg of lamb cut into 2 cm (³⁄₄ in) pieces
1 bone from the lamb's knuckle end (optional)
700 ml (25 fl oz) water
1 tsp salt
1 large cinnamon stick
1 onion (about 85 g/3 oz,) peeled and sliced
　　into half-moon shapes
1 tsp flour
¹⁄₂ tsp white pepper
1 tbs lemon juice

Remove outer leaves until you reach the base. Remove inner choke and trim the base with a sharp knife; rinse and rub with a piece of lemon to prevent discolouration.

Trim excess fat from lamb pieces. Combine with bone, water and salt. Place over high heat. Before it boils fiercely, skim the foam off the surface. Boil, add the cinnamon stick and onions. Reduce the heat to medium–low, cover and simmer for 50–60 minutes or until tender. After that add the artichokes and flour, season with white pepper and remaining salt. Bring to the boil, cover and simmer over medium–low heat for 15–20 minutes longer or until artichokes are tender. Turn off the heat, add the lemon juice and leave covered for 2 minutes, allowing the flavours to blend.

Serve hot with rice and lemon wedges.

Pea Stew
Yakhnet al-bazela

Pea seeds were found among the ruins of Troy, which indicates that they were cultivated before the Christian era. Peas, however, were until the 16th century dried and cooked. The court of Louis XIV is said to have taken great pleasure in eating fresh peas. Peas have a good concentration of protein and various benefits are attributed to them, including that they act as a contraceptive.

This stew is quick to assemble, with lovely vivid colours, and scented with fresh herbs and spices that blend superbly with tomato paste. Prepared meatless, this stew is ideal for vegetarians especially with Vermicelli Rice (using brown rice) as an accompaniment.

Ingredients

1 tbs olive oil
1 onion (about 140 g/5 oz), peeled and finely chopped
225 g (8 oz) ground meat
2–3 cloves of garlic, peeled and crushed
350 ml (12 fl oz) water
2 tbs double-concentrate tomato paste
1 carrot (about 115 g/4 oz) peeled and cut up
450 g (1 lb) peas, fresh and shelled or frozen
a handful of coriander, rinsed and chopped
¼ tsp cinnamon
1 tsp salt, or to taste
¼ tsp black pepper or to taste

Heat the oil in a pan over moderately high heat; when oil is hot enough add the onions and meat. Cook until browned (about 3–4 minutes), stirring constantly, add the garlic and stir for a few seconds longer. Add the water, bring to the boil, add the tomato paste, carrots, peas, coriander, cinnamon, salt, and black pepper. Bring to the boil again, reduce heat to medium–low, cover and simmer for 10–15 minutes.

Serve hot; eat with rice.

Broad Bean Stew
Yakhnet al-foul

It is preferable to prepare this stew when broad beans are in season, since nothing can compare with fresh vegetables. The broad, or fava, beans are shelled, although young and tender ones are left in their pods, and cooked until tender.

Scented with fresh coriander and enhanced with a touch of lemon, this stew is irresistible, deep and satisfying. Brown rice goes well with it, adding a nutty flavour and a wealth of essential nutrients.

Ingredients

350 g (12 oz) meat from a leg of lamb, cut into $2\frac{1}{2}$ cm (1 in) pieces
1–2 bones from lamb knuckle (optional)
575 ml (20 fl oz) water
$1\frac{1}{4}$ tsp salt or to taste
1 onion (about 125 g/$4\frac{1}{2}$ oz), peeled and finely chopped
2 large cloves of garlic, peeled and crushed
4–5 sprigs of coriander (about 115 g/4 oz) roots cut off, rinsed, chopped
675 g ($1\frac{1}{2}$ lb) young broad beans, both ends trimmed, strings removed
$\frac{1}{2}$ tsp allspice
$\frac{1}{4}$ tsp black pepper
1 tsp extra virgin olive oil

In a pan combine the meat, bones if used, cinnamon stick, water and salt. Set over medium–high heat, skim the foam from the surface of the water and bring to the boil. Add the onion, reduce heat, cover and simmer until meat is nearly soft (about 20 minutes).

Add the garlic, coriander and beans. Season with the allspice and black pepper, add the oil, bring to the boil and simmer for about 30–40 minutes.

Serve hot with rice and lemon wedges.

Spinach Stew

Yakhnet al-sabanekh

Spinach, which is said to have originated in Persia, was introduced into North Africa via Syria and Arabia, then the Moors took it to Spain in 1100 AD. This carotene-rich vegetable is a good source of folic acid, vitamins C and E and iron; cooked without meat, it is recommended for vegetarians.

In this recipe the spinach is cooked with ground meat, rather than pieces, which I find more suitable for the texture of spinach. The fresh-scented herbs and lemon juice make it particularly delightful and delicate.

Ingredients

$1\frac{1}{2}$ tbs olive oil
1 onion (about 170 g/6 oz) peeled and finely chopped
225 g (8 oz) ground meat, preferably lamb
450 g (1 lb) spinach, rinsed, coarsely chopped
1 tsp salt
$\frac{1}{4}$ tsp cinnamon
$\frac{1}{4}$ tsp black pepper
2–3 cloves of garlic, peeled and crushed
15–30 g ($\frac{1}{2}$–1 oz) coriander, roots cut off, rinsed and coarsely chopped
15 g ($\frac{1}{2}$ oz) pine-nuts
200 ml (7 fl oz) water

Set a pot over moderately high heat. Add the oil; when oil is hot but not smoking, add the onions and meat, cook until browned (about 4–5 minutes), add the spinach in batches; when it reduces in size, season with the salt, cinnamon, black pepper, garlic and coriander. Add the pine nuts, pour the water over, bring to the boil, cover and simmer over a medium–low heat for 15–20 minutes.

Remove from heat, transfer to a bowl, serve immediately with Vermicelli Rice, squeezing the lemon juice on top to taste.

Aubergine Stew

Batinjan wa-lahm mafroum

Another potentially great dish made with a humble vegetable, this is very quick and easy to make. Boosted by chilli pepper to add a mild piquant flavour, it is surprisingly delicious.

Ingredients

1½ tbs olive oil
1 large onion (about 225 g/8 oz),
    peeled, finely chopped
225 g (8 oz) lean ground meat
30 g (1 oz) pine-nuts
¼ tsp cinnamon
¼ tsp allspice
¼ tsp black pepper, or to taste
1–1¼ tsp salt, or to taste
2 tbs pomegranate syrup (optional)
2 tomatoes (about 285 g/10 oz) rinsed, finely chopped
675 g (1 lb 8 oz) aubergine,
    rinsed, cut into 2½ cm (1 in) pieces
1 whole chilli pepper, rinsed
150–175 ml (5–6 fl oz) water

Set a medium-sized pot over medium heat, add the oil; when oil is hot add the onions and sauté for a few seconds, add the meat and cook until browned (about 3–4 minutes), breaking up any lumps with the edge of a wooden spoon. Stir in the pine-nuts and season with the cinnamon, allspice, black pepper and salt. Add the pomegranate syrup (if used) and tomatoes and stir well, add the aubergine, chilli pepper and the water. Bring to the boil, reduce heat to medium–low, cover and simmer for 30–35 minutes.

Discard the chilli and serve hot with Vermicelli (or plain) Rice.

Potato Stew

Yakhnet al-batata

Hearty and earthy. Ground or diced meat, onions and potatoes are fried separately, after which they are allowed to simmer over a low flame in the juice of ripe tomatoes, producing a concentrated sauce with an intense flavour. In Lebanon tomatoes are abundant, cheap and have a long season; here, I use tomato past instead of fresh tomatoes. I also omit the traditional frying of the potato.

Ingredients

285 g (10 oz) meat from leg of lamb, cut into 2½ cm (1 in) pieces
1.3 l (48 fl oz) water
1 onion (about 85 g/3 oz), peeled and chopped
1 cinnamon stick
1¼ tsp salt or to taste
675 g (1 lb 8 oz) potatoes, washed, scrubbed, cut into 4 cm (1½ in) cubes
2 tbs double-concentrate tomato paste
3 cloves of garlic, peeled and crushed
½ tbs extra-virgin olive oil
¼ tsp allspice
¼ tsp black pepper
¼ tsp cinnamon
1 tbs lemon juice
a large handful of parsley leaves, rinsed, drained and chopped

Combine the meat and water, bring to the boil over high heat, skimming the foam from the surface. Add the onions and the cinnamon stick and season with salt. Reduce heat to medium–low, cover and simmer for 50 minutes or until meat is slightly tender. Add the potatoes, tomato paste, garlic and oil. Season with the allspice, black pepper and cinnamon. Bring to the boil, cover and simmer over medium heat for 15–20 minutes or until potatoes are tender. Add the lemon juice and parsley, taste and adjust the seasonings and leave to simmer for 1 minute longer. Discard cinnamon stick and serve hot.

Eat with rice and radishes.

Yoghurt

Yoghurt
Laban

Yoghurt is a sour, fermented liquor made from milk. It is highly nutritious, rich in protein, B vitamins and calcium, and is believed to rejuvenate and prolong life; whether or not this is so, I think that yoghurt is one of the super foods. In Lebanon, where mountains crowned with snow white as *laban* gave the country its name (Loubnan), and in the Arab world, it is used a lot, as a soothing drink, in cooking or as a harmonious complement to cooked food.

Yoghurt is economical to make and can also be turned into a fresh white cheese with a pleasant sourness. Below is the traditional yoghurt recipe that I learned from my mother.

Ingredients

1.1 litre (40 fl oz) milk
3 tbs live yoghurt

Place the milk in a stainless steel pan and heat to just below boiling, making sure it does not scorch (you can place a ring-stand underneath the pan to separate it from the heat). Leave to cool to 43° C (107° F), or better still, until you can put your finger in the milk and hold it there to a count of ten.

Using a small cup, thin the yoghurt with a little (about 2 tbs) of the hot milk and stir thoroughly into the milk. Cover and wrap in a woollen blanket. Leave to rest undisturbed for 8 hours. Half an hour before the end of the required time remove the lid and leave until the half hour is up. After that refrigerate and eat chilled.

Note : For a thicker, creamier yoghurt combine thoroughly 2 tbs of powdered milk with the milk before adding the yoghurt.

Yoghurt Soft Cheese
Labneh

This is one of the easiest and quickest cheeses produced by the Lebanese. It has a creamy texture with a mild tartness. To make *labneh*, sheep's, cow's or goat's yoghurt is used depending on the region. *Labneh* is spread on pitta or *markouk* bread, topped with a little olive oil; sometimes it is flavoured with fresh mint leaves or eaten with black or green olives. In villages it is also used as a filling to be folded into a bread dough and cooked on the hot stove until done, then eaten hot.

Ingredients

850 ml (30 fl oz) live yoghurt
1½ tsp sea salt or to taste

In a mixing bowl put the yoghurt, sprinkle with salt and mix well. Pour the yoghurt into a cheesecloth bag, place it over a sieve set over a bowl and leave in a cool place to drain for 8 hours or overnight.

Remove the resultant *labneh* from the cheesecloth bag and store covered in the refrigerator. Serve as suggested above.

Yoghurt Cheese Balls in Oil
Labneh makbouseh bi-zeit

Labneh cheese balls are rapidly prepared and delicious to eat, and a fine option when you're too lazy to cook. With an accompaniment of good wheat bread, cut-up tomato, cucumber, some fresh mint and olives, they make an inexpensive, refreshing and nutritious meal. Cheese balls can be equally well prepared with cow's, sheep's or goat's yoghurt, but I have found that mixture of sheep's and goat's yoghurt yields a succulent, tart flavour.

Ingredients

450 ml (15 fl oz) live sheep's yoghurt
450 ml (15 fl oz) live goat's yoghurt
2¼ tsp coarse salt free of additives

Place both yoghurts in a mixing bowl, season with salt and mix thoroughly. Put this mixture in a cheesecloth bag, place over a sieve set over a bowl and refrigerate. Allow 2–3 days to drain and dry.

Remove, then take a small amount at a time and roll the resulting *labneh* into 2½ cm (1 in) balls. Repeat with remaining *labneh*. Cover a cookie tray with 2 layers of kitchen paper. Place the balls over the paper and put in the fridge to drain of their moisture and dry completely, changing the kitchen paper from time to time. After that place the cheese balls in an airtight jar, fill with extra virgin olive oil and refrigerate. Use as necessary.

Yoghurt Fermented Cheese with Dried Thyme and Chilli Pepper
Shankleesh

This is a specialty prepared in the hilly northern part of Lebanon. It is highly valued as an accompaniment to a drink. Served with chopped tomatoes, onions and a drizzle of olive oil *shankleesh* is a pleasant dish that takes only minutes to prepare.

Ingredients

1.1 l (40 fl oz) live cow's yoghurt
½ tsp cayenne pepper
¼ tsp white pepper
2½ tsp sea salt or to taste
4 tbs plain *zaatar* (thyme)

Set the yoghurt in a stainless steel pan, bring to the boil until it curdles and the whey (liquid) separates. Draw out the curdled yoghurt from the whey and cool. Season with cayenne pepper, white pepper and salt to taste then put in a cheesecloth bag in a sieve set over a bowl and allow to drain for 3–4 days in a cool place. After this time, remove and roll a small portion at a time into 4½ cm (1½ in) balls. Take each ball and dip in thyme (*zaatar*), covering all sides, then leave in a sterilized jar in the fridge. Use as necessary.

Kishk

A delicious dish popular among mountain people, kishk is eaten with bread for breakfast, especially during winter, to provide warmth and strength throughout the day. When it is prepared for lunch, kawarma or meat is added.

Kishk is prepared in several stages, with *burghol* that is mixed with milk at first, then left for two days until the milk is absorbed; after that, yoghurt is stirred into the previous mixture and the same procedure is repeated. Then another derivative of yoghurt, *labneh* (concentrated yoghurt), is blended into the mixture and the whole batch is put in earthenware until it ferments. The time from start to finish may be up to ten days. The fermented *kishk* is then dried in the sun to be crushed afterwards, either in the traditional way, between the fingers or, nowadays, using machines. The resultant granular powder is kept ready for preparation with or without meat.

There is an anecdote about *kishk* which goes back to Ottoman rule in Lebanon. A Turkish official had the task of touring the mountain to conduct a census or collect taxes. At every village and town he visited, he was offered *kishk*. Too much *kishk* washed down with water (for that was the only drink he was allowed, apart from coffee of course) left him unsatisfied, heavy and drowsy. His hosts told him about the virtues of kishk, about how much time it takes to prepare, which is true, and how costly it is, which is vastly exaggerated.

One day the Turkish official rebelled, forgot all manners and told his hosts, 'I do not want you to go out of your way anymore to make a dish that is costly and time-consuming for you to prepare and for me to digest. I am sure that you have lighter alternatives. Next time, I assure you, a chicken will do. It is light enough to take to the air but can be in the cauldron in a matter of minutes.'

Ingredients

2 tbs extra-virgin olive oil
1 onion, thinly sliced
7 garlic cloves, peeled
½ tsp salt or to taste
125 g (5 oz) *kishk*
900 ml (32 fl oz) water

Set a pan over medium heat, add the oil, onion, garlic and salt to taste, stir well, cover and cook for 2 minutes; uncover and stir constantly for another 2 minutes or until the onions and garlic are soft and golden. Add the *kishk* and stir for 2 minutes, then add the water gradually, stirring constantly, otherwise the mixture will become lumpy. Bring to the boil, reduce heat to medium–low and simmer for 10–15 minutes. The resulting dish should be thick and cream-like.

Serve piping hot and eat with bread.

Cucumber and Yoghurt Salad
Salatet laban wa khiar

A salad that is a local interpretation of a well-known Turkish recipe, *cacik*. It can be prepared in seconds. Mint, native to the Mediterranean region, is added dry, to alleviate the sourness of the yoghurt. Yoghurt is a good source of B vitamins and calcium, soothing and easily digested. Since yoghurt can restore health-giving bacteria, it is recommended when a patient takes a course of antibiotics. Cucumber is a natural diuretic, rich in mineral salts that aid hair growth.

Cucumber and yoghurt salad is served chilled and accompanies the national dish *kibbeh*. It can also be eaten with fried aubergines.

Ingredients

1 large clove of garlic, peeled
1 tsp salt or to taste
575 ml (20 fl oz) low-fat yoghurt, strained
3 baby cucumbers, rinsed and thinly sliced
½ tsp dried mint

In a salad bowl crush the garlic with the salt until a smooth paste. Add the yoghurt and whisk well. Blend in the cucumber, taste and adjust the seasoning. Sprinkle with mint. Chill or serve immediately.

Aubergines in Yoghurt
Batinjan moufassakh bi-laban

A wonderful creation, soothing and satisfying; it can also be prepared in advance. Traditionally the slices of aubergines are fried; because they absorb a lot of oil, I grill them instead. Then the slices are arranged in one layer on a serving dish topped with the smooth yoghurt and garnished with the scented dried mint.

Ingredients

675 g (1 lb 8 oz) aubergine (about 14 slices) rinsed
salt
olive oil
2 cloves of garlic, peeled
¾ tsp salt or to taste
350–450 ml (12–15 fl oz) yoghurt
¾ tsp dry mint
½ tsp cayenne pepper (optional)

Pare both ends of the aubergine but leave the skin on. Cut, crosswise or lengthwise, at 1 cm (½ in) intervals. Sprinkle lavishly with salt and let them stand in a colander for at least 40 minutes. Rinse and pat dry between kitchen papers. Brush both sides with oil and place over a well-oiled baking sheet (to prevent sticking). Grill under a pre-heated grill until browned on both sides, about 6–8 minutes, turning them once.

Meanwhile in a bowl mash the garlic with 4 ml (¾ tsp) salt, add the yoghurt and whisk thoroughly; reserve.

Remove aubergine slices from the grill, drain on kitchen paper and arrange in one layer over a serving dish, pour yoghurt all over and sprinkle with mint and cayenne pepper, if used.

Serve with wholemeal pitta bread.

Spaghetti with Yoghurt
Macaroni bi-laban

Combining spaghetti with yoghurt may sound strange, but I assure you that *macaroni bi-laban* is delicious and is a useful dish when you are pressed for time. In Lebanon spaghetti made of white flour is used but in this recipe I use wholemeal.

Health-food shops now sell a satisfactory substitute for spaghetti, made from organic brown rice, free of gluten. This would be suitable for people on a gluten-free diet instead of white or wholemeal spaghetti.

Ingredients

225–259 g (8–8½ oz) wholemeal spaghetti
1 large garlic clove, peeled
½ tsp salt or to taste
400 ml (14 fl oz) live yoghurt

For the garnish
¹/₂ tbs olive oil
1 oz pine-nuts
a large handful of parsley or coriander leaves, rinsed,
    drained, left whole or coarsely chopped
a touch of cayenne pepper (optional)

Cook the spaghetti in boiling salted water until tender following the instructions on the packet. Meanwhile, in a serving bowl crush the garlic with salt until smooth, add the yoghurt and whisk thoroughly (if the yoghurt is too thick, thin it with 2 tbs of fresh water). Reserve.

Meanwhile heat the oil in a small frying pan and sauté the pine-nuts until golden in colour, remove and set aside, add the parsley or coriander, sauté for a few seconds or until they impart their smell. Set aside.

By this time the spaghetti should be ready. Drain and quickly add the yoghurt, toss lightly and garnish with pine nuts, parsley or coriander and a touch of cayenne pepper, if desired. Serve immediately.

Chick-Peas with Yoghurt and Minced Meat
Fattet al-hoummos bi-lahm

Dishes based on layers of cut-up toasted bread and a vegetable or a grain, with or without meat, and with or without yoghurt, are called *fatte*. All kinds of *fatte* are much loved in the Levant and constitute a meal in themselves. They should be eaten as soon as they are cooked, otherwise the bread will soak up all the yoghurt and become soft, and the yoghurt will cool the warm dish.

Fattet al-hoummos can be very rich in saturated fat if prepared by the traditional method, in which a large quantity of hot butter is poured over the yoghurt. I omit this as the dish is already rich in full-flavoured ingredients. I use ground meat, which is quick to prepare and marries well with the chick-peas.

This is a delicious and well-balanced meal, full of healthy nutrients. For vegetarians the meat can be omitted.

Ingredients

1½–2 medium-sized wholemeal bread loaves,
    cut in 2½ cm (¾ in) squares, toasted or deep-fried
115 g (4 oz) chick-peas, soaked overnight
850 ml (30 fl oz) water
2 tbs extra-virgin olive oil
30 g (1 oz) pine-nuts or almond flakes
285 g (10 oz) ground meat
a heaped ¼ tsp allspice
¼ tsp cinnamon
¼ tsp black pepper
salt
1 large clove of garlic, peeled
about 575 ml (20 fl oz) yoghurt
cayenne pepper to taste

Spread the bread evenly over a deep serving dish and reserve.

Rinse chick-peas, drain and place in a pan with the water, skim any foam forming on the surface and bring to the boil over medium–high heat, reduce heat to moderately low, cover and simmer for about 1½–2 hours or until chick-peas are very soft.

Set a heavy-bottomed pan over medium–high heat, add the oil; when oil is hot but not smoking fry the pine-nuts or almonds for a few seconds or until golden in colour;

remove with a slotted spoon, allowing the oil to drip back into the pan; reserve.

In the remaining oil cook the meat for about 6–8 minutes or until nicely browned and crisp. Season with the allspice, cinnamon, black pepper and remaining salt, stir for a few seconds; turn off heat. Reserve.

In a bowl crush the garlic with ¾ tsp salt, add the yoghurt and whisk until smooth. Reserve.

To assemble the *fatte* place the chick-peas with 3 tbs of their cooking liquid over the reserved bread and spoon the reserved yoghurt over them; top evenly with the meat. Garnish with the reserved nuts and sprinkle with cayenne pepper.

Broad beans, Yoghurt and Fried Bread
Fattet al-foul bi-roz

A combination of varied textures and perfumes, substantial, satisfying and highly valued for its nutrients, *fattet al-foul bi-roz* is easy to prepare and requires only a little oil for the frying of the bread and coriander. To cut down still more on the oil, toast the bread instead of frying it.

Ingredients

225 g (8 oz) brown rice, rinsed once
600 ml (21 fl oz) water
140 g (5 oz) onion, peeled, finely chopped
360 g (12 oz) broad beans, frozen or podded fresh
4 sprigs of coriander (about 85 g/3 oz),
    roots cut off and tough stems removed, rinsed, finely chopped
1¼ tsp salt or to taste
½ tsp allspice
½ tsp cinnamon
¼ tsp black pepper

For the yoghurt
1 large clove of garlic, peeled
1 tsp salt or to taste
450 ml (14 fl oz) low fat yoghurt

For the garnish
½ tbs extra-virgin olive oil
30 g (1 oz) hazelnut flakes
a generous handful of coriander leaves, rinsed and coarsely chopped
¼ tsp cinnamon (optional)

For the bread
olive oil for deep-frying
about 1¹⁄₂ medium-size wholemeal bread loaves, each
    split in two and cut into 1 cm (¹⁄₂ in) squares

Put the rice and the water in a heavy-bottomed pan. Bring to the boil and add the onions, cover and simmer over medium heat for 25 minutes. When cooking time is over, add the broad beans and the coriander, season with salt, allspice, cinnamon and black pepper; stir well. Cover and simmer for 15–20 minutes longer or until the rice and beans are tender and the water is absorbed.

Meanwhile, in a bowl, crush the garlic with salt until smooth, add the yoghurt and whisk until the yoghurt is smooth. Reserve.

Then heat the oil in a heavy bottomed skillet, add the hazelnuts, stir for a few seconds and add the coriander. Stir for another few seconds, remove to a side dish.

Next, with kitchen paper wipe the frying-pan you have already used, add the oil and heat until hot but not smoking (check the heat by dropping in a piece of bread; if it comes to the surface immediately the oil is ready). Add the bread to the oil in batches at a time, and fry until golden brown. Remove with a slotted spoon and drain over kitchen paper. Reserve.

Finally, place the cooked rice and broad beans evenly over a serving dish, cover with the reserved yoghurt, garnish with the reserved hazelnuts and coriander and finally spread over the reserved bread.

Sprinkle with cinnamon, if used, and serve immediately.

Fried Bread, Aubergine and Yoghurt

Fattet al-batinjan bi-laban

Whenever I prepare this great delicacy for friends I am showered with requests for the recipe. The preparation is easy but needs a few stages, though some of the ingredients can be prepared in advance. In the traditional recipe baby aubergines are stuffed with meat, but instead I present them meatless and in slices layered over crisp fried pitta bread. I usually buy the baby breads that are found in Lebanese and Greek grocers and in well-stocked supermarkets. You can even bake your own.

Ingredients

1 large aubergine (about 550 g/1¹⁄₄ lb)
salt
3 small size ripe tomatoes (about 170 g/6 oz) rinsed
250–300 ml (9–10 fl oz) water
a pinch of allspice

a pinch of white pepper
olive oil for grilling and deep-frying
4 small pitta breads, each split in 2, fried

To prepare the yoghurt
1 large clove of garlic, peeled
$^1\!/_2$ tsp salt or to taste
3–4 tbs tomato sauce from cooked aubergines
10 tbs thick yoghurt
$^1\!/_4$ tsp cayenne pepper (optional)

Trim the ends of the aubergine, rinse and cut into 1 cm (½ in) rounds (about 8–9 slices). Sprinkle lavishly with salt on both sides, place in a colander and weight them with a heavy plate to draw out excess moisture and prevent them from absorbing too much oil. Set aside for at least 40 minutes.

Meanwhile in a small saucepan combine the tomatoes and water, bring to the boil, cover and cook over moderate heat for 5 minutes. Remove and press the tomatoes and their liquid through a fine sieve into a large pan (using the back of a spoon). Season with allspice and white pepper. Reserve.

Pre-heat the grill and pour ¼ cm (⅛ in) of olive oil on to a baking sheet. Remove the slices of aubergine from colander, rinse, pat dry between kitchen papers and dip both sides in the oil on the baking sheet. Then lay them packed closely together over the remaining oil. Grill 10 cm (4 in) away from heat until nicely browned on both sides (about 7–8 minutes; time depends on the heat of the grill), remove, drain on kitchen paper, then arrange evenly, if possible, over the reserved tomato in the pan. Bring to the boil, cover, reduce heat to low and simmer for 10–15 minutes.

Arrange the bread in a serving dish, reserve and prepare the yoghurt.

In a bowl crush the garlic with the salt. Remove about 2–3 tbs of the tomato sauce that has resulted from cooking the aubergines and stir into the garlic. Add the yoghurt and whisk well. At this point remove the aubergines one at a time with a slotted spoon, and place over the reserved bread. Repeat with all the aubergines. Cover each one with yoghurt mixture, about 1 tbs each (or more). Sprinkle with cayenne pepper (if used) and serve immediately.

Note: To fry the bread pour 1 cm (½ in) of olive oil in a medium-sized frying-pan; when oil is hot but not smoking (to check, drop a corner of a piece of bread in the oil; if the oil bubbles it is ready), put in 2–4 slices of bread at a time, cook until deep golden in colour and crisp. Remove with a slotted spoon, drain over kitchen paper.

Spinach in Yoghurt
Fattet al-sabanekh

Rich and lustrous, a really succulent dish, made of super ingredients that promote good health and longevity. Spinach is said to have originated in Persia and was introduced into North Africa via Syria and Arabia, then taken by the Moors to Spain in 1100 AD. This vegetable is recommended for vegetarians as it contains large amounts of vitamins and minerals. In this easy recipe, the cooked spinach is served over toasted bread and topped with yoghurt.

Ingredients

2 medium-sized pitta breads, cut into 2½ cm (1 in)
    squares, toasted or fried
1 onion (about 115 g/4 oz), peeled, finely chopped
175 ml (6 fl oz) water
1 tsp extra-virgin olive oil
675 g (1 lb 8 oz) spinach, rinsed, tough stems removed,
    coarsely chopped or cut into 1 cm (½ in) ribbons
1 tsp salt
¼ tsp cinnamon
¼ tsp black pepper
2 cloves of garlic, peeled and crushed
½ bunch of coriander (about 100 g/3½ oz),
    roots cut off and discarded, tough stems removed,
    rinsed, drained and finely chopped
30 g (1 oz) flaked almonds

To prepare the yoghurt
1 large clove garlic, peeled
½ tsp salt, or to taste
450 g (1 lb) strained low fat yoghurt
2 tbs *tahini* (optional)

Place the fried or toasted bread in a deep serving dish and reserve.

In a pan combine the onions, water and oil and set over medium–high heat. Bring to the boil, cover and simmer over medium heat for 10 minutes. Remove the lid and in batches add the spinach. As spinach reduces in size season with salt, cinnamon and black pepper and bring to the boil. Add the garlic, coriander and flaked almonds. Cover and simmer over medium–low heat for 10–12 minutes longer.

Meanwhile in a bowl crush the garlic with salt until creamy, add the yoghurt, *tahini* (if used), and whisk until a smooth consistency.

To serve: Spread the spinach over the reserved bread in the dish and finally pour over the yoghurt; serve immediately. It makes an unusual starter as well as a main dish.

Variation: For deeper flavour sauté in oil for a minute 2 large cloves of garlic, peeled and crushed, and a large handful of coriander leaves. Sprinkle over the yoghurt.

Note: To keep the bread crunchy for longer, spread it evenly over the yoghurt.

Sweets

Nearly all celebrations in Lebanon are religious and are deemed incomplete without a number of sweetmeats prepared especially for the occasion. Although all kinds of sweets are piled high in sweet shops, some varieties are prepared and eaten only for a particular religious occasion, which may be paying homage to a real or legendary saint.

It is impossible to enumerate all the sweets that can be found in Lebanon. This tiny country has an enormously varied range of climate and terrain from a mild coast to high, snowy mountains. Moreover it is inhabited by more than 17 religious communities and sects, most of whom came to escape persecution, and some of whom kept alive links with their original religious centres. In addition Lebanon was part of the Ottoman Empire for nearly 400 years, but it was never cut off for long from Western influence. For all these reasons, the Lebanese sweets are rich and varied.

One way of identifying the origin of some of the sweets is to follow the trail of the major religious feasts celebrated annually by, respectively, Muslims and Christians, who quite often join in a common celebration. A large concentration of the Muslim population lives in the coastal towns and was under direct Ottoman control and influence, much more so than the inhabitants of the mountains, mostly Christians and Druses.

The town dwellers were also more affluent than other communities and this is reflected in their traditional sweets. Sweets eaten during the month of Ramadan (the month of fasting for Muslims), ʿId al-Fitr (a celebration of the end of fasting) and ʿId al-Adha (the commemoration of Abraham's sacrifice of the ram) are of a distinct Ottoman inspiration and are more expensive to prepare than those consumed by the inhabitants of the mountain villages. During the month of Ramadan, and as soon as the sun has disappeared over the horizon, thick crêpes filled with cheese, cream or crushed walnuts, all covered with syrup, are laid on the table to tempt people who have been fasting during the hours of daylight.

These delicacies are known as *kataef bi-jibn, kataef bi-koshta* and *kataef bi-joz*. A salad of dried fruits with almonds, walnuts and pine kernels often adorns the dining table.

The new moon indicates the end of the fast and is followed by ʿId al-Fitr, an occasion for joy, celebration and more sweets. A favourite is *kanafe bi-jibn*, which consists of layers of *akkawi* (a white cheese) and semolina cooked in the oven and eaten with syrup and a girdle of sesame bread. *Kanafe bi-jibn* is also a popular breakfast.

At 'Id al-Adha and Easter, pastries filled with dates reduced to a paste, or with crushed walnuts or pistachios, are enjoyed and offered to well-wishers together with baklava and sweets of Western origin.

The two festive occasions that are celebrated by most Lebanese are Christmas, without a religious connotation for the Muslims, and New Year. The sweets served on these occasions would normally include those you would find laid on any French table at those times. Indigenous recipes are found mainly during minor religious celebrations. Each village in the mountains has its patron saint, annually celebrated with one- or two-day fairs where sweets are abundantly on offer.

Most of us indulge in sweets at one time or another and no cook book is complete without their recipes. However, sweets should be regarded as a special treat and consumed in strict moderation. Overeating foods high in fat and sugar may be harmful to health.

Il n'y a rien que les hommes aiment mieux conserver
et qu'ils ménagent moins que leur santé.

(There is nothing that people want more to save,
yet look after less, than their health.)

La Bruyère

Crêpes
Kataef

Kataef are a popular treat all over the country, but especially in coastal towns, where, after sunset during the holy month of Ramadan, the tables are laid out with several dishes. These crêpes are made like Western crêpes, except that no dairy produce is used and they are slightly thicker. *Kataef* come with different fillings. The ones filled with *kashta* (cream) are eaten 'nature' (without further cooking), those with cheese are fried, whereas *kataef bi-joz* can be either 'nature' or fried. My favourites are the fried varieties. Baked *kataef* also taste heavenly.

Preparing *kataef* does not require any culinary experience and is quite fun.

Ingredients

For the syrup
285 g (10 oz) sugar
200 ml (7 fl oz) water
1 tsp lemon juice
1–1½ tsp flower water
1–1½ tsp rose water

For the crêpes
1 tsp dried active yeast
1½ tsp sugar
125 g (4½ oz) flour
250 ml (8 fl oz) water
3 tsp baking powder

In a small saucepan, combine sugar with water. Set over high heat and stir to dissolve the sugar completely. Bring to the boil, add the lemon juice and reduce the heat to moderate; simmer for 7–10 minutes, or until it thickens to a syrupy consistency. Add the flower and rose waters, boil once and turn the heat off. Pour into a serving jug and keep for later use.

Dissolve the yeast in a small cup with 2 tsp tap water. Stir in the sugar, cover and leave in a warm place while preparing remaining ingredients. Sift the flour in a mixing bowl; gradually add the water and the yeast mixture, whisking well to prevent any lumps from forming. Finally sprinkle with baking powder and beat vigorously until the batter is smooth, bubbly and free of any lumps and with the consistency of cream. Cover with a cloth and leave for 1½–2 hours to rise. When rising time is over, lightly oil a small, thick-bottomed, non-stick frying-pan, set over medium heat. Using a whisk, beat the *kataef* batter vigorously and from this batter measure about 3 tbs into a small cup (you can vary this if you want the *kataef* bigger or smaller). Pour into the centre of the hot pan and immediately tilt the pan slightly from side to side to distribute the mixture evenly. Cook

Flour and rice puffs *(awamat)*

for about 30 seconds or until the base is golden and the surface is dry. Remove to a tray. Repeat with remaining batter, re-oiling the pan after every one or two crêpes (use an oil-damped piece of cotton wool). Cover the crêpes well with a damp cloth or cling film. If you are filling them do this as soon as they have cooled; if not, stack them with their top surfaces, not the browned sides, touching. Seal with plastic, otherwise they will dry and the edges of the crêpes will not seal properly to enclose the filling. Crêpes can be refrigerated for no more than two days. Below is a list of different fillings to choose from.

For the walnut filling
140 g (5 oz) walnuts, crushed medium–fine
2½ tbs honey or 3 tbs sugar
1 tbs flower water
1 tbs rose water
peanut or olive oil for frying

Place the walnuts in a small mixing bowl. Dissolve the honey in flower and rose waters and combine thoroughly with the walnuts in the mixing bowl. Then take one of the prepared crêpes (*kataef*) and fill with a level 2 tbs of walnut filling (more or less, depending on the size of crêpe). Lift the edges and bring together. Gently pinch to seal. Place on a side dish and cover with plastic. Repeat with other crêpes until they are all ready. In a pan heat the peanut or olive oil (traditionally unsalted butter), fry the crêpes until golden-brown, remove and drain over kitchen paper. Serve immediately with syrup. If preferred, brush the stuffed crêpes all over with unsalted butter and bake in a preheated oven at 200° C (400° F/gas mark 6) until golden in colour. Remove and serve, spooning about 1 tbs of the syrup over each crêpe.

Cheese filling
200 g (7 oz) *akkawi* or mozzarella cheese,
    rinsed, drained and very finely shredded
½ tbs flower water (optional)

Traditionally *akkawi*, a delicious white cheese, is used. It needs soaking in several changes of water to rid it of the high quantity of salt. Taste to make sure it's not salty before using. Mozzarella cheese is a good alternative.

If using flower water, mix this into the cheese. Prepare as for walnut crêpes.

Cream filling
200 g (7 oz) ricotta cheese
1 tbs *fromage frais*
½ tbs flower water
2 tbs syrup, or to taste

In a food processor blend the ricotta with the *fromage frais*, flower water and syrup until smooth and creamy, using more syrup if necessary, but make sure it does not become too liquid. Fill the crêpes and serve immediately with the syrup.

Wheat or Barley in Orange-Blossom Water
Kamhiye

Kamhiye, *awamat* and *maacaroun* are the mouth-watering sweets eaten during the celebration of Saint Barbara, which falls on 4th December. This saint, who lived in the 4th century, was the daughter of a heathen; she converted to Christianity, rejecting all suitors proposed by her father. She used to put on a disguise to make herself unattractive and go through the wheat fields to a grotto to get away from the cruelty of her father. It is said that the wheat would grow to hide her as she ran through it. Eventually Saint Barbara was caught and, at the moment her father was about to strike off her head, a sudden flash of lightning laid him dead.

In the West Saint Barbara is invoked against lightning and is the patron saint of arsenals, artillery and firemen. In Lebanon her commemoration is the opportunity for the children to masquerade and go from door to door in their neighbourhood chanting, dancing and waiting for a little reward, either in sweets or money.

Kamhiye is also prepared when a baby's first tooth appears—then it is called *snyniya*. In this recipe organic barley may be used instead of the traditional wheat. Whole barley is full of flavour but takes a little longer to cook than the processed variety, from which all the bran has been removed.

Ingredients

1 l (35 fl oz) water
200 g (7 oz) whole wheat grains or barley
1½ tbs flower water or to taste
1 tbs rose water or to taste
honey or sugar to taste
30 g (1 oz) pine nuts, soaked for one hour and drained
30 g (1 oz) blanched almonds, soaked for one hour and drained
30 g (1 oz) pistachio nuts, soaked for one hour and drained
4 tbs sweet pomegranate seeds (optional)

Combine the water and whole wheat grains in a large saucepan and set over high heat. Bring to the boil and reduce the heat to moderately low. Cover and simmer for 60–70 minutes. If using barley, add 75 ml (3 fl oz) more water than listed in the Ingredients, bring to the boil and simmer for 35–45 minutes or until the cereal is soft. Remove and pour into a serving bowl, add the honey or sugar, flower and rose waters and stir to incorporate. Garnish with pine-nuts, almonds, pistachios and pomegranate seeds (if used). Serve immediately.

Flour and Rice Puffs in Syrup
Awamat

The baptism of Christ is celebrated by Christians on 6th January with the preparation of *awamat* and *maacaroun*. During that night a piece of bread dough, taken from a previous batch, is put in a fine, white, cloth bag, which is then suspended from a tree. Sometimes silver currency is inserted into the dough, in the belief that the piece of dough helps the bread to rise and also expands money and other provisions in the household.

Awamat are really tasty and worth trying. They are beautiful to look at and embellish the table for a party.

Ingredients

For the dough
1 tsp dried yeast
2 tsp water
45 g (1½ oz) fine ground rice
350 ml (12 fl oz) water
225 g (8 oz) flour
olive or peanut oil for deep-frying

For the syrup
800 g (1 lb 8 oz) sugar
350–400 ml (12–14 fl oz) water
1 tbs lemon juice
1–1½ tbs flower water
1½ tbs rose water

Combine yeast and water, stir to dissolve, cover with plastic and leave in a warm place for a little while. Put the rice in a small saucepan, measure 200 ml (7 fl oz) water, add to the rice in the saucepan and bring to the boil. Then cover and simmer over low heat until

Walnut, pistachio and date pastries (*maamoul*)

water is fully absorbed and rice looks like porridge (keep your eye on it because the water is quickly absorbed). Cool slightly for a minute or two.

Meanwhile sift the flour over a mixing bowl, add the yeasted water and cooked rice, mix thoroughly then gradually add the remaining water (it should look a little thicker than yoghurt); cover with a clean cloth and keep in a warm place for about 3 hours.

While the dough is rising prepare the syrup, as it will need to cool thoroughly before it is used; unless it is cold the hot *awamat* will not absorb it properly.

Combine the sugar and water in a saucepan over high heat, stir until sugar is completely dissolved, bring to the boil, add the lemon juice and leave to simmer over medium heat about 8–10 minutes or until it thickens to a syrupy consistency. Add the flower and rose waters, stir, remove from heat and cool thoroughly.

When the dough has risen, after 2–3 hours, prepare the *awamat* balls. In a small saucepan heat the oil over medium heat, and on the side have ready a teaspoon and a cup filled with water. To make each *awamat* ball, dip the teaspoon in the water, just to wet it (the film of water helps the dough to slide off without sticking to the spoon), then scoop a level teaspoonful of dough and gently drop it in the oil. Make the balls in batches of 10–12. The balls will rise to the surface of the oil in a matter of seconds; stir and cook them until they are golden-brown in colour on all sides, remove with a slotted spoon and dip in the syrup. When you have fried each batch, leave the balls in the syrup for a minute or two, then remove to a side dish with a clean slotted spoon.

Serve warm or, better still, at room temperature.

Macaroon

Maacaroun

Maacaroun are festive treats. They are pleasantly flavoured with aniseed and are slightly sticky, having been immersed in the classic, fragrant syrup used for many sweets. *Maacaroun* are simple to prepare and are ideal for dinner parties because they can be made in advance, which also gives time for their flavour to develop after cooling.

Ingredients

For the syrup
350 g (12 oz) sugar
200 ml (7 fl oz) water
1 tsp lemon juice
1 tbs flower water
½ tbs rose water

For the macaroons
7 tbs water

1 tbs whole aniseed
125 g (4½ oz) flour
125 g (4½ oz) fine semolina
½ tsp baking powder
¾ tsp ground *mahlab*
¼ tsp nutmeg
2 tbs peanut oil
3 tbs extra-virgin olive oil
1 tsp vanilla
olive or peanut oil for deep-frying

In a saucepan combine sugar with water, stir until sugar is completely dissolved. Bring to the boil, add the lemon juice and bring back to the boil. Skim the froth from the surface and leave over medium heat for 8–10 minutes, add the flower and rose waters, boil once and reserve.

In a small coffee-pot combine water with whole aniseeds. Bring to the boil and simmer for ½ minute over medium–low heat, making sure that water does not overflow the pot. Remove from heat, cover and infuse for 15 minutes.

Meanwhile, sift the flour and semolina over a mixing bowl. Add *mahlab*, nutmeg, peanut and olive oil and rub the mixture thoroughly. Add vanilla essence and strain the aniseed water through a fine sieve over the ingredients in the mixing bowl, extracting as much water as possible before discarding the whole aniseeds. Knead well until you have a smooth, fairly firm dough.

Divide dough into 20 walnut-sized portions (or more but smaller portions if you prefer). Roll each portion under your fingers into a roll about 5 cm (2 in) long and, using your fingers, swiftly but gently press and flatten each portion against a rough surface such as a carrot-grinder or colander, bringing the dough towards you and curling it back over itself. Repeat with remaining dough.

In a small saucepan heat the oil but do not let it smoke; fry batches of 4–5 at a time over medium heat for about 1–1½ minutes or until golden-brown. Remove with a slotted spoon, drain on kitchen paper and immerse in the cooled syrup for about 1 minute. Fry another batch, remove the ones in the syrup, place in a colander set over a clean bowl to drain off excess syrup. Repeat until all the portions are cooked and thoroughly drained of excess syrup, then transfer to a serving dish.

Serve at room temperature.

Note: *Maacaroun* can be baked in a preheated oven at 200° C (400° F/gas mark 6) for 30 minutes or until golden. Remove and immerse in the syrup for 2 minutes, drain as above and serve.

If you prefer not to use syrup, add 2–3 tbs honey, dissolve with the water (listed in the ingredients for macaroons) and incorporate in the dough. Then proceed as above.

Walnut, Pistachio and Date Pastries
Maamoul

These festive delicacies were traditionally made only during 'Id al-Adha and Easter. Consumer society has made things readily available all year round, however, and, in the process, deprived us of the joyful expectation that these sweets, although not lasting long, would be made and enjoyed again the following year.

Maamoul are very special, and favourites of mine. The same crumbly dough is stuffed with three succulent fillings and, to differentiate between them, they are moulded in three different traditional shapes—round for dates, oblong for pistachios and dome-shaped for walnuts. Digressing slightly from tradition, I sweeten the filling with honey instead of sugar, but the option to use sugar is just as good if you prefer.

Ingredients

For the dough
255 g (9 oz) fine or coarse semolina
45 g (1½ oz) flour or fine semolina
100 g (3½ oz) clarified butter (ghee)
    or unsalted butter, melted and cooled, or a mixture of the two
4 tbs rose water
1 tbs flower water
½ tsp easy-blend yeast

For the walnut filling
100 g (3½ oz) walnuts, crushed to medium–fine
2 tbs clear honey or 5 tbs icing sugar
1 tsp rose water
1 tsp flower water
icing sugar to decorate

Place the fine or coarse semolina and flour or fine semolina in a mixing bowl. Add the butter and, with fingertips, mix this mixture thoroughly. Warm the rose and flower waters over low heat for a few seconds, add to the semolina mixture and knead it for 2–3 minutes to bind into a dough. Cover with a clean cloth and leave to rest for 10 hours. By then the dough will be hard; dissolve the yeast in about 1 tbs of warm rose or flower water, add to the dough and knead until dough is soft. Cover and leave to rest for 10 minutes. Divide it into 18–20 equal parts, each about the size of a walnut. Take each part and roll between the palms of your hands to form a ball. Hold the dough in one hand and with the index finger of the other poke a hole into the centre; with the index finger and thumb work around the inside and outside of the dough, until you form a medium–thick shell. Push in 1 tsp of the filling, bring the edges of the dough together and gently pinch

Creamy pudding rice (*mouhallabieh*)

to enclose the filling. Press into the mould, smoothing the pinched side. Turn the mould upside down and tap it flat on the palm of your hand. Place on a lightly floured baking sheet.

Preheat the oven to 180° C (350° F/gas mark 4) and bake for about 15–17 minutes. Remove and while still hot dust with icing sugar.

Cool before serving or storing in an airtight container.

Variations

For the pistachio filling
85 g (3 oz) pistachios, roughly chopped
1½ tbs honey or 5 tbs icing sugar
1½ tsp rose water
1 tsp flower water

Mix all these ingredients and follow the recipe above, but use an oblong shape.

For the date filling
140 g (5 oz) dates, pitted and chopped
15 g (½ oz) unsalted butter (optional)
2 tbs water or as necessary
1 tbs flower water
½ tbs rosewater
¼ tsp ground *mahlab*

Place butter (if used), dates and water in a saucepan set over medium–low heat and, using a fork, mash them until smooth, adding water as necessary to achieve a smooth paste; add the flower and rose waters and *mahlab*, mix and keep mashing the dates until you have a soft mixture. Cool and prepare as above, except that the dough is made into a round shape, about 1 cm (½ in) thick, and needs baking for a longer time, about 20 minutes or until golden-brown.

Shortbread Rings
Ghoraibeh

Delicious shortbread rings with a white velvety surface, tinged with green from pistachio, and a crunchy inner texture. Fat is important in these biscuits, and the richer they are, the tastier they will be. It is best to avoid overindulging in saturated fats and one should therefore eat them as a treat only.

Ghoraibeh are simple to make and use ingredients found normally in every household. A touch of *arak* (a drink distilled from grapes and flavoured with aniseed) is an addition to the traditional method and provides a flavour that distinguishes these from other similar biscuits. As with many Lebanese sweets, the taste develops always after they have been cooled.

Ingredients

85 g (3 oz) clarified butter (*ghee*)
80 g (2¾ oz) icing sugar (sifted)
170 g (6 oz) flour (sifted)
1 tbs *arak*

In a mixing bowl cream the sugar and butter until white, smooth and fluffy. You can use a wooden spoon or a food processor. Then add the flour and knead until it has all been mixed in, add the *arak* to bind into a smooth dough. Place in a polythene bag and refrigerate for 1 hour. Remove the dough from the fridge and knead again until it becomes soft and manageable. Preheat the oven to 160° C (325° F/gas mark 3).

Divide the dough into 12–14 equal parts about the size of a walnut, roll each into a roll about 12½ cm (5 in) long. Bring both ends together and pinch lightly to seal. Push one pistachio nut into the top of each shortbread ring and place the rings on a baking sheet, leaving a little space between them. Repeat with the remaining dough and bake for 10–12 minutes. Remove and cool before serving.

Variation: Flake about 45 g (1½ oz) or more pistachio nuts and roll each portion of *ghoraibeh* dough into the nuts. Shape into a ring or a flat round and bake as above.

Creamy Pudding Rice
Mouhallabieh

This is a variation on a Lebanese sweet pudding prepared with whole rice. Ground rice is used, which gives the pudding a creamier texture. *Mouhallabieh* tastes better when chilled and eaten with a little of either of the two local jams, the succulent dates in syrup or the tasty apricot jam. *Mouhallabie*h is often prepared at home, especially for large families, because it is nourishing, inexpensive and satisfying to those with a sweet tooth. It also provides children who don't like milk with some of the calcium they need.

Mouhallabieh prepared in the traditional way with ground rice (Method I) needs a lot of patience. Because only a little rice is used, it takes 25–30 minutes to thicken and requires constant stirring, but the result is rewarding. Make it when you are calm and have something pleasant to listen to. You might be hooked on it—or never want to do it again. If in doubt try Method II, which is easier and equally mouth-watering.

Method I: Ingredients

50 g (2 oz) ground rice (very fine)
75 ml (3 fl oz) hot water
1.1 litre (40 fl oz) milk, whole or semi-skimmed
100 g (3½ oz) sugar
1 tbs flower water
1 tbs rose water
30 g (1 oz) whole or halved blanched almonds,
     soaked in water for at least one hour
30 g (1 oz) pistachio nuts or 2 tbs ground pistachio
¼ tsp *miskee* pieces, ground with 1 tsp sugar

Soak the rice in water in a small bowl for about 15–20 minutes. In the meantime put the milk in a stainless-steel pan and set over medium heat (take care or the milk may scald) and allow to boil rapidly. At this point stir the soaked rice and water into the boiling milk, stirring with a wooden spoon. Keep stirring all the time in the same direction until the pudding thickens: be patient, this takes about 25–30 minutes. Keep stirring until the pudding starts bubbling and coats the spoon. At this point, add the sugar, stir for 5 minutes longer, add the flower and rose waters, stir once or twice and turn the heat off. Sprinkle on the *miskee* (if used) and very quickly stir. Pour the pudding instantly (before it sets) into a serving bowl, allow to cool and chill.

     Serve garnished with whole almonds or ground pistachio nuts or a mixture of the two.

Method II: Ingredients

850 ml (30 fl oz) milk, whole or semi-skimmed
55 g (2 oz) cornflour
85 g (3 oz) sugar or to taste
1 tbs flower water
¼ tsp *miskee*, ground with 1 tsp sugar

Measure 5 tbs of the milk, combine with the cornflour in a cup and dissolve completely. Put the remaining milk in a saucepan, then strain the cornflour mixture over the milk in the saucepan, add the sugar and stir for ½ minute. Next, set the pan over medium heat, stirring all the time with a wooden spoon, until milk mixture boils and thickens. Remove a little to a side dish, taste to adjust the sugar if necessary. Still stirring, add the flower water and ground *miskee*/sugar mixture. Stir vigorously and immediately turn off the heat. Pour into a serving dish, cool and chill. Serve garnished as above.

Cheese Sweet
Halawet al-jibn

Tripoli, the northern second city of Lebanon, is the undisputed origin of this refined and seductive delicacy. For me as a child, and for many others, Tripoli was the city of magnificent shops full of unfamiliar sweets. Forget about the majestic Crusaders' castle, the bustling Mamluks' *souks*, the colourful orchards and the deep blue sea: what we were after when we were taken for a drive to the north of Lebanon—mostly for the purpose of running in a new car—was *halawet al-jibn* and other delicacies.

The preparation needs some effort and attention. *Akkawi* is the traditional, delicious white cheese used to make this *halwa* (sweet). Because of its high salt content it has to be soaked a long time in several changes of water. Mozzarella cheese is a readily available and satisfactory alternative. If you are a cheese-lover, not averse to generous quantities of rose water, and have energy and time to spare, you will not regret trying this recipe.

Ingredients

For the syrup
400 g (14 oz) sugar
250 ml (8 fl oz) water
1 tsp lemon juice
½ tbs flower water
½ tbs rose water

For the dough
500 g (1 lb 1 oz) *akkawi* or mozzarella cheese
110 ml (4½ fl oz) syrup
225 g (8 oz) fine semolina
120 ml (4 fl oz) rose water

For the garnish
ground pistachio nuts (optional)

If using *akkawi* cheese, soak it in several changes of water, then pat it dry and shred it very finely. If using mozzarella, no need to soak.

In a saucepan combine sugar with water. Stir until sugar dissolves completely. Bring to the boil, add the lemon juice and simmer over medium heat for 8 minutes or until it thickens to a syrupy consistency. Add flower and rose waters. Stir, boil for a few seconds, turn the heat off and leave aside.

Meanwhile, set a thick-bottomed pan (preferably non-stick) over low heat, add the cheese and allow to melt. While cheese is melting measure 110 ml (4½ fl oz) of the syrup and reserve. Spread some of the remaining syrup over a clean 45 x 45 cm (18 x 18 in) working-surface. When cheese has melted, add the reserved syrup to the cheese in the pan, stirring vigorously; add the semolina and rose water, still stirring vigorously all the time, until the dough pulls away from the sides of the pan. Remove cheese mixture and, while still hot, place on the syrup on the working-surface. Moisten a rolling-pin with a little syrup, roll out the cheese dough into a rectangular shape ⅓ cm (⅛ in) thick and leave to cool. Cut across the dough at 3¾ cm (1½ in) intervals, then cut lengthwise at 5 cm (2½ in) intervals; roll each into a bite-size, small, fat sausage, place on a serving dish or roll it again into ground pistachio nuts if used. Repeat with others.

Serve, or cover and chill.

Note: These can be filled with *kashta* (cream), made as the Cream filling described in the recipe for Crêpes (*kataef*). Then make them larger, tucking the sides of cheese dough over cream, then roll.

Ramadan Walnut Lozenges
Hadef Ramadan

Most sweets, even those associated with a particular celebration, are nowadays available all year round, but *hadef* are still prepared only during the holy month of Ramadan. The reason is that *hadef*, which means 'small and thin'—and indeed they are tiny, light and made of paper-thin layers—were ordered by the well-off to be distributed to the poor and old, so that everyone could take part in the joy after a day of fasting. Goodwill and *hadef* thus continue to typify Ramadan.

Ingredients

For the syrup
350 grams (12 oz) sugar
200 ml (7 fl oz) water
1 tsp lemon juice
½ tbs flower water
½ tbs rose water

For the filling
170 g (6 oz) walnuts, crushed medium–fine
2 tbs honey or 2–3 tbs sugar
1 tbs flower water (optional)

For the lozenges
12 leaves of filo pastry (45 x 35 cm/19 x 12¹⁄₂ in)
120 ml (4 fl oz) clarified butter (ghee)
    or unsalted butter, melted

In a saucepan, combine the sugar and water. Stir until sugar is completely dissolved. Bring to the boil, add the lemon juice, skim any scum from the surface and leave to simmer for 7–10 minutes or until the mixture thickens to a syrupy consistency. Add the flower and rose waters, boil and turn the heat off. Leave to cool. In a bowl place the walnuts; add the honey, dissolved in flower water, or the sugar, and mix thoroughly to blend. Then place the filo leaves on your working-surface. Slice down the middle to cut the leaves in half. Cover with a damp cloth, otherwise the pastry dries very quickly. Take a rectangular baking dish larger than the halved filo leaves, brush the inside with butter, then take one piece of filo leaf at a time, place on the baking dish and brush lightly with butter all over its surface. Repeat with filo leaves until you have 12 half-leaves placed one on top of the other; spread the walnut mixture evenly over the top layer and cover with the remaining 12 filo half-leaves, preparing them as before. With a sharp knife, make a series of parallel cuts down through the leaves and another series, at an angle to the first, to make small lozenges. Bake in a preheated oven at 160° C (325° F/gas mark 3), for 30 minutes or until nicely browned. Turn up the heat to 230° C (450° F/gas mark 8), bake for a further 5–8 minutes. Remove and pour the cooled syrup all over, return to oven, then turn the heat off and leave for about 20 minutes. Remove, cool and serve.

Note: For baklava, follow as above, but for filling use prime nuts or a mixture of pine nuts and almonds. Bake until golden.

Pastry with Cheese
Kanafe bi-jibn

I have heard many Westerners complain about the excess of sugar in Lebanese sweets. This recipe could be the answer to those critics. Pastry with Cheese is considered, more than any other sweet, a real treat; it is a mouth-watering delicacy that most people find irresistible at any time of the day. Here is my own recipe, a succulent combination of semolina dough and cheese which I believe matches the ones found on offer in sweet shops.

Ingredients

325 g (11 oz) regular cream of wheat or coarse semolina
125 g (4½ oz) unsalted butter, melted
75 ml (3 fl oz) warm water
½ tsp easy-blend yeast (instant)
120 ml (4 fl oz) milk

For the syrup
285 g (10 oz) sugar
200 ml (7 fl oz) water
1 tsp lemon juice
1½ tsp flower water
1½ tsp rose water

For the filling
325 g (11 oz) *akkawi* or mozzarella cheese
1½ tsp flower water (optional)

Heat the butter until very hot but not smoking, pour over the cream of wheat or semolina, mix well, add the warm water and yeast, mix thoroughly, then add the milk; keep mixing until you form a moist dough. Cover and refrigerate for 4 hours or overnight.

Meanwhile prepare the syrup: Combine sugar with water in a small saucepan, bring to the boil, add the lemon juice and simmer over medium heat for 8–10 minutes or until it thickens to a syrupy consistency. Add the flower and rose waters, boil once and turn the heat off. Pour into a jug and leave until it is time to serve.

Remove *kanafe* dough from fridge. Allow few minutes to reach room temperature. Then take small portions at a time and, using both fingers and the heel of your hand, flatten and smooth a very thin layer against the bottom of a baking dish (21.5 x 21.5 cm/8½ x 8½ in), moistening hands with water as necessary. Repeat until the base of the dish and 2 cm (¾ in) of its sides are covered. This layer will protect the cheese from browning. Preheat the grill, place the baking dish under it and brown this layer of *kanafe* well, taking care that it does not burn. Remove and leave to cool.

Meanwhile, if using *akkawi* cheese, soak it for several hours in several changes of water to rid it of excess salt. If using mozzarella, rinse and pat dry. Make sure that the cheese does not taste salty, then shred, mix thoroughly with flower water, if used, and spread over the cooled *kanafe* layer in the baking dish. Press the cheese lightly and cover with a slightly thicker layer of *kanafe* dough preparing it as before. Preheat the oven to 180° C (350° F/gas mark 4) and bake for 20 minutes. Remove from oven and place under a hot grill to brown the top (this will greatly enhance the flavour). Watch it or it is burn within seconds.

Sultanas and raisins in fragrant syrup (*khasshaf*)

Remove and serve immediately, using a knife and a spatula. Quartered sesame pitta bread—found in Lebanese food stores—can be served as an accompaniment.

A quicker and delicious variation for *kanafe*:
kataifi (shredded wheat) (about 75 g/2½ oz)
250 g (8½ oz) mozzarella cheese, rinsed, drained and finely sliced
1 tbs flower water
about 50 g (2 oz) unsalted butter, melted

Gently loosen the *kataifi* and spread a layer (about 30 g/1 oz) in a baking dish. This layer will protect the cheese from browning. Hold the *kataifi* with your fingers at one end and, with a brush, dot with butter to coat *kataifi* threads; changing the position of your fingers, keep dotting with butter until all *kataifi* threads are coated. Spread the cheese over evenly and sprinkle with flower water. Loosen the remaining *kataifi* to fully cover the cheese layer. Again, dot with butter to coat the entire surface of the *kataifi*. Bake in a preheated oven at 200° C (400° F/gas mark 6) until golden, about 12–15 minutes.
    Serve immediately with syrup.

Note: For a golden brown top, place the dish under a hot grill for about ½–1 minute (no longer, or the top will burn).

Sultanas and Raisins in Fragrant Water
Khasshaf

A refreshing, fragrant salad derived from a traditional recipe. It consists of raisins and sultanas immersed in a pleasantly-scented fresh water until they swell. A handful of different nuts is added; I also add pumpkin and sunflower seeds to the traditional recipe, as well as fruits which provide energy and interest: the lychees that marry delightfully with the texture and flavour of sultanas, the velvety juiciness of ripe papayas and the sweetness of bananas. This dessert salad sparkles like jewels, and with a bit of imagination you might think it looks like Ali Baba's treasure.

Ingredients

170 g (6 oz) sultanas, rinsed
115 g (4 oz) raisins, rinsed
600–700 ml (21–25 fl oz) water
2 tbs honey or to taste
1 tbs flower water or to taste
1 tbs rose water or to taste
30 g (1 oz) pistachios, soaked in water and chilled for 2 hours or overnight

30 g (1 oz) almonds, soaked in water and chilled
    for 2 hours or overnight
30 g (1 oz) pine-nuts, soaked in water and chilled
    for 2 hours or overnight
50 g (2 oz) halved walnuts, soaked and chilled
    for 4 hours or overnight, changing the water at least twice
2 tbs sunflower seeds
2 tbs pumpkin seeds
8 lychees, shelled, left whole or cut in half
1 medium-sized, ripe papaya, peeled, de-seeded
    and cut into $2\frac{1}{2}$ cm (1 in) pieces

In a serving bowl combine the sultanas, raisins, water and honey. Stir until the honey is completely dissolved. Chill covered for 12 hours. The following day add the flower and rose waters to this mixture, stir, taste and, if necessary, adjust the flavourings.

Then immerse the sunflower and pumpkin seeds, do not stir. Cover and chill until serving time. Just before serving drain the pistachios, almonds, pine-nuts and walnuts, mixing them lightly into the salad. Top with lychees and papaya. Serve immediately.

Spiced Rice Pudding
Mighli

A festive sweet that was traditionally prepared when a boy was born, offered to well-wishers and distributed among the neighbours. Nowadays girl babies are similarly honoured. *Mighli* is also appearing more and more at dinner parties and at Christmas to celebrate the birth of Christ. *Mighli* is a pudding rice, highly flavoured with exotic and aphrodisiac spices, simmered with water until it forms a smooth, brown-coloured mixture. This mixture is poured into a serving dish; when cool it develops a velvety surface which is then sprinkled with a touch of desiccated coconut and topped with a large handful of nuts. The amount and variety of the nuts used to depend on the wealth of the family of the new-born baby, as did the serving bowls and plates, which ranged from simple china to silver. *Mighli* is inexpensive, nutritious and delicious, though it is an acquired taste owing to its spices.

Ingredients

a heaped tbs aniseed, boiled in 100 ml (4 fl oz) water

170 g (6 oz) powdered rice

1 tbs cinnamon

1 tbs ground caraway seeds

1.75 l (60 fl oz) water

225 g (8 oz) sugar or to taste

For the garnish

3–4 tbs desiccated coconut

30 g (1 oz) pine-nuts, soaked i
    n water for at least 1 hour

30 g (1 oz) pistachios, soaked
    for 2 hours or overnight

30 g (1 oz) blanched almonds, soaked for 1 hour or overnight

45 g (1½ oz) walnuts, halved or roughly
    chopped and soaked for at least 2 hours

Boil aniseed with water for a minute, making sure it does not overflow. Cover and leave to infuse for 20 minutes. Meanwhile in a pan combine the rice with the cinnamon and ground caraway seeds. Gradually add the water; set the pan over high heat, stirring all the time until it boils. Reduce heat to medium and simmer uncovered for 15 minutes, stirring occasionally to prevent it from sticking to the bottom of the pan. After the 15 minutes, and while stirring, add the sugar, simmer until pudding thickens (about 10 minutes longer). When the pudding is ready it should coat the back of the spoon. Taste and adjust the sugar if necessary.

Remove from heat, pour immediately into a serving dish, or in separate, small bowls, and leave to cool completely. Chill to allow the full flavour to develop. Just before serving, sprinkle the coconut all over and spread the pine-nuts, pistachio nuts, almonds and walnuts evenly on top.

Sesame and Hazelnut Candies

Soumsoumia wa boundoukia

This delicacy is seldom prepared in domestic kitchens, but it used to have prime place during most festivities held in the villages to mark a saint's day. Pedlars prepared *soumsoumia* and *boundoukia* at home and brought them to the church courtyard where the annual fair was to take place. There they would place their candies on stalls among the candy-floss sellers, the showman with the magic lantern and a dozen entertainers and sweet vendors. The vendors of these candies became a fixture in some locations, the most

Anise cakes (*kaak bi-yansoun*)

famous being the alley leading to Wadi Zahle, where there is one cafe on top of another on both banks of the river Burdawni. I decided, nevertheless, to include the recipe in this book, having in mind especially expatriate and nostalgic Lebanese. The candies are delicious and easy to prepare.

Ingredients

175 g (6½ oz) sesame seeds
butter to grease pan
100 ml (4 fl oz) honey
85 g (3 oz) sugar
2 tbs water
½ tbs lemon juice

Put the sesame seeds in a thick-bottomed frying pan set over medium heat. Toast the seeds, stirring, at first occasionally and then constantly, until they become golden brown in colour. Remove, spread over a tray or dish and allow to cool.

Meanwhile, grease a deep, medium-sized, rectangular dish with butter. Then, in a saucepan, combine honey, sugar, water and lemon. Set over medium–high heat and stir all the time until sugar dissolves completely and the liquid thickens to a syrupy consistency (about 3–5 minutes from boiling point). At this point add the toasted sesame and boil over medium heat for 5 minutes. Remove and pour into the greased dish. Leave to set and cool slightly. Then cut into squares the size you like. Store in a container, placing waxed paper between layers.

Variation: For the hazelnut candy (*boundoukia*): 255 g (9 oz) hazelnuts
Heat oven to 180° C (350° F/gas mark 4) and roast the hazelnuts for 20–30 minutes or until nicely browned. Remove from oven, cool slightly and remove their outer skins by rubbing them between the palms of your hands. Then continue as for *soumsoumia*, except that for sugar add 100 g (3½ oz) instead of 85 g (3 oz).

Note: You can use un-toasted sesame seeds and different nuts, for instance toasted peanuts.

Girdle Cakes with Milk
Kaak bi-haleeb

This delicacy could well have its origins in Byzantine times, although it is very much appreciated by mountain dwellers of all denominations. The Druses particularly are fond of it and prepare it during 'Id al-Adha, calling it *kaak al-id* ('girdle of the feast'). These cakes have a subtle taste and are delicious with coffee or tea.

Ingredients

300 g (10½ oz) flour
150 g (5½ oz) fine semolina
½ tbs ground lavender
½ tsp easy blend yeast (instant)
½ tsp baking powder
½ tsp ground *mahlab*
¼ tsp ground nutmeg
¼ tsp ground cloves
150 ml (5 fl oz) milk
200–210 g (7–7½ oz) sugar
75 g (2½ oz) unsalted butter

In a mixing bowl sift the flour and combine with semolina. Add the lavender, yeast, baking powder, *mahlab*, nutmeg and cloves. Reserve for a short time.

In a saucepan over medium heat warm the milk. When milk is warm add the sugar and butter, stir for a minute then turn the heat off; keep stirring until sugar is completely dissolved then pour this mixture over the reserved ingredients in the mixing bowl. Mix them well for about 3–5 minutes to form a smooth dough. Cover with a clean cloth and leave to rest for several (4) hours.

When the resting time of the dough is over, preheat the oven to 180° C (350° F/gas mark 4). Then from dough take small portions, each the size of a walnut, roll each portion under the palm of your hand to form a medium–fine thick roll about 10–15 cm (4–5 in) long. Bring both ends together, pinch gently to seal and place over a baking sheet. Repeat with remaining dough until it is used up. Bake for 10–15 minutes or until golden. Remove, cool and place in an airtight tin.

Anise Cakes
Kaak bi-yansoun

Small ring-shaped cakes with a refreshing taste. These cakes are generally served with coffee or tea; they are simple to make and are useful to have on hand for unexpected guests, because they keep for a long time in an airtight container. They may be sweetened with honey or with sugar, as in the traditional recipe. In Ancient Rome anise cakes used to be served as an aid to the digestion of rich foods. All the more reason for you to indulge in one or two of these delicious cakes.

Ingredients

140 g (5 oz) cake flour (sifted)
¼ tsp baking powder
¼ tsp *miskee*, ground with ¼ tsp sugar
¼ tsp ground *mahlab*
¼ tsp ground nutmeg
1 tsp whole aniseeds
2–3 tbs honey or 50 g (2 oz) sugar
50 ml (2 fl oz) olive oil
2–3 tbs warm water

In a mixing bowl combine the flour with baking powder, ground *miskee*, *mahlab*, nutmeg, aniseeds, honey or sugar and oil. Mix the ingredients thoroughly before you add the water; gradually add the warmed water and knead until you form a smooth dough. Preheat the oven to 180° C (350° F/gas mark 4). Divide the dough into 12–14 pieces and roll each piece into a sausage shape about 10–12 cm (4–5 in) long; curve into a ring shape and press gently on the ends to join. Place the rings on an ungreased baking sheet and bake for about 15–18 minutes or until nicely browned. Cool before serving, otherwise the taste will be doughy.

Cream of Wheat or Semolina Cake
Nammoura

Nammoura is easy to prepare, inexpensive and popular, and used to be obtainable from street vendors who set up their stalls in strategic locations, such as near schools and cinemas.

For this recipe a medium-grain semolina is best. Farina (cream of wheat) makes an excellent substitute, especially if the only semolina available is the fine variety. Traditional *nammoura* uses much more sugar than in this recipe, and is thus stickier.

Ingredients

For the syrup
350 g (12 oz) sugar
225 ml (8 fl oz) water
¾ tsp lemon juice

Biscuits in sesame seeds and pistachio nuts (*barazek*)

$^1/_2$ tbs flower water
½ tbs rose water

For the cake
5–6 tbs *tahini*
350 g (12 oz) cream of wheat or coarse semolina
140 g (5 oz) unsalted butter, melted
450 ml (15 fl oz) soured cream
3 tbs sugar
2 tsp baking powder
125 g (4½ oz) flaked almonds

Combine the sugar and water in a saucepan over medium–high heat and stir until the sugar dissolves. Bring to the boil, add lemon juice and leave to simmer about 8–10 minutes or until the liquid thickens to a syrupy consistency. Add the flower and rose waters, stir, bring to a boil, then remove from heat and leave to cool.

Grease a rectangular 25 x 35 cm (10 x 14 in) pan with 2 tbs *tahini*. Reserve. Preheat the oven to 180° C (350° F/gas mark 4). Then put the cream of wheat or semolina in a mixing bowl, add the hot butter and mix thoroughly. In another bowl combine the soured cream with the sugar and remaining *tahini*, stir vigorously for a few seconds, add this mixture to the cream of wheat or semolina in the mixing bowl and mix thoroughly; add the baking powder, stir well and instantly pour the batter over the reserved pan. Smooth the surface, wetting your hand with water if necessary. Sprinkle the flaked almonds evenly over the surface, pressing them firmly into the batter.

Bake for 50–60 minutes or until nicely browned. Turn oven heat off, remove the semolina cake, cut in a criss-cross pattern to make lozenges (see recipe for Ramadan Walnut Lozenges), then pour the cooled syrup all over, return to the oven and leave for about 15 minutes, Remove, cool and serve.

Note: For a richer and crunchier cake, mix ingredients except for butter. Bake the cake as above, but after 30 minutes, remove from oven and pour about 200 g (7 oz) melted butter all over. Return to the oven and continue baking time.

Biscuits in Sesame Seeds and Pistachio Nuts
Barazek

Although the dough used here is nearly the same as tart dough, the sesame seeds and flaked pistachios give these biscuits end product a distinctive flavour. They have a crunchy texture and keep for a long time if stored in an airtight container.

Ingredients (for about 28 biscuits)

100 g (3½ oz) clarified butter (*ghee*), melted and cooled
85 g (3 oz) icing sugar
1 whole free-range egg
1 tsp vanilla
1 tsp white vinegar (preferably cider vinegar)
200 g (7 oz) flour, sifted
a pinch of salt
½ tsp baking powder
1 tbs egg white, lightly mixed with 1 tbs very cold
    water and ¾ tsp white vinegar (optional)
sesame seeds, toasted (about 85 g/3 oz)
pistachio nuts (about 55 g/2 oz), flaked and toasted

In a mixing bowl cream the butter and sugar together thoroughly. Add the egg, vanilla and vinegar; stir to mix. Then add the flour, salt and baking powder. Mix thoroughly to form a soft dough, cover with a cloth or plastic and refrigerate for about 30 minutes or until it is easy to work with. The dough is delicate because of the quantity of butter in it. Work with half of the dough at a time, leaving the rest in the refrigerator until you are ready to use it .

Preheat the oven to 180° C (350° F/gas mark 4) and grease a baking sheet. From the dough take small portions, shape between the palms of your hands into thin circles, about 5 cm (2 in) in diameter. Dip one side of the circle into pistachio flakes, press lightly with four fingers, then lightly smooth the other surface of the circle with the egg-white mixture (if used) and dip it into the sesame seeds. Using your finger, gently smooth the top to remove excess seeds. Gently remove and place on the baking sheet. Repeat with remaining dough. Bake for 15–18 minutes or until the biscuits are golden-brown in colour. Remove baking sheet from the oven and, with a spatula, gently remove *barazek* while still hot. Place on a serving dish and leave to cool for at least 2 hours before serving.

Note: To toast sesame seeds place them in a heavy-bottomed, non-stick frying-pan, set over medium heat, stir until golden-brown, remove and spread over a tray or dish so that they do not darken further. Cool, then store in a glass jar. Use when necessary.

To flake the pistachios, place whole nuts in a polythene bag and gently pound and roll with a rolling-pin. Toast in a preheated oven at 220° C (425° F/gas mark 7) for about 10–15 minutes, or until lightly browned.

Turmeric Cakes
Sfouf

Sfouf are a feature of mountain home cooking. For some people the taste needs to be acquired because of the distinctive flavouring of turmeric. *Sfouf* are simple and inexpensive to make, with ingredients that are standard in most kitchens. In addition, *sfouf* have a light, spongy texture that makes them suitable for older people. When sugar was expensive—such as in times of war—molasses was used as a substitute. My grandmother told me this, adding, quite rightly as we now know, that molasses is healthier than sugar.

Ingredients

1½ tbs light *tahini*
175 g (6½ oz) flour
2 tsp baking powder
1½ tbs turmeric
255 g (9 oz) fine semolina
75 ml (3 fl oz) olive oil
2 tbs melted butter
350 ml (12 fl oz) milk
3 tbs water
250 g (8½ oz) sugar
30 g (1 oz) pine nuts

Grease base and sides of a rectangular pan (26 x 20 cm/10½ x 8 in) with *tahini*; reserve. Sift the flour, baking powder and turmeric over a mixing bowl and combine with semolina, oil and butter. Preheat the oven to 180° C (350° F/gas mark 4). Then, in another medium-sized mixing bowl, combine milk, water and sugar; stir until sugar is completely dissolved and gradually add to the ingredients in the other mixing bowl. Mix them thoroughly until you have a smooth batter. Pour this batter into the reserved pan and sprinkle all over with pine-nuts.

Bake for 30–40 minutes. After 30 minutes insert a wooden tooth pick or skewer into the centre of the cake: if it comes out clean, the cake is ready. Remove, cool and cut into 5 cm (2 in) squares. *Sfouf* keep well if they are stored in an airtight container to prevent drying.

Quince preserve *(m'rabba al-safarjal)*

Baked Date or Walnut Cake
Maamoul mad

This preparation of *maamoul* is really delicious, and also nourishing, provided it is eaten in moderation, because it is calorific.

Preparation takes a little care and patience, as the dough needs to rest for several hours.

Ingredients

310 g (11 oz) semolina
2 tbs wholemeal or white flour
150 ml (5 fl oz) clarified butter *(ghee)*
2 tbs live yoghurt
2 tbs honey or sugar
½ tsp baking powder
2 tbs warm flower water
2 tbs warm rose water

For the date filling
200 g (7 oz) dates, finely chopped if dry
6 tbs water or as necessary
1 tsp ground *mahlab*
2 tbs flower water

For the walnut filling
170 g (6 oz) medium–fine crushed walnuts
2½–3 tbs honey or sugar to taste
1 tbs flower water
1 tbs rose water

In a mixing bowl combine the semolina and wholemeal or white flour with the butter; work them well with your fingertips. Add the yoghurt, honey or sugar and baking powder; mix well to form a crumbly dough. Add the warmed flower and rose waters and knead well. Cover and leave to stand for 6 hours. Meanwhile prepare one of the fillings.

For date filling: Place dates with water in a saucepan set over medium–low heat, mash them with a fork until smooth. Then add the *mahlab* and flower water, mix well and turn the heat off.

For walnut filling: Place walnuts in a small mixing bowl; dissolve honey in flower and rose waters, add to the walnuts in the mixing bowl and mix thoroughly to blend.

After the dough has rested place it on a working-surface and knead (if necessary add a very small amount of rose water). Divide dough into two equal portions and from one portion take small lumps at a time, pat and press each lump down against the base of a lightly greased 21 x 21 cm (8½ x 8½ in) baking dish; repeat until you have formed a bottom layer. Over this layer spread the filling of your choice evenly. Prepare the remaining dough in the same way and use to form a top layer.

Bake in a preheated oven at 180° C (350° F/gas mark 4) for 30–35 minutes or until nicely browned. Remove and leave to cool about 2 hours. Then cut into squares about 5 cm (2 in) or smaller and gently remove with a spatula to prevent breaking. Serve or place in an airtight container.

Salep Ice Cream
Bouza sahlab

Sahlab, a starchy powder obtained by grinding the dried tubers of wild orchids, is used for the preparation of delicacies much in favour in Turkey. In Lebanon *sahlab* is used to make a hot drink and an ice-cream, both very popular. The hot drink, dusted with a little cinnamon, is taken in winter by early risers before they walk to their jobs in town or travel to the Bekaa Valley or Syria.

Ingredients

255 g (9 oz) sugar
2 tbs *sahlab* powder
1 litre (35 fl oz) milk
1 tbs flower water
½ tbs rose water
¼ tsp *miskee* pieces, ground with ½ tsp sugar

In a saucepan combine the sugar with *sahlab*. Gradually add the milk while stirring so that *sahlab* powder does not form any lumps. Keep stirring until sugar and *sahlab* are well incorporated into the milk. Then set the saucepan over medium heat, stirring all the time, until it thickens to resemble milk rice pudding (*mouhallabieh*). At this point add the rose and flower waters and *miskee* if desired. Mix to blend.

If you have an ice cream maker pour the mixture in and blend for 15 minutes. If not, place in a dish in the freezer. Remove from freezer several times while it is freezing and mix with a whisk.

Conserves and Jams

Fresh fruits in season are not only full of flavour, but also abundant in valuable vitamins and minerals. The Lebanese love all kinds of fruits, with their different colours, textures and flavours. Those fruits that have a short season or are over-ripe are revived by cooking. Our grandmothers and mothers used to spend long, pleasurable hours in the making of mouth-watering conserves and jams. Nowadays, few people have time for this activity and fruits tend to be identified as much with laboratory-made rejuvenating creams as with food.

Most fruits can be used to prepare jam; but some set more easily than others because of their high pectin content—for example citrus fruits and quinces—while others, such as strawberries, over-ripe plums and apricots, need some help in setting. One method of doing this is to put the seeds of fruits such as lemons, oranges, apples or quinces in a Muslim bag to simmer with the principal fruit.

The utensils you will need are a large, heavy-bottomed stainless-steel pan, a long-handled wooden spoon and sterilized jars. Strict cleanliness is essential throughout the process. Wash the fruits thoroughly to remove any harmful substances and wash the jars in hot, soapy water, rinse well and invert over a clean cloth. Prepare the fruit, cool and pour into sterilized jars, then cover with an airtight seal. To inactivate harmful organisms, which cause spoilage, set a wire rack in a large pan. Place the sealed jars on the rack and fill the pan with hot water. Bring to the boil, cover and leave to boil gently for 30 minutes. Carefully remove the jars, cool and store.

Remember that jams are high in calories, and should be eaten in moderation. They should never be regarded as a substitute for fresh fruits, which should be a part of everyone's daily diet.

Seville Orange Preserve
M'rabba abou sfair

Seville Orange Preserve is one of the tastiest of all preserves. It is simple to make but takes time as the fruit has to be scrubbed and peeled. Seville oranges are in season in winter. As with all jams and preserves the amount of sugar used and the details of preparation may vary from one household to another. Some people like the oranges caramelized which increases the length of the cooking time.

Ingredients

1 kg (2 lb 2 oz) Seville oranges (about 8–10 oranges)
500 g (1 lb 1 oz) sugar
500 ml (16 fl oz) water
2¹/₂ tbs lemon juice

Lightly grate the oranges, cut the peel into quarters and put in a saucepan with water to cover, bring to the boil and simmer for 5 minutes over medium heat. Remove from heat and drain, then place in a bowl with cold water to cover. Leave to stand for 18–24 hours, changing the water several times (at least 3 times daily) to rid them of their bitterness. When soaking time is over, drain well, then take one orange peel, roll, squeeze off excess water; put a thread through it, to keep it in its rolled shape; pack the peels one against the other, to form a necklace. Reserve for a short while.

In a saucepan combine the sugar with the water and stir to dissolve the sugar completely. Bring to the boil over high heat, add the lemon juice, stir, then skim the froth from the surface of the water. Reduce the heat to medium and simmer for 10 minutes or until the mixture thickens slightly. Place the reserved orange peel in the saucepan with the syrup, bring to the boil, add the cloves and simmer over medium–high heat for about 3–5 minutes. Reduce the heat to medium and simmer for 20–30 minutes longer or until syrup had reduced and thickened. Turn the heat off, cool, then unthread the oranges and place in a sterilized jar, pour over the reduced syrup, seal and process in boiling water for 30 minutes. Cool and store.

Date Preserve
M'rabba al-balah

Because of the availability of good-quality jams in supermarkets, many people in Lebanon have stopped making them, but this wonderful, succulent preserve, the Seville Orange Preserve and Fig Jam are exceptions and, indeed, very special. In the Middle East dates are regarded as a gift from heaven, for they are energizing and an excellent source of minerals. They have a short season but any fresh dates, the dark red ones or the golden-yellow, are good for preserving, to be enjoyed all year round.

Ingredients

About 50 fresh, red or yellow dates (ripe but firm)
50 whole blanched almonds
50 tiny strips of Clementine zest
450 g (1 lb) sugar
8 cloves
2 tbs lemon juice
juice of 1 Clementine

Thinly peel the dates, place in a pan covered with water by 5 cm (2 in). Bring to the boil and skim off the scum as it forms. Simmer the dates over medium heat until they are slightly soft and their pits can be easily removed (about 5–10 minutes). With a slotted spoon remove the dates to a side dish and turn the heat off, reserving the water in the pan. Hold one date in one hand and with the other hand insert a wooden pick and gently push the pit out from the other end. Take one almond with one Clementine zest and push into the side of the date that has the larger hole. Repeat with remaining dates and reserve.

Re-heat the reserved date water in the pan, then add the sugar and the cloves. Stir until sugar is completely dissolved. Bring to a boil, skim off the scum and drop in the reserved stuffed dates one by one. Add the lemon and Clementine juices, bring to the boil again and simmer for 50–60 minutes or until the liquid has thickened slightly. Ladle into sterilized jars. Cool, seal and process for 30 minutes in boiling water. Cool and store.

Quince Preserve

M'rabba al-safarjal

Quinces are delicious, especially when prepared as jam. The quince was associated in Greek mythology with love, marriage and fertility. Nowadays, its importance is in its flavour and its high vitamin C content. Cooking, however, decreases the vitamin and the addition of sugar tops up the calories. It is therefore advisable to eat this jam strictly in moderation.

Ingredients

1 kg (2 lb 2 oz) quinces
575 ml (20 fl oz) water
550 g (1 lb 4 oz) sugar
2½ tbs lemon juice

Peel the quinces, cut in half, core and cut again so that each fruit is quartered. Place in a saucepan with the water and bring to the boil over high heat. Reduce the heat to medium, cover and simmer for 10 minutes or until quinces are slightly soft. With a slotted spoon, remove to a side dish.

To the water in the saucepan add the sugar, stir until it dissolves completely, bring to the boil, add the lemon juice and bring to the boil again. Skim off any froth and drop in the cooked quinces. Bring to the boil and simmer over medium heat for 1 hour or until quinces turn red. For the last 2 minutes only, turn the heat up to moderately high; reduce the heat if the mixture is boiling too vigorously. Put in sterilized jars, cool, seal tightly, then process in boiling water for 30 minutes. Cool and store.

Apricot Conserve

Apricot Conserve is a good source of nutrients and is easy to prepare. In Lebanon apricots are simmered over a low flame to keep the maximum freshness and flavour, after which they are spread on shallow trays and put outside the house or on the roof, to dry in the sun; after a day excess moisture evaporates while the beautiful, orangey apricot colour remains.

Ingredients

900 g (2 lb) apricots, ripe but firm, rinsed and drained
450 g (1 lb) sugar

Wash the apricots, halve and remove the stones. Place them in a bowl, cover with sugar and leave to stand overnight. This preparation allows excess moisture to be released from the apricots. The following day put the apricot mixture into a pan over medium–low heat. Stir with a wooden spoon until sugar is completely dissolved. Bring slowly to the boil until it starts to bubble. Simmer for 30 minutes or until it thickens. Ladle into sterilized jars and process in boiling water until excess moisture evaporates from the jam. Cool well, seal and process in boiling water for 30 minutes. Another method is to put the apricot jam over cheese cloth in a sieve set over a pan and allow excess moisture to drain before sealing and processing.

Dried Fig Jam

M'rabba al-teen al-nashef

A delicious jam; dried figs are used, which are more readily obtainable than fresh figs. One way of serving the jam is to simmer it over low heat in unsalted butter, stirring all the time, then to spread it in a serving dish. Another, less familiar method—a favourite of mine, and known mostly in the mountains—is to spread some of the jam in a dish, sprinkle it evenly with halved walnuts and then cover it with light *tahini*. This makes an irresistible dish but remember it is highly calorific, so a little will be more than enough.

Ingredients

1 kg (2 lb 2 oz)) good-quality, organic dried figs
½ kg (1 lb 1 oz) sugar
700 ml (25 fl oz) water
2 tbs lemon juice
3–3½ tsp whole aniseeds
50–85 g (2–3 oz) toasted sesame seeds
½ tsp *miskee*, gently pounded with ½ tsp sugar

Check the figs; make sure they are clean inside, remove their tough stems, wash and drain. Chop them roughly or blend in a food processor for a few seconds. In a saucepan combine the sugar and water, bring to the boil, add the lemon juice, stir, and skim any foam from the surface. Throw in the aniseeds, allow them to boil for 1 minute, then drop in the chopped figs. Cook for about 20 minutes over medium heat or until water is completely absorbed, stirring constantly to prevent the mixture from sticking to the pan; use a long-handled wooden spoon as the figs may spatter and burn you while they are cooking. After 20 minutes add the sesame seeds, stirring all the time for another 10–15 minutes or until the jam has thickened and easily coats the back of the spoon. Turn the heat off and very quickly add the *miskee*, stirring vigorously. Cool, then put the jam into sterilized jars, seal and process in boiling water for 30 minutes. Cool and store.

Pickles

Pickled Olives

In early autumn olive picking is a feature of village life; it makes a a charming spectacle but is hard work for those doing it.

The olive tree grows on coastal plains and hills, mostly up to a maximum height of 500 metres (1640 ft) above sea-level. Olive fruits vary in flavour and size as well as in colour. They provide a good quantity of vitamins and minerals and are high in monounsaturated fatty acids, but they also have a high sodium content and calorific value, so people who are watching their weight or their salt intake should eat them in moderation. Below are some traditional ways of preparing green and black olives.

To make crushed green olives (*zaytoon akhdar marsous*), wash the olives and soak for two days in several changes of water. Then crush them with a pebble or a pestle. Sprinkle the olives lavishly with sea salt (free of any additives) and leave for four days to mature. Stir and mix them four times a day. After that, place the olives in a container; this may be of any material but earthenware preserves the flavour of the olives best. At this point the olives are ready to eat and should be consumed within a week, or at most two weeks, if they are still hard enough.

If you have a freezer, you can use the following method of making crushed olives last longer than a week. To prepare, soak the green olives in several changes of water for two days, drain and lightly crush with a clean pebble or wooden pestle (make sure not to break the stone).

Place the crushed olives in a polythene freezer bag and store in your freezer. When needed, remove the desired quantity, sprinkle with sea salt (free of any additives) and leave for 3–4 days to mature, stirring them 3–4 times a day. Then eat within two weeks. They will have an exceptional, bitter, slightly salty taste as if they have just been freshly picked off the tree. These olives are delicious to eat with *labneh* (concentrated yoghurt), fresh *zaatar* (thyme), tomatoes or pepper grass. If *labneh* is not available white cheese will do.

Olives can also be pickled in brine (one cup salt to 6 cups water).

Ingredients:

900 g (2 lbs) green olives
l lemon with skin on, rinsed and cut into 4–6 pieces
2–3 green chillies, rinsed (optional)
1–2 sprigs of coriander, rinsed (optional) or
a handful of dill, rinsed (optional)
700 ml (25 fl oz) water
140 g (5 oz) coarse sea salt
4 tbs extra virgin olive oil

Slit each olive longitudinally on the surface. Soak in several changes of water for 2 days to rid them of their bitterness. Drain and pack into a sterilized 1¾–2 litre (60–72 fl oz) glass jar; if you are using lemon pieces, chillies, coriander or dill, intersperse these among the olives. Boil the water, add the salt and stir until it dissolves completely. Leave to cool, then pour over the olives and remaining ingredients in the jar to cover fully. Top with the olive oil. Seal and leave in a kitchen cupboard. Eat after one month.

The most frequently used black olives are *al-jarjir,* also known as bitter olives. These olives are picked already ripened and are characterized by their wrinkled skin. To prepare, salt them lightly (optional) and place them with a little olive oil in a container, preferably earthenware. These olives are ready to be used straight away. *Jarjir* are especially delicious when served with *labneh* (concentrated yoghurt). They are on sale at most Lebanese food stores.

Black olives need time to mature. They are rinsed in several changes of water, drained, lavishly sprinkled with sea salt and left in an earthenware container for 10 days. After the 10 days they are packed in a jar half-full of water that has been boiled and cooled and extra-virgin olive oil is added to cover the contents fully. Red chillies can be added if you wish.

Another interesting way of preparing black olives is to add vinegar or lemon juice. Follow the same procedure for black olives, then combine about 100 ml (3½ fl oz) wine vinegar or lemon juice with 200 ml (7 fl oz) boiled, cooled water. Pour this over the black olives in the jar, then fill the jar with extra-virgin olive oil. The olives are ready to eat after 21–28 days.

Other Pickled Vegetables
Moukhallal

The Lebanese pantry is packed with jars filled with local produce. A great variety of hand-picked vegetables are pickled in brine with or without vinegar. Pickling gives the vegetables an appetizing flavour and most importantly a long life span. Remember, however, that vegetables lose much of their nutritional value in pickling and should be avoided by ulcer sufferers.

The vinegar used in pickling fresh vegetables, such as turnips, cucumber, green beans, okra, onions and peppers, stops the growth of bacteria. Nevertheless, strict hygiene is required during the preparation. The glass jars should be washed with hot, soapy water and rinsed very well, then sterilized by placing them in a pan, covering them with warm water and boiling them over medium–low heat for about 10 minutes. The jars must be removed a little before you need them, giving them enough time to drain, inverted over a clean cloth.

The ratio of vinegar to water varies from one household to another; I have found that for turnips 1 cup vinegar to 2 cups water is adequate. For cucumbers I use 1 cup vinegar to 1 cup water. For each kg (2 lb 2 oz) of vegetables, use 60 g (2 oz) rock salt, free of additives, or the vegetable will spoil. Organic cider vinegar gives a clean fresh taste to the vegetables.

Pickled Cucumber
Moukhallal al-khiar

It is not known whether the beauties who lived in India and Burma, where the plant originated 9000 years ago, used cucumbers as a facial treatment like their modern counterparts. Whether they did or not, my concern here is strictly with cucumbers for eating. The cucumbers that grow in Lebanon are small with a very tasty flesh. They are picked young and preserved to lengthen their life. Pickled cucumbers are easy to make and good ingredients make for delicious results. These pickles are perfect to serve with a drink or to enliven sandwiches, especially roast meat and chicken.

Ingredients

500 g (1 lb 1 oz) small cucumbers, rinsed
200 ml (7 fl oz) organic cider vinegar
about 1 tbs rock salt free of any additives

Barely trim both ends of cucumber, position them upright in a sterilised jar. Then completely dissolve the salt in 250 ml (8 fl oz) boiling water, cool slightly and combine with vinegar. Pour this liquid over the cucumbers to cover fully, then seal. Place the jar in a dark kitchen cupboard and leave to stand for one week before using.

Pickled Turnips
Moukhallal al-lift

Turnips are the pickles most favoured by the Lebanese and hardly a house is without them. Their preparation may vary from one household to the other, for instance they can be sliced or left whole, peeled or unpeeled. Depending on the quantity of beetroot used, they may be ruby red or rosy pink in colour.

In this recipe I follow my mother's method, which is to leave the turnip whole and unpeeled, but to make criss-cross in it. I use a small amount of beetroot to give the pickles an agreeable colour.

Ingredients

500 g (1 lb 1 oz) white turnips (preferably small), rinsed
20 g (¾ oz) beetroot, peeled and cut into 3 pieces
1½ tbs rock salt
150 ml (5 fl oz) organic cider vinegar
1–2 chilli peppers (optional)

Trim off both turnip ends and leave unpeeled. Slice at ½ cm (¼ in) intervals the length of the turnip, but leave it whole. Pack the turnips with beetroot quarters and chillis (if used) in between, into a sterilized glass jar. Dissolve the salt into 400 ml (14 fl oz) boiled water. Cool, stir in the vinegar, and pour over the turnips, beetroot and chillis in the jar to cover fully. If desired, add a thin film (2–3 tbs) of olive oil to prevent them from spoiling. Seal and keep in a dark kitchen cupboard. Use after 10 days–2 weeks.

Pickled Aubergines with Walnuts
Makdouss al-batinjan

Makdouss is a delicacy much appreciated for it contains a subtle and expensive filling not found in our other pickles.

People of my mother's generation were quite fussy about the aubergines they used for pickling, which had to be tiny and seedless. Nowadays we make do with what is available but the baby variety is definitely easier on the palate and the eye. The aubergines are stuffed with a beautiful mixture of crushed walnuts, garlic and chilli, to be fully covered with pure olive oil. They are very simple to make and very pleasant served with a convivial drink.

Ingredients

300 g (10½ oz) baby aubergines about 5–6 cm (2–2½ inches) long,
    rinsed and stem trimmed
575 ml (20 fl oz) water
100 g (3½ oz) halved walnuts, crushed into medium–fine
2–3 cloves of garlic, peeled and crushed
1 tsp pure sea salt

1 red chilli pepper, deseeded, rinsed, finely crushed
2 whole red chilli peppers, rinsed and patted dry
extra-virgin olive oil to cover aubergines

Combine aubergines and water in a saucepan. Set over high heat and bring to the boil. Reduce heat to medium, cover and simmer for about 6 minutes or until aubergines are half cooked. Remove and drain. Meanwhile in a small bowl combine well the walnuts, garlic, salt and crushed chilli; reserve this walnut mixture. Then take one aubergine at a time and, using a pointed knife, make a slit lengthwise; push about 1 tsp, more or less, of the reserved walnut mixture (depending on the size of each aubergine) into the slit. Place into a sterilized jar and repeat with remaining aubergines. When they are all ready, partially cover the jar and place it upside-down over a small dish for 24–36 hours. This traditional method is said to rid the aubergines of excess moisture and prevent them from spoiling.

After the 24–36 hours upturn the jar again and intersperse the whole chillis between the aubergines. Pour over olive oil to cover completely. Seal and place in a kitchen cupboard. Use within 10 days–2 weeks.

Note: An alternative method is to drain the aubergines well in a colander before stuffing.

Sauces

The following sauces are included in this book because they are particular to the Lebanese cuisine. They enhance the flavour of food without masking it.

Sauce for Salads
Salset al-salayet

A basic and healthy dressing normally used for fresh and cooked salads. It is made of garlic, a little salt, olive oil and lemon juice. Cider vinegar can be substituted for lemon juice, but it is always better to taste the dressing while adding the vinegar.

Ingredients

1 small clove of garlic, peeled
1 tsp salt or to taste
5 tbs extra-virgin olive oil
6 tbs lemon juice

In a small mixing bowl crush the garlic with salt until smooth. Add the olive oil and gradually add the lemon juice, whisking constantly. Taste: if it is too sharp add a very little oil and whisk again.

Creamed Sesame Sauce
Tahini Sauce

This is an essential sauce in the Lebanese cuisine. *Tahini* sauce is eaten as a dip with dishes such as *shawarma*, *falafel*, or baked fish; or is used in cooking with foods such as *arnabie* and *tagen*; or is an ingredient of some sweets, such as *nammoura*. It is easy to make and very nutritious, but also highly calorific.

Ingredients

½ small clove of garlic (optional)
$^1\!/_2$ tsp salt or to taste
150 ml (5 fl oz) light *tahini*
6–7 tbs lemon juice
6–7 tbs water

If using the garlic, crush it in a mixing bowl with the salt until smooth; add the *tahini* and mix. Gradually add the lemon juice and water. Use a whisk, to prevent any lumps forming. Keep whisking until the sauce has the consistency of cream. Taste and adjust the lemon or salt.

Variation: To *tahini* sauce add a large handful of parsley, rinsed and finely chopped; or pitted green olives (about 10), each cut in half; or slice the white ribs of Swiss Chard, boil until tender, drain and mix with the sauce.

Tahini with Onions
Tagen

This can be made up to two days ahead of time, if stored in the refrigerator. It is served with *sayadieh* and baked fish. It is also eaten on its own, with bread, at room temperature. Sometimes leftover fish is added towards the end of the cooking time; or a handful of coriander leaves may be simmered with the *tahini*.

Ingredients

For the onions
2 medium onions (about 300 g/ 10 H oz), peeled and thinly sliced
1 tbs extra-virgin olive oil
175 ml (6 fl oz) water
1 tsp salt or to taste

For the tahini
200 ml (7 fl oz) white *tahini*
150 ml (5 fl oz) lemon juice
100 ml (3 ½ fl oz) water

For the garnish
45 g (1 ½ oz) pine-nuts
½ tbs extra-virgin olive oil

¼ tsp cayenne pepper or to taste
a handful of chopped parsley, rinsed and drained (optional)

In a medium saucepan coat onions with the oil, saute for a minute or two and add the water and salt. Bring to the boil, reduce the heat to medium–low, cover and simmer for 10 minutes or until onions are soft.

Meanwhile prepare *tahini* sauce: In a small mixing bowl put the *tahini* and lemon juice and stir. At first it will thicken. Gradually add the water, whisking constantly, until you have a smooth *tahini* sauce. When the onions are soft add *tahini* sauce. Still stirring, bring to the boil, reduce heat to low and simmer for 10 minutes, remove from heat and pour into a serving dish.

In a small frying pan saute the pine-nuts in the olive oil until golden brown, remove and drain over kitchen paper. Garnish the sauce with these. Sprinkle with cayenne pepper and parsley if used.

Index